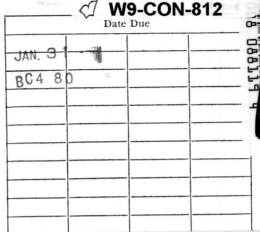

Canadian Indians and the Law: Selected Documents, 1663-1972

edited and with an introduction by
Derek G. Smith

The Carleton Library No. 87
McClelland and Stewart Limited

THE CARLETON LIBRARY

A series of Canadian reprints, original
works, and new collections of source material
relating to Canada, issued under the editorial
supervision of the Institute of Canadian Studies
of Carleton University, Ottawa.

© *McClelland and Stewart Limited, 1975*

ALL RIGHTS RESERVED
0-7710-9787-5

The Canadian Publishers
McClelland and Stewart Limited
25 Hollinger Road, Toronto 374

Printed and bound in Canada

TABLE OF CONTENTS

SECTION B: PRE-CONFEDERATION LEGISLATION, 1663-1916   26

Preface

THE primary purpose of this volume is to draw together and make readily available to the public a selective compilation of legal documents concerning Indians in Canada. Many of the documents are extremely difficult to track down, especially for the layman, and many can only be found in major legal libraries. It is my hope that more ready access to these documents will assist interested Canadians in making themselves familiar with the historical basis of Indian/non-Indian relations in this country, and will help the informed layman to appreciate the immensity and complexity of the legal confrontations over Indian matters which must face all Canadians in coming years.

Naturally the items selected for this volume are only a small portion of the relevant materials, and readers may wish that one selection or another was included or deleted. However, I have tried very hard to ensure that there is a reasonably fair representation in the available space of all the main types of documents and the issues they define. Judicial decisions, a most important category of documents, have been reserved for a separate volume with an introduction by a qualified lawyer. Also, French legislation until 1763 deserves considerably more attention than can be given here. Somehow Canadians have been inclined to shrug off the French Indian legislation as dead history with no modern relevance. However, such issues as the formation of Métis communities and their dispersion cannot be dissociated from the pre-1763 French policy and practice. The French period deserves very close attention and research; it can only be touched in passing in this volume.

Many of the older pieces of legislation represented here have been repealed, and are principally of historical interest; others (such as Jay's Treaty) have been the focus of continuing debate over their current legal status—a point of conflict between Indians and various governments still. Whether a piece of legislation is currently in force or not, an examination of the selections in this volume shows that it is clear that over time there have been some remarkable continuities of Indian policy and legislation; it is clear too that major questions now looming on the horizon can only be considered in deep historical perspective. This volume has attempted to provide items, which illustrate these points.

The Introductory essay is not a technical legal one. It is an overview of what I feel to be the main social implications of principal points in Canadian Indian legislation. I have also tried to point out where certain sociological and anthropological concepts may fruitfully be brought to bear on these points.

Special thanks must be given to the Librarian of the Library of the Supreme Court of Canada in Ottawa. He and his staff facilitated the tracking down of some of the rarer but more important items. Claire Fassett assisted in translating the items from the French regime.

Derek G. Smith
Ottawa
June, 1974

Introduction

TRADITIONALLY, Canadian anthropologists have been most concerned with detailed description and analysis of socio-cultural organization among Canada's Indians and Eskimos. Their preference for community studies and participant observation techniques has fostered an emphasis on group and community differences among Native people. With some exceptions, it is only in recent years that they have begun to consider more systematically those features which relate Canadian Native peoples considered as a more general ethnic group (or groups) to the structure and dynamics of Canadian society as a whole. The recent upsurge of interest among Native peoples and other Canadians concerning Indian land claim settlement and the recognition of aboriginal rights has caused many anthropologists to consider more carefully than heretofore the historical, legal, and constitutional position of Native people in the Canadian polity.

It is naturally with trepidation that an anthropologist tries to deal with the role of law in Canadian society, although it has been a crucial factor in shaping the social phenomena he studies. Perhaps increasingly he cannot avoid dealing with it directly. His interest is not in its legal technicalities *per se*. He is interested in knowing how the law, as only one of several important societal phenomena, has historically directed, sustained, or modified patterns of social interaction between the heterogeneous segments of Canadian society. He may ask about the social values, beliefs, attitudes, opinions and sentiments which underlie Canadian law concerning Native people. He may wish to assess the extent to which these relate to such matters as social stratification, poverty, social prejudice and discrimination, or the formation of Native political movements. These questions are not easy to analyze and evaluate. Their solution requires much more than a consideration of legal history; but perhaps legal history has not always been considered carefully enough.

In North America the sociology of law has tended to be oriented to what we may call a "sociology of jurisprudence", with a considerable bent to practical legal-social issues. This has been true too of Social Anthropology, represented by its many cross-cultural studies of court systems and litigation procedures. In Europe, on the other hand, rather than the development of a special sociological science of law, the sociology of law has been much more a part of a general sociological science of society. Perhaps what is required now is that a degree of *rapprochement* be sought between these divergent emphases. Surely, as Gurvitch[1] has so cogently argued, the sociology of law must comprehend the full social reality of the law, ranging from (a) its tangible expressions in legal institutions and organizations, through (b) its role in social control and social integration, to (c) jural values and ideas and the collective beliefs and intuitions which the law both reflects and helps to shape. Social anthropologists should have a particular interest in the latter, primarily cultural, dimension of the law and its symbols. Such a study is not even in its infancy in Canada, but were it so it could shed much light on the legislation regarding Indians.

II

This volume presents a selection of historically important or historically illustrative legal documents bearing on the legal position of Indians in Canadian society. They are divided into four major categories, the definition of which is somewhat arbitrary, but which are of use to us here in identifying prominent issues and historical trends.

Section A: The Early British Colonial Period, 1760-1826

This section consists of proclamations, government instructions, and international treaties or agreements which represent (a) unilateral enactments by colonial powers regarding Indian matters; and (b) transactions between colonial powers which place the Indians "off-stage" as a passive third party, but which have been crucial in determining the future course of legal and social interaction with Indians.

Already here one sees the emergence of a pattern of relations which has tended to dominate the history of dealings with Indians in Canada—namely that the bulk of legislation, litigation, and politico-legal process over Indian matters has been between colonial governments, government jurisdictions (e. g. Federal/Provincial after Confederation), or between private groups such as businesses or missionary organizations. There is nothing new in all this. It is a legacy of colonial regimes everywhere. But sociologically it is a parade example of one of the classic structures of conflict situations as described by Simmel.[2] This style of conflict theory has not yet been applied to the Canadian Indian situation. It is worth pursuing.

Among the principal issues reflected in this section are the following.

Clearly implicit, sometimes very explicit, in these documents is the concept that Indians constituted separate and sovereign peoples subject to their own law, who were capable as nations and tribes of forming and breaking alliances with colonial powers, and who had national or tribal territories under their control. Yet this sovereignty was not without substantial qualifications since the beginning of British Colonial rule, and was virtually completely eroded by 1826. While sovereign powers in their own right in many respects, Indian tribes and nations were nevertheless "under Royal protection", a position *broadly* analogous to the Protectorates under indirect rule in late British colonial policy in Africa. Being "under protection" meant that domestic legal arrangements were the concern of Indians themselves, but foreign policy regarding the British and other colonial powers was under British control.

The Indians were not considered to constitute a single powerful entity, but were constantly referred to as "the several nations and tribes". Under early colonial rule they emerge as a number of minor, fragmented, quasi-autonomous units with no precisely defined socio-political boundaries—a vulnerable position indeed *vis-á-vis* colonial powers.

After 1763 there were repeated demands by the colonial administration for a systematic listing of the nations and tribes "under protection", for estimates of their population numbers, for delineation of the territories occupied by them. There were also requests for details "of the manner of their lives, and the Rules and Constitutions, by which they are governed or regulated" (A. 3, item 61). Instructions for administering Indian matters are issued which attempt to be responsive to the information gathered about the Indian groups.

While Indians were considered to have absolute title in land and territory, which could not be permanently occupied by settlers without Royal permission and purchase from the Indians, Indian territory was progressively eroded by e. g. the Hudson's Bay Charter and the apparently constant ignoring by settlers of the official policy recognizing Indian title. Indian title is repeatedly reasserted in the face of Indians being "molested and disturbed" in their possession of territory (cf.A.2). Settlement on lands still under Indian title is strictly forbidden. This reflects a prime principle of British colonial policy: sovereign nations and tribes (even "under protection and dominion") held sovereign territories. Yet this principle had important qualifications, too, which facilitated the erosion of Indian control. Missionaries and fur-traders under Royal permission and licence were to be admitted to Indian territories. Authority was reserved for Crown agents to seize and apprehend in these territories fugitives from British justice who had committed crimes within non-Indian territory. The sale and traffic of

intoxicants in Indian territories was forbidden. Non-Indians committing criminal and civil offenses within Indian territory were to be tried
before British courts—that is, they were not subject to Indian legal
process. Offenses between Indians, within either British or Indian
territory, were not considered fully subject to British legal process until
1826 (cf. A.10).

In 1826 the first warrant for execution of an Indian was issued.
The Indian in question had murdered another Indian in broad daylight
in the streets of Amherstburg. But the important decision taken in this
case came only after extensive discussion between the local and Imperial powers. It marks a crucial turning point in Canadian Indian legal
history (cf. A.10a,b,c). Henceforth Indians were to be subject to
British and Canadian law. Erosion of Indian sovereignty was now
well-nigh complete.

Until 1826, British policy in these matters differed markedly from
the previous French regime. French colonial authorities considered
Indians fully subject to French civil and criminal law. French Indian
legislation has not received nearly enough sociological attention. It is a
field for much fruitful research.

Until the American Revolution, Indians in what is now Canada
were subject to an Indian Affairs administration located in what is now
up-state New York. There, Indian administration was effectively con-
trolled by military authorities. After the American Revolution there
was intense discussion in Canada whether Indians should be administered by civil rather than military authority (A. 8a,b,c). The decision
that the civil administration *must* be the controlling agency was issued
by Royal Instruction in 1796. Full control by civil authorities, however, was only achieved by about 1845. In the United States Indians
continued under military administration. The social implications of this
contrast in policy are not yet fully understood, and this is another
fruitful field for future research. While there is a good deal of myth in
the idea of Canadian "peaceful penetration" of Indian territory, the
situation in Canada does contrast with the bloody and legendary events
of American Indian history (e.g. the Custer Affair, the handling of the
Sioux outbreaks, and the military pacification of the American South-
west). There has been too ready a tendency to analogize superficially
the Canadian and American situation.

Section B: PreConfederation Legislation, 1663-1916

This section consists of a selection of legislative documents enacted by
the various colonial regimes, crown colonies, and provinces until their

entry into Confederation (or, in the case of the French regime, until the so-called conquest).

The French regime[3] from early times considered itself authorized to legislate regarding relations both between Indians and non-Indians and between Indians themselves. This, as we have noted, contrasts with early British policy. Legislation interdicting the traffic of intoxicants with Indians, so prominent a feature of Indian policy in Canada until the 1950's, is already well established (B.1, B.3, B.4). Indians are considered subject to French criminal law (B.2). Indian slaves, mostly taken by capture or purchase from groups in the Mississippi River valley, are subject to French colonial law (B.5).

Pre-Confederation British legislation continues the interdiction of alcohol (e.g. B.6, B.10, B.18). Legislation is recurrently enacted to reassert Indian land title (e.g. B.7 to B.13). Indian rights of usufruct over unoccupied lands are affirmed. At least limited Indian subsurface rights are recognized (B.8, Section V). Legislation defining "Indian Status", a prominent feature of Post-Confederation enactments, begins to appear (B.10, B.12). Lands for the use of Indians, foreshadowing the reserve system of later treaties and Indian policy, appear as early as 1829 (B.7). Provision is made for Indians to choose for the "removal of all legal distinctions" (enfranchisement) by 1857 (B.15). The principal elements of Indian policy, which will later be consolidated without any major modification in the Post-Confederation *Indian Act*, are by now well established.

Of considerable importance, although their social implications have never been fully analyzed, are a number of items of legislation representing what we may call the "moral premise" of much of Canada's Indian policy. This "moral premise" takes a variety of forms, but in general terms it states that Indians who choose to live an Indian style of life are to be considered "uncivilized" (cf. B.15, B.17). They are therefore culturally and morally different from other British subjects, and therefore require special legislation, among other things, for (a) their protection from (particularly unscrupulous) others, (b) for the restraint of moral vices, and (c) to regulate their passage from an "uncivilized" to a "civilized" state. This premise clearly underlies the long-established proscription of the use of alcohol by Indians. It underlies the recurrent questioning of the acceptability of testimony given under oath by Indians (e.g. B.17). It underlies the legal proscription of the potlatch, the Sun Dance, and certain other ceremonials as heathen and wasteful. (Laviolette[4] has an extended discussion of these matters.) It underlies, too, the insistence for a time that Indians should be encouraged to develop "agriculture and other civilizing pursuits" (B.12, section VIII) as a means of moving them more quickly from barbarism to civilization. Too, in order to apply for enfranchisement in 1957 (B.15, section III) an Indian must be

> ... of the male sex, and not under twenty-one years of age ... able to speak, read and write either the English or the French language readily and well, and ... sufficiently advanced in the elementary branches of education ... and of good moral character and free from debt. ...

One wonders how many non-Indian Canadians of the period who were presumably "civilized" possessed these qualities in order to qualify for full civil rights.

It is far too easy and superficial to dismiss these matters as racism. But they identify a premise of inequality in Canadian society which has had profound consequences for stratification. The early legislation on qualifications for enfranchisement continues throughout the Post-Confederation *Indian Acts*.

In Pre-Confederation times the Indian land question develops quickly and in a very complex fashion. Quite early (cf. B.9) lands appropriated for the occupation, benefit, and use of Indians are not considered to be under Indian title. They are held in perpetual trust by the Crown. Several corollaries of considerable social importance derive from this, for since Indians do not have title in these lands:

> (a) they are not subject to land taxes on them (cf. B.10, section IV);
>
> (b) the land may not be leased by Indians, nor may these lands be seized in a lien for non-payment of debts (cf. B.10, section III);
>
> (c) income from rents, leases, or utilization of the land's resources must be received and administered by a Crown agent for the collective benefits of Indians (B.9, section III);
>
> (d) Indians may not enter into contracts for the purchase or sale of these lands without permission from the Crown (B.10, section I).

It is exactly around the issue of land held in trust and the management of equity in its benefits that the backbone of Indian administration has developed since the *Act of Union*. The question of land and its administration has become so basic that it has become a key element in defining "Who is an Indian" (cf. e.g. B.9, B.10, B.12). Land and "Indian identity" are intimately linked, as much a consequence of Canadian policy as the persistence of aboriginal sentiments of affinity with the land. This question is also a basic one for the Metis and "non-status Indian" problem, and has been since long before the Riel Rebellions. It cannot be ignored socially, politically, or legally. Its sociological consequences are deep and comprehensive for Indians in Canadian society.

Since the early colonial period with its modicum of sovereignty for Indians, the period especially since 1845 saw a progressive development of the status of Indians as one of "wardship". The term "wardship" is one which Canadian officials have been hesitant to use, although some have designated it as a policy of "guardianship"[4]. It accorded Indians a special and unique position in Canadian society, both constitutionally and legally[5] and also in a broader social sense. The shaping of the policy in Pre-Confederation times determined many of the main lines of Post-Confederation legislation. Laviolette[6] sees the wardship policy emerging from the early colonial period with three major components.

First there is a system of land reserves set aside in Crown trust for the exclusive use of Indians assigned to them. This entailed the development of a complex Indian Affairs administration around the administration of the land and equity in its benefits, with the delegation of only minor decision-making powers to Indian bands.

Secondly, the concept of wardship envisages a rather high degree of Indian self-sufficiency and self-support based on the land and its benefits. Hence agriculture is encouraged, and the Indians are given for collective benefit income accruing from surface and subsurface resource use. This policy appears to have intended a curtailment of Indian dependence on facilities and resources external to the bands and their lands. Only in later years did a general government policy of individualized social welfare through statutory payments and health programmes begin to alter appreciably the self-support policy.

Thirdly, wardship necessitates a clear legal concept of "Indian Status". Legal rights and obligations differed for Indians and non-Indians. Indian status was not one of full Canadian citizenship, but it was not the manifest intent of policy to perpetuate this situation indefinitely. Through education, and to some degree by Christianization, as well as curtailment of aboriginal subsistence patterns by encouragement to develop agriculture, it was hoped to "civilize" the Indian population gradually. Then Indians would enjoy full civil rights: the vote, the right to consume alcohol, the right to hold land in fee simple, the obligation to pay land taxes, etc. The enfranchisement legislation (e.g. B.15) clearly expresses an optimism for the gradual assumption by Indians of full citizenship—but history has shown the reality to be otherwise. Enfranchisement policy undergoes a degree of continual development, so that in the last major revision of the *Indian Act* (1951) provision was made for the enfranchisement of whole bands and their conversion into local municipalities. In fact, this has occurred in only a few cases. Enfranchisement policy has certain affinities with other colonial policies, such as the *évolué* concept which has enjoyed such notoriety in Africa.

Understanding the social implications of wardship requires a penetrating analysis of much more than a selection of legislative documents, but these help to define a distinctive order of social relations in Canada.

In wardship, Indians were subject to a "pluralistic" relationship with other Canadians. By "pluralism" I do not intend the concept as applied by American political scientists to describe social systems in which there is

> . . . a balance of power among overlapping economic, religious, ethnic, and geographical groupings. Each "group" has some voice in shaping socially binding decisions; each constrains and is constrained through the process of mutual group adjustment; and all major groups share a broad system of beliefs and values which encourages conflict to proceed within established channels and allows initial disagreements to dissolve into compromise solutions.[7]

Many equate such situations with the ideal realization of liberal democracy,[8] and find that

> . . . pluralism of institutions, conflict patterns, groupings, and interests makes for a lively, colorful, and creative scene of political conflict which provides an opportunity for success of every interest that is voiced.[9]

The concept of pluralism as used in anthropology differs considerably from this position. Here it denotes social systems which contain culturally and socially differentiated societal sections which are hierarchically arranged in a system of stratification and are "integrated" not by the members of the sections sharing common basic values but by regulation of inter-sectional relations by authority and power exercised by dominant sections.[10] Legal or constitutional definition and recognition of sections in a plural society are important elements in regulating and maintaining the characteristic social cleavages and hierarchical arrangements of such an order. One perhaps cannot properly characterize Canadian society as a whole as a plural society. It is perhaps more appropriate to describe the quality of the relationships between certain sections of Canadian society as highly pluralistic (e.g. English/French, Indian/non-Indian). Each set of pluralistic relationships will be distinctive. French/English and Indian/non-Indian relations in Canada are both intensely pluralistic, but differ considerably in detail. Since such relationships constitute a special though variable type which have specific historical outcomes for stratification, sectional political entities, the development of characteristic modes of inter-sectional conflict, etc., it would be well to look carefully at Indian/non-Indian relations over a long historical time-span (focusing especially on legal events and such phenomena as wardship) with the aid of this historical framework. This must be done at a societal level. Application of the framework within small regional areas, as I have done in some of my own work,[11] is simply inadequate to understanding this important feature of Canadian policy and social practice regarding Indians.

Section C: The British North America Act, The Indian Acts, and Allied Documents

This section contains selections from the B.N.A. Act and its allied documents as they bear on Indians. The major revisions of the Indian Act, which derives its authority from the B.N.A. Act, are given in full.

Section 91 of the B.N.A. Act (C.1) places Indians, the only named group other than "aliens", indisputably under Federal jurisdiction. This section includes matters which are "of national importance and have attained such dimensions as to affect the body politic of the Dominion."[12] As with other matters covered by Section 91 (Federal jurisdiction) and Section 92 (Provincial jurisdiction) there has been considerable Federal-Provincial disagreement and differences of interpretation since Confederation. Perhaps this is as it should be. Continual inter-jurisdictional dialogue must be maintained in order to readjust continually the delicate and dynamic balances and accommodations required to maintain a Federal union of this kind. However, this process has tended to place Indians "off-stage" to many of the principal Federal-Provincial disputes concerning them. It has been a relatively powerless position for Indians. One need not look far for examples. Clause 13 of the 1871 Order-in-Council admitting British Columbia into the Union (C.6) stipulated that the charge of Indians and Indian lands would be a Federal Government responsibility, and the Federal Government pledged to follow a policy "as liberal as that hitherto pursued by the British Columbia government."

Laviolette[13] argues that the effect of this clause (and the events rising from it) was that

> . . . the Indian was denied the opportunity to share or participate in the appreciation of land values as a result of settlement. White

men could pre-empt 320 acres and purchase as many more. Some Indians were assigned as little as nine acres, almost none were acquainted with pre-emption laws, and in any case few had the necessary capital for purchasing land. In a different perspective, it could be said that again the white man visualized no future for the Indian.

Less than two years later, a Dominion Order-in-Council of March 21, 1873 recommended that the provincial government assign eighty acres of land to every Indian family of five persons. The provincial government refused to follow this recommendation and suggested that twenty acres for each family of five was more appropriate. In 1874 the Indians began a long series of protest petitions to the Federal Government. Now there was a three-way deadlock between the two levels of government and Indian protest groups. Out of this deadlock eventually came, in 1887, a joint Federal-Provincial Royal Commission assigned to review the issues. This commission sat doggedly for nearly twenty years, riddled with internal dissension, and caught between opposing policies. Its report in four volumes was published in 1916.[14] It was during this period that the British Columbia Government took the unprecedented move of appointing an Indian Commissioner for the province, despite the stipulation of Section 91 of the B.N.A. Act that Indian matters were under Federal jurisdiction.

Another major source of difficulty between the government of British Columbia and the Dominion was the issue of "reversionary interest" in Indian lands. Imperial policy had assumed Indian lands as vested in the Crown. The Government of British Columbia, however, insisted that the title of alienated Indian lands must revert to the province. In a Dominion Order-in-Council of November 5, 1875, the Federal Government recognized the provincial reversionary interest. Now in addition to Indian anxiety about acreage and location of lands precipitated by Clause 13 of the Order admitting British Columbia to the Union, Indians were faced with the additional problem of having any lands they might seek to alienate revert to a government whose Indian policies they already opposed.

Policy disagreement between levels of government since Confederation varies considerably by the region involved. These disagreements have been *one* important factor in the whole complex of issues which have helped to retard the settlement of Indian land claims. There were serious problems regarding Indian lands between the governments of Ontario and the Dominion (cf. C.11). References to Indian lands in the Manitoba and Saskatchewan Natural Resources Acts (C.12. C.14) and the *Railway Belt and Peace River Block* Act (C.13) are potential sources of difficulty in the same vein.

The major revisions of the Indian Act and their immediate con-
geners in previous Confederation legislation are presented here in their
entirety in order to facilitate comparison for the reader. While there is
considerable repetition between them, there are subtle shifts of emphasis in policy reflected throughout, often dependent on the placing of
a preposition or phrase. Nearly any selective procedure would serve to
obscure these. Above all, the Indian Acts are unique among Canadian
statutes. They are among the largest and lengthiest pieces of legislation
and are consequently of considerable complexity; they function as a
repository for policies derived from long historical trends in Canadian
society; and finally, they undertake to circumscribe and direct on a
comprehensive basis virtually every feature of Indian social life in
Canada.

In the years immediately following the B.N.A. Act of 1867,
Indian matters continued to be regulated by Pre-Confederation Legislation with the addition of a series of statutes largely focused on administrative procedures required to administer them in the context of Confederation. In the nine years between the B.N.A. Act (1867) and the
first *Indian Act* (1876), no basic new social policies were introduced
except for some further definition of band councils and their legislative
responsibilities (C.3, sections 10-12); it was essentially a period of
administrative housekeeping. Indians were now the principal statutory
responsibility of the Secretary of State, and the basis for the pattern of
Indian Affairs administration which has essentially continued to the
present time is now complete.

The first Indian Act (1876) (cf. C.8) has the full title *An Act to
Amend and Consolidate the Laws Respecting Indians*. Indeed the
emphasis is on consolidation; most of the amendments involved simply
serve to integrate and make consistent legislative material covering a
considerable time-span enacted by a variety of legislative bodies.

A major revision of the *Indian Act* in 1880 (C.10) made very
explicit some of the policies which we have already identified as the
"moral premise" in Canadian Indian legal history. In addition to
elaborating the sections dealing with intoxicants, two lengthy sections
(95, 96) concerning sexual promiscuity and prostitution are introduced.
It was under the *Indian Act* (1880) that attempts were eventually made
to suppress the potlatch, spirit-dancing, and other ceremonies. It was
only with the revision of the *Indian Act* in 1951 (C. 15) that these were
no longer legally proscribed. Here we may see the classic "pater-
nalism" of which Canadian Indian policy has so often been accused.
While intended to "protect" Indians, it can readily be argued that
curtailment of civil liberties was involved. Something of the same may
be seen in Sections 32 and 33 of the *Indian Act* (1951). To prevent
exploitation of Indians farming in the prairies provinces, Indians were

TABLE 1:

Location of Principal Issues in the Indian Acts of 1876, 1880, and 1951, and their Precedents in other Legislation.

Topic	Indian Acts			Sample of Precedents*
	1876 (C.8)	1880 (C.10)	1951 (C.15)	
	Sections	Sections	Sections	
Indian "Status"	3.3-3.5, 64-73	2, 11-14, 75-80, 81-89	5-17, 42-45, 48-50, 87-90, 103-108	B.9, B.12, B.15, B.16, C.2, C.3, C.7
Enfranchisement	3.5, 86-94	99-107	109-113	B.15, C.2, C.3
Reserve Lands	4-22	15-43	18-31, 35-36, 124	B.8, B.9, B.10, B.13, B.16, C.2, C.3
Management, Sale, Lease of Lands	25-44	46-55	37-41, 53-60, 124	B.8, B.9, B.10, B.16, C.2, C.3
Management, Sale, Lease of Resources	45-57	27, 56-71	32-33, 71, 93	B.8, B.9, B.10, C.2, C.3
Intoxicants	79-85	79, 90-94	94-102	B.1, B.3, B.4, B.6, B.16, B.18, C.2, C.3, C.7
Band Structure and Powers	23-24, 58-60, 61-73	72-74	34, 61-69, 74-86	C.2, C.3
Admissibility of Indian Evidence Under Oath	74-78	85-89	—	B.17, C.7

*Reference numbers are to items included in this volume.

not allowed to sell farm stock or produce to non-Indians without prior written consent of the Indian Superintendent. The effect was to prevent Indians from taking best advantage of agricultural markets open to other prairie farmers. These sections have since been repealed. Certainly, too, the proscription of intoxicants can well be argued to have curtailed Indian civil liberties. This has been argued before Canadian courts.

The *Indian Act* was, and is, constantly being revised. It is not possible here to examine all of these revisions, let alone examine the Indian Acts themselves with the attention they deserve. Table 1 indicates some of the principal topics covered by the various Indian Acts and indicates some of their historical sources in preceding legislation. Considerable continuity will be noted since the union of Upper and Lower Canada. However, several trends of change may be noted briefly:

1. The question of Indian "status" becomes progressively more elaborate and precise. It bears close affinity to the question of land, band organization, and participation in band equity accruing from land and resource sales and leases.
2. Legislation to facilitate both individual and band enfranchisement becomes progressively elaborated and detailed. These must be considered in any study of "assimilation" and "integration" policies.
3. The structure of band councils and their responsibilities are progressively refined, and progressively more responsibility and power is handed over to local bands.
4. Legislation reflecting the "moral premise" reaches a peak in the *Indian Act* (1880); with the exception of legislation on intoxication, other issues (e.g. prostitution, potlatch and spirit-dancing, and the admissibility of Indian evidence under oath in courts of law) are rapidly attenuated in the legislation since.

Section D: Indian "Treaties"

The question of "Indian treaties" is extremely complex, not least because the words are used to denote documents of several distinctive kinds. Only a few examples of "treaties" are given here, but in them may be found most of the key features (and their variations) of this kind of document.

The "Selkirk Treaty" of 1817 (D.1) is simplest in structure, and is similar to many previous North American treaties. It is clearly a bill of surrender of a specified tract of land in return for an annual quit-rent payment. One may easily question the justice of the quit-rent consisting of two hundred pounds of tobacco *per annum*. Much more important in a structural sense is the decision to pay a quit-rent rather than a full purchase price over a specific period of time. Quit-rents or annual ''presents'' or payments are a common feature of Indian treaties since earliest times. Since the amounts are usually fixed by agreement, they are not responsive to economic inflation and changing values, and have been a continuous source of grievance for Indians. For example, Treaty Number Eleven (1921) grants an annual payment of ''equipment, such as twine for nets, ammunition and trapping [sic] to the value of three dollars per head to each Indian who continues to follow the vocation of hunting, fishing and trapping'' (D.4). In 1921, three dollars purchased a considerable amount of such commodities. Today, it purchases less than one-quarter of a standard fish net. Grievances over such arrangements cannot fail to become a chronic source of discontent, for they are annual reminders in perpetuity of perceived injustices.

The ''Robinson Superior Treaty'' of 1850, important as a model for Post-Confederation treaties, is a direct surrender of rights in a specified area of land. An initial payment is made in addition to annual payments. Unlike the ''Selkirk Treaty,'' the ''Robinson Superior Treaty'' specifies that subsurface resources will be sold for the benefit of the band as a whole, and this only by order of the Superintendent-General of the Indian Department. It also grants continuing rights of usufruct over unsettled portions of the ceded territory. It clearly vests the land title in the Crown. In addition, specific reserves for the exclusive use of Indians are set aside within the territory.

''Treaty Number One'' (D.3) of 1871, the first of the treaties concluded after Confederation, is in many ways closely patterned on late Pre-Confederation treaties (e.g. ''The Robinson Superior Treaty''). However, it adds certain significant new elements. It specifies that a council of chiefs and councillors be authorized by the Indians both to negotiate the treaty and to assist in its subsequent administration. This insistence on band structures is a prominent feature of the Post-Confederation Indian Acts and treaties. The treaty specifically proscribes intoxicants, both within and without the ceded territory. Like other Post-Confederation treaties, it guarantees provision of educational facilities. Others also guarantee at least minimal medical services. Finally, there are several mentions in the document that the treaty is to be an agreement of ''perpetual peace''.

''Treaty Number Eleven'' (D.4), concluded in 1921-1922, one of the latest Post-Confederation Treaties, is closely patterned on ''Treaty Number One''. It is also of interest since it shows clearly the method by which local bands and groups subsequently made adhesion to it. It includes a most significant feature of late treaties, that is the cession not only of the rights to a specific tract of land but also of "the Indian rights, titles and privileges whatsoever to all other lands wherever situated in the Yukon Territory, the Northwest Territories or in any other portion of the Dominion of Canada." While a promise is made to set aside reserve lands under this treaty, in fact the reserves have not yet been allocated.

Cumming and Mickenberg[15] show that so-called "Indian treaties" conform closely to neither of the two common meanings in law of the word "treaty", although they combine elements of both these meanings. In one meaning, a "treaty" denotes a compact or agreement between two or more sovereign nations. In the other meaning, in private law, "treaty" denotes "the discussion of terms . . . immediately prior to the making of a contract."[16] As Cumming and Mickenberg show, historically and legally Indian treaties have not been recognized as having the status of international treaties between two or more separate and sovereign nations.[17] Yet in the list of characteristics we give below, certain features of Indian treaties clearly evince elements of international treaties.

In certain situations, on the other hand, judicial decisions have recognized the analogy between Indian treaties and private agreements, "offers to treat", and contracts.[18]

In our view, the fully-developed "Indian treaty" in Canada consists of some or all of at least the following elements or characteristics:

1. an agreement of peace and amity;
2. the cession of land, both as specific tracts or as rights to all lands in the Dominion;
3. initial payments to Indians, either to each individual "taking treaty" or to bands as corporate bodies;
4. the designation of chiefs and councillors to negotiate the treaty, and to assist in its subsequent administration;
5. small annual payments in cash and/or goods variously described as quit-rents, presents, or gifts (these derive historically, at least in part, from the practice of making annual gifts of "grace and favour" or "bounty and benevolence", a prominent feature of Indian/non-Indian relations in early contact times in North America);
6. guarantee of rights of usufruct over unoccupied territories, either or both within or without tracts ceded in treaties;
7. guarantee of lands reserved for the use of Indians;
8. promises to provide health, educational, or other services.

These, then, are complex and varied documents. While the components are inter-related, each one in itself is fertile ground for social and legal conflict.

Finally, while these documents clearly reflect national policy towards Indians, especially when viewed in historical perspective, it can never be assumed that these truly reflect the agreement and understanding of the Indians. In coming years, these treaties and the historical legislation to which they are related bode well to become burning political and legal issues. The resolution of these issues are moral, political, and legal imperatives which Canadians cannot escape.

FOOTNOTES

[1] Georges Gurvitch, *Sociology of Law* (London: Routledge and Kegan Paul, 1947).

[2] Georg Simmel, "Conflict," in *Conflict and the Web of Group Affiliations*, trans. Kurt R. Wolff (Free Press, 1955), esp. pp.13-28,35-48. Further development of Simmel's work on conflict may be found in Lewis H. Coser, *The Functions of Social Conflict* (New York: Free Press, 1956).

[3] Valuable insight into French Indian policy can be found in: J.H. Kennedy, *Jesuit and Savage in New France* (New Haven: Yale University Press, 1950); Bruce Trigger, "The French Presence in Huronia: The Structure of Franco-Huron Relations in the First Half of the Seventeenth Century, *Canadian Historical Review*, vol. XLIX (1968), pp. 107ff.; Yves Zoltvany, "The Frontier Policy of Philippe de Rigaud de Vaudreuil, 1713-1725," *Canadian Historical Review*, vol. XLVIII (1967), pp.227ff.; G.F.G. Stanley, "The Policy of 'Francisation' as Applied to the Indians during the Ancien Regime,: *Révue d'Histoire de l'Amerique Francais*, vol. 3 (1949), pp. 333ff.; G.F.G. Stanley, "The First Indian 'Reserves' in Canada," *Révue d'Histoire de l'Amérique Francaise*, vol. 4 (1950), pp.169ff.; Peter A. Cumming and Neil H. Mickenberg, *Native Rights in Canada* (2nd. ed.) (Toronto: The Indian-Eskimo Association of Canada and General Publishing Co. Ltd., 1972), esp. Ch. 11, pp.75-91.

[4] F.E. Laviolette, *The Struggle for Survival* (Toronto: University of Toronto Press, 1961), esp. Ch's 2 and 3.

[5] Kenneth Lysyk, "The Unique Constitutional Position of the Canadian Indian," *Canadian Bar Review*, vol. 45 (1967), pp.513-553.

[6] F.E. Laviolette, *op. cit.*, pp. 14-15.

[7] W.E. Connolly (ed.), *The Bias of Pluralism* (New York: Atherton, 1969), p.3.

[8] Raymond Aron, "Social Structure and the Ruling Class," *British Journal of Sociology*, vol. 1 (1950), pp.1-16; Edward A. Shils, *The Torment of Secrecy* (London: Heinemann, 1956), pp.55ff., 207; W.Kornhauser, *The Politics of Mass Society* (London: Routledge and Kegan Paul, 1960), p.104.

[9] Ralf Dahrendorf, *Class and Class Conflict in Industrial Society* (Stanford: Stanford University Press, 1959), p.317.

[10]J.S. Furnivall, *Colonial Policy and Practice* (London: Cambridge University Press, 1948); Leo Kuper and M.G. Smith, *Pluralism in Africa,* (Berkeley: University of California Press, 1969); M. G. Smith, *The Plural Society in the British West Indies* (Berkeley: University of California Press, 1965).

[11]Derek G. Smith, *Natives and Outsiders: Pluralism in the Mackenzie River Delta*, unpub. Ph.D. dissertation, Harvard University, 1971; "The Implications of Pluralism for Social Change Programs in a Canadian Arctic Community," *Anthropologica*, n.s.,vol. XIII, No's. 1-2 (1971), pp. 193-214.

[12]Bora Laskin, *Canadian Constitutional Law*, 4th. rev. ed. (Toronto: Carswell, 1973), p.119.

[13]F.E. Laviolette, *op.cit.*, pp. 111-112.

[14]*Report of the Royal Commission on Indian Affairs for the Province of British Columbia*, 4 vols. (Victoria: Acme Press, 1916).

[15]Peter A. Cumming and Neil H. Mickenberg, *op.cit.*, esp. Ch.9, pp.53-62 ("The Legal Nature of Indian Treaties")

[16]Peter A. Cumming and Neil H. Mickenberg, *op.cit.*, p.54.

[17]Peter A.Cumming and Neil H. Mickenberg, *loc. cit.*

[18]Peter A. Cumming and Neil H. Mickenberg, *op.cit.*, p.56.

Section A

The Early British Colonial Period, 1760-1826

A1.

Articles of Capitulation Between their Excellencies Major-General Amherst, Commander-in-Chief of his Brittanic Majesty's Troops and Forces in North America, on the One Part, and the Marquis de Vaudreuil, Governor and Lieutenant-General for the King in Canada on the Other. Montreal, September 8, 1760. (Extracts)

* * *

Article VIII.

The Officers, Soldiers, Militia, Seamen and even the Indians, detained on account of their wounds or sickness, as well as in the hospital, as in private houses, shall enjoy the privileges of the cartel, and be treated accordingly.—"The sick and wounded shall be treated the same as our own people."

Article IX

The British General shall engage to send back, to their own homes, the Indians, and Moraignans, who make part of his armies, immediately after the signing of the present capitulation, and, in the mean time, the better to prevent all disorders on the part of those who may not be gone away, the said Generals shall give safe-guards to such persons as shall desire them, as well in the town as in the country. "The first part refused."—There "never have been any cruelties committed by the Indians of our army: "and good order shall be preserved."

* * *

Article XL

The Savages or Indian allies of his most Christian Majesty, shall be maintained in the Lands they inhabit; if they chuse to remain there; they shall not be molested on any pretence whatsoever, for having carried arms, and served his most Christian Majesty; they shall have, as well as the French, liberty of religion, and shall keep their missionaries. The actual Vicars General, and the Bishop, when the Episcopal see shall be filled, shall have leave to send to them new Missionaries when they shall judge it necessary.—"Granted except the last article, which has been already refused."

* * *

Article XLVII

The Negroes and panis of both sexes shall remain, in their quality of slaves, in the possession of the French and Canadians to whom they belong; they shall be at liberty to keep them in their service in the colony or to sell them; and they may also continue to bring them up in the Roman Religion—"Granted, except those who shall have been made prisoners."

A2.

Royal Proclamation, October 7, 1763. (Extract)

* * *

And whereas it is just and reasonable, and essential to our Interest, and the Security of our Colonies, that the several Nations or Tribes of Indians with whom We are connected, and who live under our Protection, should not be molested or disturbed in the Possession of such Parts of our Dominions and Territories as, not having been ceded to or purchased by Us, are reserved to them, or any of them, as their Hunting Grounds.—We do therefore, with the Advice of our Privy Council, declare it to be our Royal Will and Pleasure, that no Governor or Commander in Chief in any of our Colonies of Quebec, East Florida, or West Florida, do presume, upon any Pretence whatever, to grant Warrants of Survey, or pass any Patents for Lands beyond the Bounds of their respective Govern-ments, as described in their Commissions; as also that no Governor or Commander in Chief in any of our other Colonies or Plantations in America do presume for the present, and until our further Pleasure be known, to grant Warrants of Survey, or pass Patents for any Lands beyond the Heads or Sources of any of the Rivers which fall into the Atlantic Ocean from the West and North West, or upon any Lands whatever, which, not having been ceded to or purchased by Us as aforesaid, are reserved to the said Indians, or any of them.

And, We do further declare it to be Our Royal Will and Pleasure, for the present as aforesaid, to reserve under our Sovereignty, Protection, and Dominion, for the use of the said Indians, all the Lands and Territories not included within the Limits of Our said Three new Governments, or within the Limits of the Territory granted to the Hudson's Bay Company, as also all the Lands and Territories lying to the Westward of the Sources of the Rivers which fall into the Sea from the West and North West as aforesaid;

And We do hereby strictly forbid, on Pain of our Displeasure, all our loving Subjects from making any Purchases or Settlements whatever, or taking Possession of any of the Lands above reserved, without our especial leave and Licence for that Purpose first obtained.

And, We do further strictly enjoin and require all Persons whatever who have either wilfully or inadvertently seated themselves upon any Lands within the Countries above described, or upon any other Lands which, not having been ceded to or purchased by Us, are still reserved to the said Indians as aforesaid, forthwith to remove themselves from such Settlements.

And Whereas great Frauds and Abuses have been committed in purchasing Lands of the Indians, to the great Prejudice of our Interests, and to the great Dissatisfaction of the said Indians; In order, therefore, to prevent such Irregularities for the future, and to the end that the Indians may be convinced of our Justice and determined Resolution to remove all reasonable Cause of Discontent, We do, with the Advice of our Privy Council strictly enjoin and require, that no private Person do presume to make any Purchase from the said Indians of any Lands reserved to the said Indians, within those parts of our Colonies where, We have thought proper to allow Settlement; but that, if at any Time any of the said Indians should be inclined to dispose of the said Lands, the same shall be Purchased only for Us, in our Name, at some public Meeting or Assembly of the said Indians, to be held for that Purpose by the Governor or Commander in Chief of our Colony respectively within which they shall lie; and in case they shall lie within the limits of any Proprietary Government, they shall be purchased only for the Use and in the name of such Proprietaries, conformable to such Directions and Instructions as We or they shall think proper to declare and enjoin, that the Trade with the said Indians shall be free and open to all our Subjects whatever, provided that every Person who may incline to Trade with the said Indians do take out a Licence for carrying on such Trade from the Governor or Commander in Chief of any of Our Colonies respectively where such Person shall reside, and also give Security to observe such Regulations as We shall at any Time think fit, by ourselves or by our Commissaries to be appointed for this Purpose, to direct and appoint for the Benefit of the said Trade:

And we do hereby authorize, enjoin, and require the Governors and Commanders in Chief of all our Colonies respectively, as well those under Our immediate Government as those under the Government and Direction of Proprietaries, to grant such Licences without Fee or Reward, taking especial Care to insert therein a Condition, that such Licence shall be void, and the Security forfeited in case the Person to whom the same is granted shall refuse or neglect to observe such Regulations as We shall think proper to prescribe as aforesaid.

And we do further expressly enjoin and require all Officers whatever, as well Military as those Employed in the Management and Direction of Indian Affairs, within the Territories reserved as aforesaid for the use of the said Indians, to seize and apprehend all Persons whatever, who standing charged with Treason, Misprisions of Treason, Murders, or other Felonies or Misdemeanors, shall fly from Justice and take Refuge in the said Territory, and to send them under a proper guard to the Colony where the Crime was committed of which they stand accused, in order to take their Trial for the same.

Given at our Court at St. James's the 7th Day of October 1763, in the Third Year of our Reign.

GOD SAVE THE KING

A3.

Instructions to Governor Murray, December 7, 1763. (Extract)

* * *

60. And whereas Our Province of Quebec is in part inhabited and possessed by several Nations and Tribes of Indians, with whom it is both necessary and expedient to cultivate and maintain a strict Friendship and good Correspondence, so that they may be induced by Degrees, not only to be good Neighbours to Our Subjects, but likewise themselves to become good Subjects to Us; You are therefore, as soon as you conveniently can, to appoint a proper Person or Persons to assemble, and treat with the said Indians, promising and assuring them of Protection and Friendship on Our part, and delivering them such Presents, as shall be sent to you for that purpose.

61. And you are to inform yourself with the greatest Exactness of the Number, Nature and Disposition of the several Bodies or Tribes of Indians, of the manner of their Lives, and the Rules and Constitutions, by which they are governed or regulated. And You are upon no

Account to molest or disturb them in the Possession of such Parts of the said Province, as they at present occupy or possess; but to use the best means You can for conciliating their Affections, and uniting them to Our Government, reporting to Us, by Our Commissioners for Trade and Plantations, whatever Information you can collect with respect to these People, and the whole of your Proceedings with them.

62. Whereas We have, by Our Proclamation dated the seventh day of October in the Third year of Our Reign, strictly forbid, on pain of Our Displeasure, all Our Subjects from making any Purchases or Settlements whatever, or taking Possession of any of the Lands reserved to the several Nations of Indians, with whom We are connected, and who live under Our Protection, without Our especial Leave for that Purpose first obtained; It is Our express Will and Pleasure, that you take the most effectual Care that Our Royal Directions herein be punctually complied with, and that the Trade with such of the said Indians as depend upon your Government be carried on in the Manner, and under the Regulations prescribed in Our said Proclamation.

* * *

A4(a).

Instructions to Governor Carleton, January 3, 1775. (Extract)

* * *

32. It is Our Royal Intention, that the Peltry Trade of the interior Country should be free and open to all Our Subjects, Inhabitants of any of Our Colonies, who shall, pursuant to what was directed by Our Royal Proclamation of 1763, obtain Licences from the Governors of any of Our said Colonies for that purpose, under penalties to observe such Regulations, as shall be made by Our Legislature of Quebec for that purpose; Those Regulations therefore, when established, must be made public throughout all Our American possessions, and they must have for their object the giving every possible facility to that Trade, which the nature of it will admit, and as may consist with fair and just dealing towards the Savages, with whom it is carried on. The fixing stated times and places for carrying on the Trade, and adjusting modes of settling Tariffs of the prices of Goods and Furs, and above all the restraining the Sale of Spirituous Liquors to the Indians will be the most probable and effectual means of answering the ends proposed. These and a variety of other regulations, incident to the nature and purpose of the Peltry Trade in the interior Country, are fully stated in a Plan proposed by Our Commissioners for Trade and Plantations in 1764, a

copy of which is hereunto annexed, and which will serve as a Guide in a variety of cases, in which it may be necessary to make provision by Law for that important Branch of the American Commerce.

* * *

A4(b).

Plan for the Future Management of Indian Affairs, Referred to in the Thirty-second Article of the Foregoing Instructions to Governor Carleton, January 3, 1775.

1. That the Trade and Commerce with the several Tribes of Indians in North America under the protection of His Majesty shall be free and open to all His Majesty's subjects, under the several Regulations and Restrictions hereafter mentioned, so as not to interfere with the Charter to the Hudson's Bay Company.

2. That for the better Regulation of this Trade, and the Management of Indian Affairs in general, the British Dominions in North America be divided into two Districts, to comprehend and include the several Tribes of Indians mentioned in the annexed Lists A. and B.

3. That no Trade be allowed with the Indians in the southern District, but within the Towns belonging to the several Tribes included in such District; and that in the Northern District the Trade be fixed at so Many Posts, and in such Situations, as shall be thought necessary.

4. That all Laws, now in Force in the several Colonies for regulating Indian Affairs, or Commerce, be repealed.

5. That there be one general Agent or Superintendant appointed by His Majesty for each District.

6. That the Agent or Superintendant for the Northern District shall be allowed three Deputies to assist him in the Administration of Affairs within his District; and that the Agent or Superintendant for the Southern District shall be allowed two Deputies.

7. That there shall be a Commissary, Interpreter, and Smith, appointed by His Majesty to reside in the Country of each Tribe in the Southern District, and at each Post in the Northern District.

8. That it be recommended to the Society for the propagation of the Gospel in foreign parts to appoint four Missionaries in each District, to reside at such places, as the Agent or Superintendant for each District shall recommend.

9. That the Commissaries, Interpreters, and Smiths in each District do Act under the immediate Direction and Orders of the Agent or

Superintendant, who shall have a power of Suspending them in Case of Misbehaviour, and, in Case of Suspension of a Commissary, or of a Vacancy by Death, or Resignation, the Office shall be executed, until the King's pleasure is known, by one of the Deputies to the Agent or Superintendant.

10. That the said Agent or Superintendant shall have the Conduct of all public Affairs relative to the Indians; and that neither the Commander in Chief of His Majesty's Forces in America, nor any of the Governors and Commanders in Chief of any of the Colonies, or persons having military Commands in any of the Forts within each of the said Districts, do hold any General Meetings with the Indians, or send any public Talks to them without the Concurrence of the Agent or Superintendant, unless in cases of great Exigency, or when the said Agent or Superintendant may be in some remote part of his District.

11. That the said Agents or Superintendants do in all Affairs of political consideration, respecting peace and war with the Indians, purchases of Lands, or other Matters, on which it may be necessary to hold any general Meetings with the Indians, advise and act in concert with the Governors, (or the Governors and Councils, as the Occasion may require), of the several Colonies within their respective Districts; And that the said Agents or Superintendants shall be Councillors extraordinary within each Colony in their respective Districts, in like manner as the Surveyors General of the Customs for the Northern and Southern Districts of America.

12. That the Governor or Commander in Chief of every Colony be directed to communicate to the Agent or Superintendant of that District, within which his Government lyes, all such Information and Intelligence, as he may receive respecting Indian Affairs; And that the Agents or Superintendants shall in like manner communicate to the Governors all Intelligence and Information, respecting the State of Indian Affairs, which may in any wise regard the Security and Interest of the said Colonies.

13. That no Order shall be issued by the Governor or Commander in Chief of any of His Majesty's Colonies, or by any Officer having Military Command in any Forts within the Indian Country, for stopping the Trade with any Tribe of Indians in either of the said Districts, without the Concurrence and Consent of the Agent or Superintendant for Indian Affairs.

14. That the said Agents or Superintendants shall by themselves, or sufficient Deputies visit the several Posts or Tribes of Indians within their respective Districts once in every year, or oftener, as Occasion shall require, to enquire into, and take an Account of the Conduct and Behaviour of the subordinate Officers at the said Posts, and in the

Country belonging to the said Tribes; to hear Appeals; and redress all Complaints of the Indians; make the proper Presents; and transact all Affairs relative to the said Indians.

15. That for the maintaining peace and good Order in the Indian Country, and bringing Offenders in criminal Cases to due Punishment, the said Agents or Superintendants, as also the Commissaries at each Post, and in the Country belonging to each Tribe, be empowered to Act as Justices of the Peace in their respective Districts and Departments, with all powers and priviledges vested in such Officers in any of the Colonies; and also full power of Committing Offenders in Capital Cases, in order that such Offenders may be prosecuted for the same; And that, for deciding all civil actions, the Commissaries be empowered to try and determine in a Summary way all such Actions, as well between the Indians and Traders, as between one Trade and another, to the Amount of Ten Pounds Sterling, with the Liberty of Appeal to the Chief Agent or Superintendant, or his Deputy, who shall be empowered upon such appeal to give Judgement thereon; which Judgement shall be final, and process issue upon it, in like manner as on the Judgement of any Court of Common Pleas established in any of the Colonies.

16. That for the easy attainment of Justice, the evidence of Indians, under proper Regulations and Restrictions, be admitted in all Criminal as well as civil causes, that shall be tried and adjudged by the said Agents or Superintendants, or by the said Commissaries; and that their Evidence be likewise admitted by the Courts of Justice in any of His Majesty's Colonies or Plantations in Criminal cases, Subject to the same Pains and Penalties in Cases of false Evidence, as His Majesty's Subjects.

17. That the said Agents or Superintendants shall have power to Confer such Honors and Rewards on the Indians, as shall be necessary; and of granting Commissions to principal Indians in their respective Districts to be War Captains or Officers of other Military Distinctions.

18. That the Indians of each Town in every Tribe in the Southern District shall choose a beloved Man to be approved of by the Agent or Superintendant for such District, to take care of the Mutual Interests both of Indians and Traders in such Town; and that such beloved Men, so elected and approved in the several Towns, shall elect a Chief for the whole Tribe, who shall constantly reside with the Commissary in the Country of each Tribe, or occasionally Attend upon the said Agent or Superintendant, as Guardian for the Indians and Protector of their Rights, with Liberty to the said Chief to be present at all Meetings and upon all Hearings or Trials relative to the Indians before the Agent or Superintendant, or before the Commissaries; and to give his Opinion upon all Matters under Consideration at such Meetings or Hearings.

19. That the like Establishments be made for the Northern District, as far as the Nature of the Civil Constitution of the Indians in this District, and the Manner of Administering civil affairs will admit.

20. That no person having any Military Command in the Indian Country shall be capable of Acting as Commissary for the Affairs of the Indians; in either of the above mentioned Districts respectively; nor shall such person having military Command be allowed to carry on trade with the Indians, or to interpose his Authority in any thing, that regards the Trade with, or civil Concerns of the Indians; but to give the Commissary or other Civil Magistrate all Assistance in his power, whenever thereunto required.

21. That the said Commissaries shall keep exact and regular Accounts, by way of Journal, of all their Transactions and Proceedings, and of all Occurrences in their respective Departments, and shall by every opportunity communicate such Transactions and Occurrences to the Agent or Superintendant in their respective Districts; which Agent or Superintendant shall regularly by every Opportunity correspond with the Commissioners for Trade and Plantations.

22. That the Agent or Superintendant, to be appointed for each District, as also the Commissaries residing at the Posts, or in the Indian Country within each District, shall take an Oath before the Governor or Chief Judge of any of the Colonies within their respective Districts, for the due Execution of their respective Trusts; and they and all other subordinate Officers, employed in the Affairs of the Indians, shall be forbid, under proper Penalties, to carry on any Trade with them, either upon their own Account, or in Trust for others, or to make any Purchase of, or accept any Grants of Lands from the Indians.

23. That for the better regulation of the Trade with the said Indians, conformable to their own Requests, and to prevent those Frauds and Abuses, which have been so long and so loudly complained of in the manner of carrying on such Trade, all Trade with the Indians in each District be carried on under the Direction and Inspection of the Agents or Superintendants, and other subordinate Officers to be appointed for that purpose, as has been already mentioned..

24. That all Persons intending to trade with the Indians shall take out Licences for that purpose under the Hand and Seal of the Governor or Commander in Chief of the Colony, from which they intend to carry on such Trade, for every of which Licences no more shall be demanded or taken than two Shillings.

25. That all persons taking out Licences shall enter into Bond to His Majesty, His Heirs, and Successors in the Sum of   with one Surety in the Sum of   for the due observance of the Regulations prescribed for the Indian Trade.

26. That every Person willing to give Security, and finding a

Security willing, if required, to take an Oath, that he is possessed of property to double the value of the Sum he stands security for, shall be intitled to a Licence.

27. That every such Licenced Trader shall at the time of taking out the Licence, declare the Post or Truck house, at which or the Tribe of Indians with which he intends to trade, which shall be specified in the Licence itself.

28. That no Licence be granted to continue longer than for one Year.

29. That no Person trade under such Licence, but the person named in it, his Servants, or Agents, whose Names are to be inserted in the Margents; and in Case any of the Servants or Agents named in such Licence shall die, or be discharged, the same shall be notified to the Governor, by whom the Licence was granted, or to the Commissary of the Post, or in the Tribe, where such Trader carries on Trade, to the end that the Name or Names of any other Servants or Agents, employed by the said Trader in the place of those dead or discharged, may in like manner be inserted in the Margent of the Licence.

30. That all Licences be entered in the Secretary's Office, or other proper Office of Record in each Colony, where they are taken out; for which Entry no more shall be demanded or taken than Six pence for each Licence; and all persons to have free Liberty to inspect such Entry, paying a Fee of Six pence for the same.

31. That Persons trading with the Indians without a Licence, and without giving the Security above required, or trading at any other Posts or places, than those expressed in their Licences, do forfeit all the Goods they shall be found then trading with, and also pay a Fine of   to His Majesty, His Heirs, and Successors, and suffer   Months Imprisonment.

32. That all Traders immediately upon Arrival at the posts or Truck houses in the Northern district, or in the Tribes in the Southern district, for which Licences have been taken out, and before any Goods are sold to, or bartered with the Indians, do produce such Licences to the Commissaries appointed for the Direction and Inspection of the Trade at such posts, or Truck houses, or in such Tribes.

33. That all Trade with the Indians shall be carried on by Tariffs, to be settled and Established from time to time by the Commissaries at the several Posts, or Truck houses, or in the Countries belonging to the several Tribes in Concert with the Traders and Indians.

34. That the Commissaries appointed to direct and inspect the Trade at each Truck house in the Northern District, shall be empowered to fix and prescribe Limits round each Post or Truck house, within which Limits all Trade with the Indians may be commodiously carried on in the most public Manner.

35. That all Traders have free Liberty to erect Hutts and Warehouses within such Limits, in such Order and Manner as the Commissary shall, with the concurrence of the Officer Commanding at such Post, Direct and appoint.

36. That no Trader shall Traffic, or have any Dealings with the Indians without the Limits prescribed by the Commissary or other Chief Officer appointed for the Inspection and Direction of the Trade.

37. That each Truck house or post of Trade in the Northern District be fortified and garrisoned; and that all Traders have free Liberty to retire into such Garrison with their Effects, when ever any Disturbance shall Arise, or the Commissary at such post shall represent it to be necessary.

38. That no Trader shall sell or otherwise supply the Indians with Rum, or other spirituous Liquors, Swan Shot, or rifled Barrelled Guns.

39. That in Trade with the Indians no Credit shall be given them for Goods in Value beyond the Sum of fifty Shillings; and no Debt beyond that Sum shall be recoverable by Law or Equity.

40. That all Disputes concerning Weights or Measures in the buying or selling Goods shall be decided by Standard Weights and Measures, to be kept in each Post or Truck-house in the Northern District, and in each Tribe in the Southern District.

41. That no private person, Society, Corporation, or Colony be capable of acquiring any Property in Lands belonging to the Indians, either by purchase of, or Grant, or Conveyance from the said Indians, excepting only where the Lands lye within the Limits of any Colony, the soil of which has been vested in proprietors, or Corporations by Grants from the Crown; in which Cases such Proprietaries or Corporations only shall be capable of acquiring such property by purchase or Grant from the Indians.

42. That proper Measures be the Consent and Concurrence of the Indians, to ascertain and define the precise and exact Boundary and Limits of the Lands, which it may be proper to reserve to them, and where no Settlement whatever shall be allowed.

43. That no purchases of Lands belonging to the Indians, whether in the Name and for the Use of the Crown, or in the Name and for the Use of proprietaries of Colonies be made but at some general Meeting, at which the principal Chiefs of each Tribe, claiming a property in such Lands, are present; and all Tracts, so purchased, shall be regularly surveyed by a Sworn Surveyor in the presence and with the Assistance of a person deputed by the Indians to attend such Survey; and the said Surveyor shall make an accurate Map of such Tract, describing the Limits, which Map shall be entered upon Records, with the Deed of Conveyance from the Indians.

It is estimated, that the annual Expence of supporting the Establishments, proposed in the foregoing plan, providing presents for the Indians, and other contingent Expences, may amount to about twenty thousand pounds; and it is proposed to defray this Expence by a Duty upon the Indian Trade, either collected upon the Exportation of Skins and Furs, (Beaver excepted,) from the Colonies, or payable by the Traders at the posts and places of Trade, as shall, upon further Examination and the fullest Information, be found most practicable, and least burthensome to the Trade.

A.

List of Indian Tribes in the northern District of North America.

Mohocks.	Powtewatamis.
Oneidas.	Ottawas.
Tuscaroras.	Chipeweighs, or Missisagis.
Onondagas.	Meynomenys.
Cayugas.	Folsavoins.
Senecas.	Puans.
Oswegachys.	Sakis.
Nanticokes.	Foxes.
Conoys.	Twightwees.
Tuteeves.	Kickapous.
Saponeys.	Mascoutens.
Caghnawagas.	Piankashaws.
Canassadagas.	Wawiaghtonos.
Arundacks.	Keskeskias.
Algonkins.	Illinois.
Abenaquis.	Sioux.
Skaghquanoghronos.	Micmacs.
Hurons.	Norwidgewalks.
Shawanese.	Arseguntecokes.
Delawares.	Penobscots.
Wiandots.	St Johns.

B.

List of Indian Tribes in the southern District of North America.

Cherokees.	Attucapas.
Creeks.	Bayugtas.
Chickasaws.	Tunicas.
Chactaws	Peluches
Catawbas,	Ofugulas.
Beluxis.	Querehas.

Endorsed : Drt

Instructions for Guy Carleton Esqr Govr of Quebec, Dated 3d Jany 1775.
In Order of Council of 28th Decemr 1774.

George R

C.O.

A5.

Instructions to Sir Guy Carleton, Governor-in-Chief and Captain-General, August 23, 1786. (Extract)

* * *

4th You are to obtain as soon as possible, an account of the actual Number of Our Subjects residing in Our said Province, distinguishing the Old from the New Inhabitants, and again distinguishing those who have retired from the Province, now the United States of America, and those who have been in Our Service during the late War, and whose Corps have been reduced; and you are also to Obtain the most authentick Information, whether any of the Nations of Indians in alliance and Friendship with Us, continue to reside within the Territories of the United States of America, and the Boundaries thereof, as settled by the Treaty of Peace; and whether those Indians, or any others within Our Territories, are supplied with goods from the subjects of the said United States, or have any commercial or other Intercourse with them; and You are to transmit the same to Us thro one of our Principal secretaries of State as before directed, together with any Information, or proposition, by which you may think, proper and effectual Measures may be taken, to Induce those Indians to remove within Our Territories, and to discontinue any Intercourse with the subjects or Inhabitants of the said United States, which may Lessen Our Influence with them, and be prejudicial to Our Service, and the Interest and Commerce of Our Subjects.

* * *

A6.

Instructions to Lord Dorchester as Governor of Upper Canada, September 16, 1791. (Extract)

* * *

55. It is our Royal Intention that the Peltry Trade of the Interior Country shall be free and open to all Our Subjects Inhabitants of any of Our Colonies who shall pursuant to what was directed by Our Royal Proclamation of 1763 obtain Trading Licences from the Governors of any of Our said Colonies under Penalties to observe such Regulations as shall be made by Our Legislature of Our Province of Upper Canada for that Purpose. These Regulations therefore when established, must be made public throughout all Our American possessions and they must have for their Object the giving every possible facility to that Trade which the nature of it will admit, and which may be consistent with fair and just dealing towards the Native Indians with whom it is carried on; the fixing stated times and places for carrying on the Trade and adjusting Modes of settling Tariffs or the prices of Goods and Furs and above all the restraining the Sale of Spirituous Liquors to the Indians, will be the most probable and effectual Means of answering the Ends proposed.

* * *

A7.

"Jay's Treaty" of Amity, Commerce, and Navigation, November 19, 1794. (Extract)

* * *

Article III

It is agreed that it shall at all times be free to His Majesty's subjects, and to the citizens of the United States, and also to the Indians dwelling on either side of the said boundary line, freely to pass and repass by land or inland navigation into the respective territories and countries of the two parties on the continent of America, (the country within the limits of the Hudson's Bay Company only excepted), and to navigate all the lakes, rivers and waters thereof, and freely to carry on trade and commerce with each other. But it is understood that this article does not extend to the admission of vessels of the United States into the sea-ports, har-bours, bays or creeks of His Majesty's said territories; nor into such parts of the rivers in His Majesty's said territories as are between the mouth thereof and the highest port of entry from the sea, exept in small vessels trading *bona fide* between Montreal and Quebec, under such regulations as shall be established to prevent the possibility of any frauds in this respect. Nor to the admission of British vessels from the sea into the rivers of the United States, beyond the highest ports of entry for foreign vessels from the sea. The river Mississippi shall, however, according to the treaty of peace, be entirely open to both parties; and it is further agreed that all the ports and places on its eastern side, to whichsoever of the parties belonging, may freely be resorted to and used by both parties, in as ample a manner as any of the Atlantic ports or places of the United States, or any of the ports or places of His Majesty in Great Britain.

All goods and merchandize whose importation into His Majesty's said territories in America shall not be entirely prohibited, may freely, for the purposes of commerce, be carried into the same in the manner aforesaid by the citizens of the United States, and such goods and merchandize shall be subject to no higher or other duties than would be payable by His Majesty's subjects on the importation of the same from Europe into the said territories. And in like manner all goods and merchandize whose importation into the United States shall not be wholly prohibited, may freely, for the purposes of commerce, be carried into the same, in the manner aforesaid, by His Majesty's subjects, and such goods and merchandize shall be subject to no higher or other duties than would be payable by the citizens of the United States on the importation of the same in American vessels into the Atlantic ports of the said States. And all goods not prohibited to be exported from the said territories respectively, may in like manner be carried out of the same by the two parties respectively, paying duty as aforesaid.

No duty of entry shall ever be levied by either party on peltries brought by land or inland navigation into the said territories respectively, nor shall the Indians passing or repassing with their own proper goods and effects of whatever nature, pay for the same any impost or duty whatever. But goods in bales, or other large packages, unusual among Indians, shall not be considered as goods belonging *bona fide* to Indians.

No higher or other tolls or rates of ferriage than what are or shall be payable by natives, shall be demanded on either side; and no duties shall be payable on any goods which shall merely be carried over any of the portages or carrying-places on either side, for the purpose of being immediately re-embarked and carried to some other place or places. But as by this stipulation it is only meant to secure to each party a free passage across the portages on both sides, it is agreed that this exemption from duty shall extend only to such goods as are carried in the usual and direct road across the portage, and are not attempted to be in any manner sold or exchanged during their passage across the same, and proper regulations may be established to prevent the possibility of any frauds in this respect.

As this article is intended to render in a great degree the local advantages of each party common to both, and thereby to promote a disposition favourable to friendship and good neighbourhood, it is agreed that the respective Governments will mutually promote this amicable intercourse, by causing speedy and impartial justice to be done, and necessary protection to be extended to all who may be concerned therein. . . .

* * *

A8(a).

Letter, Lord Portland to Lieutenant-Governor Simcoe Regarding Military and Civil Administration of Indian Affairs, September 3, 1795.

Whitehall, 3d. Septr. 1795.

Lt. Govr. Simcoe,

Sir,

I have received and laid before The King your Letters of the dates and numbers mentioned in the Margin with their several Inclosures.

As your Sentiments respecting the *Commissariat* and the *Indian Department* but more especially repecting the latter, are fully detailed in Nos 20 and 21, it will not be so necessary for me in my Answer to these points to advert to Nos 18 and 19, as they discuss the same Subjects.

From the terms in which I have already stated my opinion as to the Nature of those Departments, both in my Letters to Lord Dorchester and Yourself, I should hope that their execution under their present Constitution, might be carried on with the best possible effect both to The King's Service, and the Civil Interest of the Province of Upper Canada.

From the nature of those Departments they are placed, and allowed to be properly placed under the Authority of the Commander in

Chief in the first instance, with powers to be delegated by him, and executed under his directions. When Upper Canada became a separate Province, it evidently appeared that those Departments, particularly the Indian, would in many respects bear an intimate relation to, and have connection with the Civil Policy and Government of that Province. This Circumstance naturally led to representations, that the Commander in Chief, in exercising his primary Authority over those Departments, in cases where their Administration was connected with the Civil Policy and Government of Upper Canada, would of course arrange such Administration upon communication, and in concert with the Person entrusted with the Executive Authority of that Province, although the Authority over the Departments themselves continued (as it still does) to be vested in the Commander in Chief.

Having thus shortly stated the case, as it actually stands, I cannot but seriously regret the want of that Mutual Concert and arrangement which appear to me to be so easy and practicable, and which are of such Consequence at this moment, when so much depends upon a proper impression being made on the minds of the Indians within the Boundary Line of 1783, in the Upper Province. As far as my own ideas go, I should be more inclined to confine any part of the Authority of the Indian Department which might be delegated by the Commander in Chief in certain Cases touching the Civil Government of Upper Canada to the Lieutenant Governor in person, than to the Lieutenant Governor and Council. The Concert and Communication between those two great Officers would by this means be more immediate, and better kept up—And I should imagine that the same assistance might be received by the Lieutenant Governor from the Officers in the Indian Department merely as such, in Upper Canada, (in Consequence of Orders from the Commander in Chief for that purpose) as if they joined to their situation that of being Members of the Executive Council of that Province.

The Circumstances which have delayed the publication of our Treaty with America, are highly to be lamented, as no time should be lost in preparing the minds of the Indians for the Evacuation of the Posts, conformably to the Ideas expressed in my former Letters on this Subject of the 19th of November and 8th of January last.

Some of the Measures suggested in Your Letter to Lord Dorchester of the 9th of March last, especially those which relate to holding General Councils of the Indians, would I conceive, be very conducive to this purpose, and might be the means of giving them a true notion of their future situation with regard to us, and of the nature of the present Treaty, which in fact, by giving up the precarious and contingent tenure of the Posts, secures to us and the Indians, both within and without the Line of 1783, the most unrestrained intercourse and communication, and both the power and the means of trading with each other to an extent, which is denied to the Americans, from the very nature of their situation with regard to the Indians.

I am &c.

PORTLAND.

Endorsed:—Drat.
To Lt Govr Simcoe
1795.

A8(b).

Additional Instructions Relating to the Indian Department, December 15, 1796.

ADDITIONAL INSTRUCTION to the Governor Lieutenant Governor or the Person Administering the Government of Our Province of Upper Canada for the time being. Given at Our Court at Saint James's the 15th day of December 1796 In the Thirty seventh Year of Our Reign.

WHEREAS we judge it to be conducive to the better Regulation of Our Concerns with the Indian Nations within Our Province of Upper Canada, that the same should be conducted by the Person exercising the Government of Our said Province for the time being. It is therefore Our Will and Pleasure, That you do take upon you the Conduct and Management of Our Concerns with the said Indians within the Province of Upper Canada, and that you do from time to time give to all Persons whom it may concern, such Directions for the due Execution of these, Our Instructions, as occasion may require, such Directions nevertheless to be subject to any special Orders directed to you, from such Person as shall at any time be constituted & appointed by Us to be Governor General of Our Provinces in North America. And It is Our Will and Pleasure, That all Persons holding Commissions in the Indian Department within Our Provinces of Lower and Upper Canada, so far as the same relates to the Province of Upper Canada, shall follow such Orders and Directions as they shall from time to time receive from you in the Execution of this Our Instruction, any thing in the said Commissions to the contrary notwithstanding. And you are in case of any Vacancy in any Office or Place in the said Indian Department within Our Province of Upper Canada, to transmit to Us by the first opportunity thro' one of Our Principal Secretaries of State, the name of such Person, with an Account of his Character and Services, as You shall esteem to be best qualified for fulfilling the Duties of such Office, for Our further Directions therein.

GEORGE R.

A8(c).

Letter, Lord Portland to the Duke of York Regarding Military and Civil Administration of Indian Affairs, February 21, 1800.

WHITEHALL, 21st Feby 1800

SIR,—

By the Copy of His Majesty's Instructns to the Lieut. Govr, or the Person administering the Government of Upper Canada for the time being, dated the 15th Decr 1796, which I herewith beg leave to lay before Your Royal Highness, it will appear to Your Royal Highness that the Person in whose hands the Executive Authority of Upper Canada is placed, is exclusively vested with the management of the Indian Department in that Province, and the recommendation of the Officers necessary to conduct it [subject to His Majesty's approbation:] Your Royal Highness will also observe that the Instructions inclosed are formed so absolutely on that Principle, that the Power of giving any special Order with respect to that Department in case of any sudden emergency which may require it, is cautiously witheld from the Commander in Chief, and restricted to the Govr Genl in His Civil Capacity [should there be any such Officer as Govr Genl then in being] so that it will be evident to Your Royal Highness that no connection or intercourse whatever does or was intended to exist in this respect between the Departments of Commander in Chief of North America, and the Civil Government of Upper Canada: Your Royal Highness will therefore see the necessity I am under of representing to Your Royal Highness against the exercise of a Power, which I am persuaded has been inadvertently assumed By His Royal Highness The Duke of Kent in His Capacity of Commander in Chief of His Majesty's Forces in North America, by the Appointment of a Person to the Office of Deputy Superintendt Genl of Indians, which was held by the late Col. McKee, and which is, as Your Royal Highness will observe by the Instructions above referred to, an Office in the Civil Establishment of Upper Canada, & distinctly in the appointment of the Civil Government of that Province.—

I forbear from troubling Your Royal Highness with a Detail of the Duties of the Office, or with the reasons which make it indispensibly

necessary that it should be fill'd by a Person who is intimately conver-
sant with the Interest, disposition, Language & customs of the Indians
in that quarter of the World, because it will be evident to Your Royal
Highness's superior Judgement, that in this as well as in every other
instance, the Administration of His Majesty's Colonial Government
cannot be carried on with Propriety, unless the Govrs, Lieut. Govrs or
Persons administering the same, are alone responsible for the exercise
of that Authority which His Majesty has thought proper to place in their
hands, that it is therefore absolutely necessary that their responsibility
should in no degree be diminished by the interference of any other
Person, the consequence of which would be to afford & hold out a
ground of excuse or apology to be resorted to on the Part of the
Governors in the Colonies for any Act of misconduct which they might
commit in the administration of the Governments over which they
preside.

  Having felt it to be my duty to represent this case to the King, I
have received His Majesty's Commands to acquaint Your Royal Highness that it is His Majesty's Pleasure that His Royal Highness the Duke
of Kent should be forthwith informed that the Civil Concerns of all His
Majesty's North American Provinces, and the appointments to Civil
Offices of every Description within the same can only be managed and
recommended to, by the Persons administering the Civil Government
therein, submitted to the King through that Department, with which His
Majesty has directed them to correspond: and consequently that the
Office lately held by Col. McKee is now, and must be considered to all
intents and purposes as vacant, until His Majesty's Pleasure with
respect to Col. McKee's Successor be signified to the Lt Govr of Upper
Canada, whose duty it is to submit [in conformity to the inclosed
instructions] thro' one of His Majesty's Principal Sectys of State, the
Name of such Person, with an Acct of his Character & Services, as he
shall esteem to be best qualified for fulfilling the duties of such Office,
for His Majesty's further directions therein. It being His Majesty's
opinion, that a strict & invariable adherence to these Commands of His
Majesty is indispensibly necessary to preserve the conduct & Management of the Public Service in its regular & established Course.—

I am

[Signed]   PORTLAND.

H. R. H.
The Duke of York.

A9.

The Treaty of Ghent, December 24, 1814. (Extract)

* * *

Article IX.

The United States of America engages to put an end, immediately after the ratification of the present treaty, to hostilities with all the tribes or nations of Indians with whom they may be at war at the time of such ratification; and forthwith to restore to such tribes or nations, respectively, all the possessions, rights and privileges which they may have enjoyed or been entitled to in one thousand eight hundred and eleven, previous to such hostilities: Provided always that such tribes or nations shall agree to desist from all hostilities against the United States of America, their citizens and subjects, upon the ratification of the present treaty being notified to such tribes or nations, and shall so desist accordingly. And His Britannic Majesty engages, on his part, to put an end immediately after the ratification of the present treaty, to hostilities with all the tribes or nations of Indians with whom he may be at war at the time of such ratification, and forthwith to restore to such tribes or nations respectively all the possessions, rights and privileges which they may have enjoyed or been entitled to in one thousand eight hundred and eleven, previous to such hostilities: Provided always that such tribes or nations shall agree to desist from all hostilities against His Britannic Majesty, and his subjects, upon the ratification of the present treaty being notified to such tribes or nations, and shall so desist accordingly.

* * *

A10(a).

Letter, Sir Peregrine Maitland to Lord Bathurst Regarding the Status of Indians as Subject to British or Canadian Law, February 14, 1823.

Upper Canada: York,
14th February 1823.

My Lord,

I have the honor to acquaint your Lordship that at the last Assizes held in the Western District of this Province an Indian was fully convicted of the Murder of another Indian in the Streets of Amherstburg, and sentenced to suffer death. The circumstances of the case, and the causes which led the Judge of Assize to suspend the execution of the sentence, and to make a special report of the case, are fully detailed in Mr Justice Campbells Report, and in the accompanying papers.

On receipt of this Report. I caused the other Judges to be referred to: the Report of Mr Justice Boulton will be found in the enclosure No 3 and that of the Chief Justice, together with an Extract from his charge to the Grand Jury of the same District at a former Assize, in the enclosures Nos 4 and 5. A Petition from the Convict himself is also forwarded.

There being no precedent on record in this Province of a Case similar to the present, and the evident discrepancy in the sentiments of the Judges on the Policy of making individuals of the Indian Tribes amenable to our Laws for Offences committed amongst themselves, have induced me to order that the prisoner be respited until the decision of His Majesty's Government on the matter can be obtained. In order to which purpose, I have now the honor to submit the subject for your Lordship's consideration.

I have the honor to be,

My Lord,

Your Lordship's

Most Obedient

Humble Servant,

P. MAITLAND.

A10(b).

Letter, Lord Bathurst to Sir Peregrine Maitland Regarding the Status of Indians as Subject to British or Canadian Law, August 11, 1823.

DOWNING STREET

11th Augt 1823

SIR,

Having referred to the consideration of Mr. Secretary Peel your letter of the February last transmitting the case of an Indian Convicted of Murder I have now the Honor to transmit to you the Copy of a letter from Mr. Hobhouse stating that Mr Peel wishes before he takes The King's Pleasure on this case to be informed whether there exists any Such Treaty as is alluded to in Mr. Justice Campbell's letter of the

9th Septr 1822; and I am to desire that you will furnish me with the information required by Mr Peel.

I have the Honor to be
Sir,
Your most obed Servant

Bathurst

Major General
    Sir P. MAITLAND K.C.B.
        &c   &c

A10(c).

Letter, Sir Peregrine Maitland to Lord Bathurst Regarding the Status of Indians as Subject to British or Canadian Law, November 4, 1825.

UPPER CANADA
YORK, 4th November 1825

MY LORD,

With reference to Your Lordship's despatch of the 11th of August 1823, I have the honor to report that after the most diligent Search in the records of the Indian Department in this Country, there appears to exist no treaty that can give color to the idea that an Indian is not to be considered as amenable to the Law for offences committed against another Indian within His Majesty's dominions.

I have the honor to be,
My Lord,
Your Lordship's
Most Obedient
Humble Servant

P. MAITLAND.

The EARL OF BATHURST K.G.
    &c.ra   &c.ra   &c.ra

A10(d).

Warrant for the Execution of an Indian as Subject to British or Canadian Law, February 13, 1826.

WARRANT FOR EXECUTION OF INDIAN, 1826.

George R.

Whereas Shawanakiskie, an Indian of the Ottawa Tribe, was at the Assizes holden for the Western Circuit in Our Province of Upper Canada, in or about the Month of August in the year One thousand Eight hundred and twenty two, tried and Convicted of the Murder of another Indian at Amherstburgh in Our said Province and had Sentence of Death passed upon him for the same; but Execution was Respited by Our Lieutenant Governor of Our said Province, until Our Pleasure should be known, on the ground of there being no precedent on Record in that Province of a similar Case, and of doubts whether the Indians were ameanable by Law to Our Courts, for Offences committed within Our Territory, against each other.— And Whereas We thought fit to refer the Proceedings in the said Case to Our Advocate, Attorney and Solicitor General for their Opinion, who have Reported unto Us that the Conviction of said Shawanakiskie was proper; and that no valid Objection exists against the Jurisdiction of the Court before which the said Shawanakiskie was tried. Now We considering the Heinousness of the said Offence, Think it just that the said Sentence should be carried into full effect, and Our Will and Pleasure therefore is that Execution be done thereupon, unless in the case hereinafter next provided for But inasmuch as some circumstances unknown to Us may be Known to you Our Governor of Our Provinces of Upper and Lower Canada, or to you Our Lieutenant Governor of Our said Province of Upper Canada which may render it inexpedient to Execute the same, We are therefore graciously pleased to declare Our further Will and Pleasure, that if there shall appear to you or either of you to be good reason for not carrying the said Sentence into full effect, you do cause to be passed under the Great Seal of Our said Province of Upper Canada Our Most Gracious Pardon of the said Murder and Felony upon Condition that the said Shawanakiskie be Transported to New South Wales or Van Dieman's Land or some one or other of the Islands adjacent for and during the Term of his Natural Life, or be Imprisoned in some Prison in the said Province and there kept to hard Labour for the same Term, as to you or either of you shall seem most meet and agreeable to Justice.— And for so doing this shall be Your Warrant.

Given at Our Court at Carlton House, the 13th day of February 1826, in the Seventh Year of Our Reign.

To Our Right Trusty and Right Welbeloved Cousin Lieutenant General George, Earl of Dalhousie, Our Governor and Commander in Chief of Our Provinces of Upper and Lower Canada, Our Lieutenant Governor of Our Province of Upper Canada, and all others whom it may concern.

By His Majesty's Command—

Rob Peel

Warrant vesting the Governor or Lieutenant Governor of Upper Canada with discretionary Power in the case of Shawanakiskie Convicted of Murder

Section B

Pre-confederation Legislation, 1663-1916.

B1.

Decree of the Superior Council of Québec Forbidding all Persons to Trade or Give Intoxicating Liquors to Indians, September 28, 1663. (Translation)

ON what has been demonstated by the King's Attorney-General that since the founding of this colony the trading of intoxicating liquors to the Indians has always been prohibited and forbidden under penalty of discretionary fine because of the rage in which these peoples find themselves when intoxicated; and that it is established that they desire to drink only to become intoxicated; and that notwithstanding the pursuit and punishment of offenders this disorder had come to such a state that it had come to the attention of His Majesty; by decree of the King's Council of State dated March 7, 1657 it had been forbidden to deal in the said liquors with the Indians under penalty of corporal punishment. In contempt of the said prohibitions as well as censures made by the Church this wretched commerce has continued; and notably in these last two years many have taken the liberty of vying with one another due to the relaxation of bringing delinquents to punishment; and seeing the growing disorder which has resulted, and that the Indians were inclined towards drunkenness, despising the laws of Christianity and giving themselves to all sorts of vices and abandoning the hunt, by which this colony has subsisted to the present time; it is required that a suitable remedy be produced, and further having taken the advice of the Reverend Jesuit Fathers, missionaries to the said Indians, summoned for this purpose, and everything having been considered:

The prohibitions and interdictions are reiterated to all persons of whatever rank or station, neither to deal nor give directly or indirectly to the Indians any intoxicating liquors for whatever reason or under whatever pretext, not even one drink, under penalty of 300 pounds (livres) payable for the first offence, a third payable to the informer, a third to the Hôtel-de-Dieu, and a third to the Treasury (Fisc); and in the case of repeated offence flogging or banishment depending on the particulars of the case.

And this decree will be read, published and posted in the accustomed places in Québec, Trois-Rivières, and Montréal so that no person may plead ignorance.

By order, etc.,

Signed: Mézy, G.

Francois, Bishop of Pétrée

Rouer de Villeray

B2.

Decree of the Superior Council of Québec Subjecting Indians to the Penalty Carried by the Laws of France Concerning Murder and Rape, April 21, 1664. (Translation)

Present in the assembled Council: His Excellency the Governor, His Excellency the Bishop, Messrs. de Villeray and Damours, the Attorney-General of the present King, and later on the Messrs. de la Ferté and de Tilly.

On that which has been introduced by the Attorney-General of the King following the rape committed on the person of Marthe Hubert, wife of   called Lafontaine, resident of the Isle d'Orléans, by   called Robert Hache, an Indian, who for this reason was made prisoner and then escaped custody; in order to accommodate to the customs of the Indians, our allies, who are ignorant of our laws and the penalties prescribed for the punishment of the majority of crimes, notably that of rape; therehaving been assembled before the said Council: the person named Noël Tek8erimat, chief of the Algonquins of Québec; Kaetmaguechis, commonly called Boyer, chief of Tadoussac; Mangouche, chief of the Nipissing Indians; Gahyk8an, chief of the Iroquois Indians; Nauck8ape8ith, called le Saumonnier, chief of the   , and Jean-Baptiste Pipouikih, Abenaki Captain, in order to answer for the said Robert Hache and to see cause why, for the punishment of the said rape, the said Robert Hache would have deserved to have been hanged and strangled. This having been understood by the said Indians through Nicholas Marsollet, accepted as interpreter in the presence of Father Drouillettes of the Society of Jesus, the said Indians with the said Noël Tek8erimat acting as spokesman interpreted by the said Marsollet, stated that for a great many years they had always remained in with friendship with the French; that if their youths had not been able to behave so well on certain occasions which may have given cause for complaint, neither had French youths been any more blameless; that until the present they had not been led to understand that rape, but only murder, was punishable by death and so the misdeed of the said Robert Hache, the same of which he had not been proven guilty, should neither for a first offence be faced by the rigour of the law nor injure so ancient a friendship; but that for the future they would make themselves subject to the law and that to this end they requested that this be drawn up in writing so that it might be preserved for their descendants. And in order to continue to live in friendship and avoid the obstacles which may prevent it, it will be necessary to prohibit Frenchmen, creditors of the Indians, from plundering and harrassing them while in default of payment, all the more so because during this time of war it is impossible for the Indians to satisfy their debts entirely, being able to hunt only half of the time:

The Council, after having deliberated the matter, has pardoned and now pardons the said Robert Hache of the penalty which he had deserved by reason of the said rape, barring the civil interests of the said Marthe Hubert; and to prevent future such disorders, with the consent of the said Tek8erimet, Kaetmaguechis, Mangouche, Gahyk8an, Nauck8ape8ith and Pipouikh, has ordered and now orders that the said Indians submit to the penalties carried by the laws and ordinances of France concerning murder and rape, which things having been given to them to be understood through the said interpreter; and it is ordered that they make it known to all people in their nations so that none may be ignorant of it; and with regard to the constraints that the French, creditors of the said Indians, place upon them in order to be paid, it will be made lawful according to the requirements of the case.

B3.

Ordinance in Favour of the Inhabitants of Notre-Dame-des-Neiges Bearing on the Clause of Confiscation Inserted in their Contracts of Concession against those who Give Brandy to the Indians to be Null and Void, July 2, 1706, (Translation)

The inhabitants of Notre-Dame-des-Neiges and others on the Island of Montréal, having demonstrated to us that in the contracts of concession which have been made with them is inserted a clause of confiscation of their lands in the event that they give brandy and other intoxicating liquors to the Indians, to which having been liable, those who do not fall into that category will not permit themselves to be exposed daily to inconveniences that people of ill intention might cause them; in falsely supposing that they would sell the said liquors, which are so expressly forbidden by the ordinances of the King, this clause is presently useless; and after having heard le Sieur Cailhé, who told us that the seigneurs had never had the intention of benefiting from the labour of the said inhabitants by inserting this clause in their contracts, but only to assist in averting the disorders for which the ordinance of the King had provided; in consideration of which:

We order that the said inhabitants will enjoy the said concessions without the said clause being of any consequence against them, nevertheless enjoining them to observe the ordinances under penalty of punishment of the full effect of the law in the event of infraction. By order, etc.

Made and given at our Residence in Montréal, July 2, 1706.

Signed: RAUDOT

B4.

Decree of the Superior Council of Québec which Orders the Registration of the Ordinance by His Majesty, which Prohibits the Sale of Intoxicating Liquors to the Indians of this Country, October 24, 1707. (Translation)

Present in the assembled Council: Messrs. Raudot, Intendants, Messrs. de Lotbinière, Dupont, DeLino, Hazeur, Aubert, and Maccart, Councillors.

Considered by the Council was the ordinance of the King given at Versailles, the 30th of June last, by which His Majesty made very express prohibitions and interdictions to all His subjects of whatever rank or condition to neither sell to nor cause to be drunk any brandy or intoxicating liquors by the Indians of this country in future, under penalty of confiscation of the liquors, half of the value of which to be paid to the informer, and of corporal punishment in case of repeated offences; confirmed, and this demands that Monsieur Charles Maccart, Councillor, perform the function of Attorney-General to the King.

The Council has ordered and now orders that the said ordinance of His Majesty be registered with the Clerk of Court in order to be executed according to its form and terms, and that at the responsibility of the said Sieur Maccart it be read, published and posted in all the necessary and accustomed places and points.

Signed: RAUDOT

B5.

Ordinance on the Subject of Negroes and the Indians Called Panis,
April 13, 1709. (Translation)

Having a perfect knowledge of the advantage that this colony might
derive if it could securely locate here, by purchases that the inhabitants
might make of some of the Indians called Panis, whose nation is far
removed from this country, and who can only be obtained from those
Indians who go to capture them in their country and who traffic in them
most often with the English of the Carolinas and who have occasionally
sold them to people of this country, who frequently find themselves
defrauded of considerable sums they have given for them by an idea
inspired in them (the slaves) by those who have not purchased them,
which causes them almost always to leave their masters, and this under
the pretext that in France there are no slaves, which is not always true
with reference to those colonies which depend on them since on the
islands of this continent all negroes that the inhabitants purchase are
always regarded as such (as slaves); and since all the colonies must be
regarded on equal footing, and since the people of the Panis nation are
also necessary to the inhabitants of this region for the cultivation of the
land and other tasks which might be undertaken similar to those
performed by the negroes in the islands, and since these sorts of
engagements are very useful to this colony, and being necessary to
assure ownership (of slaves) to those who have purchased them and will
purchase them in the future:

We, by His Majesty's pleasure, decree that all Panis and negroes
who have been purchased and will be purchased in the future will fully
belong to those who have purchased them, as being their slaves;

We prohibit the said Panis and negroes from leaving their masters,
and anyone from enticing them to do so, under penalty of 50 pounds
(livres) fine.

We order that this decree be read and posted in the accustomed
places in the cities of Québec, Trois-Rivières, and Montréal and that it
be registered with the Clerks of the Provosts of these cities at the
responsibility of our subdelegates.

Made and given at our Residence in Québec, April 13, 1709.

Signed: RAUDOT

Read and published at the Church in Lower Town after 7 o'clock
Mass, and at the door of the Parish Church of this town of Québec after

High Mass, this 21st of April, 1709, by me, process-server and court-crier in the Provostship of Québec, there residing in Rue Saint-Pierre.

Signed: CONGNET

B6.

17 George III (1777) Cap. 7 (Province of Québec). An Ordinance to Prevent the Selling of Strong Liquors to the Indians in the Province of Québec, as also to Deter Persons from Buying their Arms or Cloathing, and for other Purposes Relative to the Trade and Commerce with the said Indians.

WHEREAS many mischiefs may be occasioned by the practice of selling rum and other strong liquors to the Indians, and of buying their cloaths and arms, and also by trading with the said Indians, or settling amongst them, without a licence; It is ordained and enacted, &c., that from and after the publication of this ordinance, no person or persons whatsoever shall sell, distribute, or otherwise dispose of, to any Indian or Indians within this Province, or to any other person or persons for their use, any rum or other strong liquors, of what kind or quality soever, or shall knowingly or willingly suffer the same, in any manner, to come to the hands of any Indian or Indians, without a special licence in writing for that purpose, first had and obtained from the Governor, Lieutenant-Governor, or Commander-in-Chief of this Province for the time being, or from His Majesty's agents or superintendants for Indian affairs, or from His Majesty's commandants of the different forts in this Province, or from such other person or persons as the Governor, Lieutenant-Governor, or Commander-in-Chief of the Province, for the time being, shall authorise for that purpose.

Every person offending herein shall, for the first offence, forfeit the sum of five pounds, and suffer an imprisonment for any time not exceeding one month, and for the second and every subsequent offence, shall forfeit ten pounds, and suffer an imprisonment for any time not exceeding two months.

If the person so offending, be a publican, innkeeper, or retailer of strong liquors, he shall, over and above the said penalty and imprisonment, be rendered incapable, from the day of his conviction, of selling or retailing liquors to any person whatsoever, notwithstanding any licence that he may have for that purpose, which licence is hereby declared to be null and void from the day of his conviction.

II. From and after the publication of this ordinance, no person or persons whatsoever shall purchase, or receive in pledge or in exchange, any cloaths, blankets, fire-arms or ammunition belonging to any Indian or Indians within this Province, under a penalty of five pounds, and imprisonment for any time not exceeding one month, for the first offence, and of ten pounds, and imprisonment for any time not exceeding two months, for the second and every other subsequent offence.

III. From and after the publication of this ordinance, it shall not be lawful for any person to settle in any Indian village or in any Indian country, within this Province, without a licence in writing from the Governor, Lieutenant-Governor, or Commander-in-Chief of the Province, for the time being, under a penalty of ten pounds for the first offence, and twenty pounds for the second and every other subsequent offence.

B7.

10 George IV (1829) Cap. 3 (Upper Canada). An Act the Better to Protect the Mississaga Tribes, Living on the Indian Reserve of the River Credit, in their Exclusive Right of Fishing and Hunting therein. /passed March 29, 1829/

WHEREAS heretofore the principal chiefs and warriors of the Mississaga Indians, that is to say, Cheehalk, Osenega, Acheton, and others of the said chiefs, for themselves and their people, did sell, make over, and surrender, by several deeds registered in the office of the secretary of the province, to his Majesty, King George the Third, his heirs and successors, divers large tracts of land lying between the river Etobicoke and the head of the lake Ontario, reserving to themselves, their people, and their posterity forever, amongst other portions of the said tracts, a certain parcel thereof on the river Credit, called in the Indian language the river Mazenahekasepa, with the sole right to the fisheries therein, which parcel of land so reserved is, in the office of the surveyor general, described as follows, that is to say; commencing in the southern boundary of the said reserve, at a large white oak squared post, planted by Mr. Wilmot, deputy surveyor, in the year one thousand eight hundred and six, standing on the bank of lake Ontario, one mile southwesterly from the said river; thence north sixty-nine degrees west, sixty-three chains, thirty-one links, more or less, to where the said boundary line forms the first angle; thence south sixty-four degrees west, one hundred and ninety-one chains, more or less, to where the said boundary line forms the second angle; thence north, forty-five degrees west, twenty chains, more or less, to within the distance of fifty chains of the eastern limit of Dundas street; thence north, thirty-eight degrees east, parallel to Dundas street, three hundred chains, more or less, to the intersection of the said line with the northern boundary line of the said reserve, produced on a course north sixty-nine degrees west, from a squared white oak post, planted in the year one thousand eight hundred and six, by the said deputy surveyor, piled with stone, near the bank of lake Ontario, one mile from the river Credit, at right angles from the general course to the first bend of the said river, which is north sixty-nine degrees west; thence along the said northern boundary line on a course south sixty-nine degrees east, one hundred and eighty-five chains, more or less, to lake Ontario, at the last mentioned squared post; thence along the water's edge of the said lake to the place of beginning, containing four thousand acres, more or less; and whereas the tribe of the said Mississagas living on the said river Mazenahekasepa, or Credit, have by petition to his excellency sir John Colborne, complained of many unwarrantable disturbances, trespasses, and vexations, practised by divers idle and dissolute fishermen, and others, upon the said reserved parcel of land and fishery aforesaid, thereby unjustly diminishing the source of their subsistence, wantonly destroying fish and game, and setting evil examples by their rudeness and ill manners towards the said worthy and unoffending people; and it is necessary to prohitbit such unwarrantable disturbances, trespasses, vexations, and evil example, in order to preserve to the said Mississaga people the quiet and peaceable enjoyment of their said land and fishery, and the rights and privileges thereunto belonging; be it therefore enacted by the King's most excellent Majesty, by and with the advice and consent of the legislative council and assembly of the province of Upper Canada, constituted and assembled by virtue of and under the authority of an act passed in the parliament of Great Britain, entitled, ''An act to repeal certain parts of an act passed in the fourteenth year of his Majesty's reign, entitled, 'An act for making more effectual provision for the government of the province of Quebec, in North America, and to make further provision for the government of the said province,' '' and by the authority of the same, That if, after the passing of this act, any person or persons whatsoever, against the will of the said Mississaga people, or without the consent of three or more of their principal men or chiefs, shall hunt or fish in any way, mode, or manner, whatsoever, for fish, or game, or fur, of any kind, upon the said reserved parcel of land and waters thereof, such person or persons so offending shall be liable to be taken by one of the principal men of the said Indian people, and one of the sworn constables of the said district, before any one of his Majesty's justices of the peace, convenient to the said reserved parcel of land, and being convicted by the oath of one or more creditable witness or witnesses, before such justice of the peace, shall be committed to prison in the next gaol, there remain for a space of time not less than one, nor more than three days; and the fish, flesh, game, and fur, taken with the offender, shall be deemed to belong to the Indians arresting and taking such offender; and the boat, skiff, canoe, net, spears, light-jacks, traps, springs, or other craft or implements in the possession of the offender at the time of the offence, or set, placed, laid, moved, or otherwise used by him in hunting or fishing on the said reserved land, and the waters thereof, against the provison of this law, shall be liable to be seized and taken by the said Indian people, and held and taken to be public property of the said Indian tribe, disposable at the discretion of their principal men or chiefs, for the public benefit of the said tribe.

II. And whereas it may be necessary to obviate all doubt or ignorance of the extent of the said right of fishing so necessary to the existence and support of the said Indian tribe living on the said river Mazenahekasepa, or Credit; be it therefore enacted by the authority aforesaid, That the said right to the sole fishery aforesaid shall be held and taken to extend through the entire stream, from Racey's line down its course, to its mouth, and from thence one mile into lake Ontario, occupying such a space thereon as may be supposed to be included in the segment of a circle, having the middle of the said river at its mouth as the centre, and the distance thence to the eastern boundary where it touches the shore as its radius, whereby to describe the said segment from the east to west boundaries thereof on the shore as aforesaid: Provided always, nevertheless, That nothing herein contained shall extend, or be construed to extend, to take away or in any wise diminish, the common law rights and remedies, which the said Indian people may at any time be desirous of availing themselves, as other subjects of his Majesty within this province, in protection of their lands from trespass, waste, or other damage whatsoever; neither shall any thing herein contained extend, or be construed to extend, to prevent or in any wise to obstruct any of his Majesty's subjects, in travelling, passing, and repassing, by themselves, their teams and carriages, by and along any public highway or road now or hereafter laid out by lawful authority, in or over any part of the said reserved land, nor to prevent or in any wise to obstruct any of his Majesty's subjects with their vessels, boats, and rafts, to navigate freely the said river and waters, for the purposes of trade or other lawful occasion.

III. And be it further enacted by the authority aforesaid, That this act shall continue in force for four years, and from thence to the end of the then next ensuing session of parliament, and no longer.

B8.

2 Victoria (1839) Cap. 15 (Upper Canada). An Act for the Protection of the Lands of the Crown in this Province from Trespass and Injury.
/passed May 11, 1839/

WHEREAS the lands appropriated for the residence of certain Indian Tribes in this Province, as well as the unsurveyed lands, and lands of the Crown ungranted and not under location, or sold or held by virtue of any lease or license of occupation, have from time to time been taken possession of by persons having no lawful right or authority so to do: *And whereas* the said lands have also been from time to time unlawfully entered upon, and the timber, trees, stone and soil, removed therefrom, and other injuries have been committed thereon; *And whereas* it is necessary to provide by law for the summary removal of persons unlawfully occupying the said lands, as also to protect the same from future trespass and injury: *Be it therefore enacted* by the Queen's most Excellent Majesty, by and with the advice and consent of the Legislative Council and Assembly of the Province of Upper Canada, constituted and assembled by virtue of and under the authority of an Act passed in the Parliament of Great Britain, intituled, "An Act to repeal certain parts of an Act passed in the fourteenth year of His Majesty's reign intituled, 'An Act for making more effectual provision for the Government of the Province of Quebec, in North America,' and to make further provision for the Government of the said Province," and by the authority of the same, That it shall and may be lawful for the Lieutenant-Governor of the Province, from time to time, as he shall deem necessary, to appoint two or more Commissioners under the Great Seal of this Province, to receive information, and to inquire into any complaint that may be made to them, or any one of them, against any person for illegally possessing himself of any of the aforesaid lands, for the cession of which to Her Majesty no agreement hath been made with the Tribes occupying the same, and who may claim title thereto; and also to inquire into any complaint that may be made to them, or any one of them, against any person for having unlawfully cut down or removed any timber, trees, stone or soil, on such lands, or for having done any other wilful and unlawful injury thereon.

II. *And be it further enacted by the authority aforesaid,* That if such Commissioners, or any one of them, shall upon investigation of any complaint made, as aforesaid, against any person for being unlawfully in possession of any of the lands herein-before mentioned, find and determine that such person is unlawfully in possession of such lands, it shall be lawful for the said Commissioners, or any one of them, to give notice to and require such person to remove from the occupation of such lands, within not less than thirty days from the day of the service of such notice; and if the person so required to remove from the occupation of such lands, shall neglect to remove from the same within the time specified in the said notice, it shall be lawful for the said Commissioners, or any one of them, to issue a warrant under their hands and seals, or the hand and seal of any one of them, directed to the Sheriff of the District wherein such lands are situate, commanding him to eject and remove the person in such warrant mentioned from the lands so unlawfully occupied by him; which warrant the Sheriff to whom the same is directed shall have full power and authority to execute, and shall execute and carry into effect, in the same manner as by law he is authorised to execute and carry into effect writs issued by Her Majesty's Courts of Law for restoring and delivering possession of lands recovered in any action of trespass in this Province.

III. *And be it further enacted by the authority aforesaid,* That if any person who shall have been removed from the lands and tenements aforesaid, in manner herein-before mentioned, shall return and unlawfully resume the occupation thereof, or any one of them, upon complaint made and satisfactory proof being adduced, that such person has returned and unlawfully resumed the occupation of the lands and tenements from which he had been removed, as aforesaid, to order and direct that he be committed to the common Gaol of the District in which such lands are situate, for a term not exceeding thirty days, and that he pay a fine to Her Majesty, Her Heirs and Successors, not exceeding twenty pounds.

IV. *And be it further enacted by the authority aforesaid,* That if any such Commissioners, or any one of them, shall upon investigation of any complaint made, as aforesaid, against any person for having unlawfully cut down or removed any timber or trees, or for having quarried upon, or removed any stone or other materials from the lands aforesaid, find the person charged with such offence guilty thereof, it shall be lawful for such Commissioners, or any one of them, to order and direct that he pay a fine to Her Majesty, not exceeding twenty pounds; and in default of paying the same, that he be committed to the common Gaol of the District, for a period not exceeding three months.

V. *And be it further enacted by the authority aforesaid,* That it shall and may be lawful for the Commissioners aforesaid, or any one of them, to order and direct that all timber and trees unlawfully cut down, or any stone quarried upon the lands aforesaid, and which have not been removed from off the same, be seized and detained, and to cause the same according to such instructions as they, from time to time, shall receive from the Lieutenant Governor to that effect.

VI. *And be it further enacted by the authority aforesaid,* That the Commissioners, or any one of them, appointed under and by virtue of this Act, shall have full power and authority to summon and call before them any person as a witness, to give evidence upon the subject of any complaint or matter the said Commissioners by this Act are authorised to investigate, and to administer in the usual form to such witness an oath, that he will true answer make to all such questions as shall be put to him in reference to the matter under investigation; and if such witness shall be guilty of wilful false swearing in giving his evidence, as aforesaid, he shall on conviction be deemed guilty of wilful and corrupt perjury, and be liable to be punished in the same manner as persons convicted of wilful and corrupt perjury are now by law liable to be punished.

VII. *And be it further enacted by the authority aforesaid,* That all monies and fines levied and collected under and by virtue of this Act shall, after deducting the expenses of collecting the same, be paid into the hands of the Receiver-General, and accounted for as part of the hereditary revenues of the Crown in this Province, or appropriated for the benefit of the Indian Tribes in this Province, in such manner as the Lieutenant Governor, by and with the advice and consent of the Executive Council of the Province shall direct, as the case may require.

VIII. *And be it further enacted by the authority aforesaid,* That when any person shall be charged with any offence against the provisions of this Act, the Commissioner appointed to examine into the same, shall before entering upon the investigation of such charge, summon the party accused to appear before him or them, at a place to be named in the said summons; and if he shall not appear there, upon proof of the due service of such summons, by delivering the same to him personally, the Commissioner or Commissioners may proceed to hear and determine the complaint *ex parte*.

IX. *And be it further enacted by the authority aforesaid,* That it shall be lawful for any Commissioner or Commissioners, duly appointed and acting under the authority of this Act, to issue any warrant or warrants under their hands and seals, directed to any Sheriff, Gaoler or Peace Officer, of the District in which any proceeding shall be had before them, commanding such Sheriff, Gaoler or Peace Officer, to carry into effect any order by them made in respect to any matter within their jurisdiction; and such warrant or warrants shall be executed by the Sheriff, Gaoler or Peace Officer, to whom the same may be directed, in the same manner as warrants issued by any of Her Majesty's Justices of the Peace are executed.

X. *And be it further enacted by the authority aforesaid,* That the Commissioners appointed under and by virtue of this Act, and all others acting under their authority, shall be entitled to the same privileges and protection in respect of any action or suit that may be instituted against them for any act by them done, that by law is granted and secured to any

Justice of the Peace, Sheriff, Gaoler or Peace Officer, against whom an action may be brought for any thing by him done in the execution of his office.

XI. *And be it further enacted by the authority aforesaid,* That in case any person shall be dissatisfied with the judgement or decision of the said Commissioners, it shall and may be lawful for him at any time, not exceeding three months from the date of such judgment or decision, upon giving fourteen days notice in writing of his intention to the said Commissioners, who shall thereupon transmit to the proper officer of the Court, for the use thereof, a copy of their judgment, together with the evidence taken before them the said Commissioners, to appeal therefrom to the Court of Chancery of this Province; and the Vice-Chancellor is hereby authorised and empowered to revise, alter, affirm or annul, the decision of the said Commissioners, or to order such further inquiry to be made, or if he shall see fit, to direct an issue to be tried at law touching the matter in dispute, and to make such orders and directions therein for payment of costs, and other matters respecting the same, as to him shall seem just and reasonable; and the decree of the said Court of Chancery to be given on such appeal shall be binding and conclusive on the party appealing, as well as on the said Commissioners.

B9.

13 and 14 Victoria (1850) Cap. 42 (Province of Canada). An Act for the Better Protection of the Lands and Property of the Indians in Lower Canada. /passed August 10, 1850/

WHEREAS it is expedient to make better provision for preventing encroachments upon and injury to the lands appropriated to the use of the several Tribes and Bodies of Indians in Lower Canada, and for the defense of their rights and privileges: Be it therefore enacted by the Queen's Most Excellent Majesty, by and with the advice and consent of the Legislative Council and of the Legislative Assembly of the Province of Canada, constituted and assembled by virtue of and under the authority of an Act passed in the Parliament of the United Kingdom of Great Britain and Ireland, and intituled, *An Act to re-unite the Provinces of Upper and Lower Canada, and for the Government of Canada,* and it is hereby enacted by the authority of the same, That is shall be lawful for the Governor to appoint from time to time a Commissioner of Indian Lands for Lower Canada, in whom and in whose successors by the name aforesaid, all lands or property in Lower Canada which are or shall be set apart or appropriated to or for the use of any Tribe or Body of Indians, shall be and are hereby vested, in trust for such Tribe or Body, and who shall be held in law to be in the occupation and possession of any lands in Lower Canada actually occupied or possessed by any such Tribe or Body in common, or by any Chief or Member thereof or other party for the use or benefit of such Tribe or Body, and shall be entitled to receive and recover the rents, issues and profits of such lands and property, and shall and may, in and by the name aforesaid, be subject to the provisions hereinafter made, exercise and defend all or any of the rights lawfully appertaining to the proprietor, possessor or occupant of such land or property: Provided always, that this section shall extend to any lands in Lower Canada now held by the Crown in trust for or for the benefit of any such Tribe or Body of Indians, but shall not extend to any lands now vested in any Corporation or Community legally established and capable in law of suing and being sued, or in any person or persons of European descent, although held in trust for or for the benefit of any such Tribe or Body.

II. And be it enacted, That all suits, actions or proceedings by or against the said Commissioner shall be brought and conducted by or against him by the name aforesaid only, and shall not abate or be discontinued by his death, removal from office or resignation, but shall be continued by or against his successor in office; and that such Commissioner shall have in each District in Lower Canada, an office which shall be his legal domicile, and whereat any process, notice or like matter may be legally served upon him, and may appoint such deputy or deputies, and with such powers as he shall from time to time deem expedient, or as he shall be instructed by the Governor to do: Provided always, that no suit or proceeding shall, during one month next after the passing of this Act, be commenced or proceeded with by or against the said Commissioner or any other party, with regard to any lands or property intended to be hereby vested in him, nor shall any prescription or limitation of time within which any proceeding or thing would otherwise require to be commenced, had or done, run or avail against the said Commissioner during the term last aforesaid.

III. And be it enacted, That the said Commissioner shall have full power to concede or lease or charge any such land or property as aforesaid, and to receive or recover the rents, issues and profits thereof as any lawful proprietor, possessor or occupant thereof might do, but shall be subject in all things to the instructions he may from time to time receive from the Governor, and shall be personally responsible to the Crown for all his acts, and more especially for any act done contrary to such instructions, and shall account for all moneys received by him, and apply and pay over the same in such manner, at such times and to such person or officer, as shall be appointed by the Governor, and shall report from time to time on all matters relative to his office in such manner and form, and give such security, as the Governor shall direct and require: and all moneys and moveable property received by him or in his possession as Commissioner, if not duly accounted for, applied and paid over as aforesaid, or if not delivered by any person having been such Commissioner to his successor in office, may be recovered by the Crown or by such successor, in any Court having civil jurisdiction to the amount or value, from the person having been such Commissioner and his sureties, jointly and severally.

IV. Provided always, and be it enacted, That nothing herein contained shall be construed to derogate from the rights of any individual Indian or other private party, as possessor or occupant of any lot or parcel of land forming part of or included within the limits of any land vested in the Commissioner aforesaid.

V. And for the purpose of determining any right of property, possession or occupation in or to any lands belonging or appropriated to any Tribe or Body of Indians in Lower Canada, Be it declared and enacted: That the following classes of persons are and shall be considered as Indians belonging to the Tribe or Body of Indians interested in such lands:

First.—All persons of Indian blood, reputed to belong to the particular Body or Tribe of Indians interested in such lands, and their descendants.

Secondly.—All persons intermarried with any such Indians and residing amongst them, and the descendants of all such persons.

Thirdly.—All persons residing among such Indians, whose parents on either side were or are Indians of such Body or Tribe, or entitled to be considered as such: And

Fourthly.—All persons adopted in infancy by any such Indians, and residing in the Village or upon the lands of such Tribe or Body of Indians, and their descendants.

VI. And be it enacted, That the Interpretation Act shall apply to this Act.

B10.

13 and 14 Victoria (1850) Cap. 74 (Province of Canada). An Act for the Protection of Indians in Upper Canada from Imposition, and the Property Occupied or Enjoyed by them from Trespass and Injury. /passed August 10, 1850/

WHEREAS it is expedient to make provision for the protection of the Indians in Upper Canada, who, in their intercourse with the other inhabitants thereof, are exposed to be imposed upon by the designing and unprincipled, as well as to provide more summary and effectual means for the protection of such Indians in the unmolested possession and enjoyment of the lands and other property in their use or occupation: Be it therefore enacted by the Queen's Most Excellent Majesty, by and with the advice and consent of the Legislative Council and of the Legislative Assembly of the Province of Canada, constituted and assembled by virtue of and under the authority of an Act passed in the Parliament of the United Kingdom of Great Britain and Ireland, and intituled, *An Act to re-unite the Provinces of Upper and Lower Canada, and for the Government of Canada,* and it is hereby enacted by the authority of the same, That no purchase or contract for the sale of land in Upper Canada, which may be made of or with the Indians or any of them, shall be valid unless made under the authority and with the consent of Her Majesty, Her Heirs or Successors, attested by an Instrument under the Great Seal of the Province, or under the Privy Seal of the Governor thereof for the time being.

II. And be it enacted, That if any person, without such authority and consent, shall in any manner or form, or upon any terms whatsoever, purchase or lease any lands within Upper Canada of or from the said Indians, or any of them, or make any contract with such Indians, or any of them, for or concerning the sale of any lands therein, or shall in any manner, give, sell, demise, convey or otherwise dispose of any such lands, or any interest therein, or offer so to do, or shall enter on, or take possession of, or settle on any such lands, by pretext or colour of any right or interest in the same, in consequence of any such purchase or contract made or to be made with such Indians or any of them, unless with such authority and consent as aforesaid, every such person shall, in every such case, be deemed guilty of a misdemeanor, and shall, on conviction thereof before any Court of competent jurisdiction, forfeit and pay to Her Majesty, Her Heirs or Successors, the sum of Two Hundred Pounds, and be further punished by fine and imprisonment, at the discretion of the Court.

III. And be it enacted, That no person shall take any confession of Judgment or Warrant of Attorney from any Indian within Upper Canada, or by means thereof, or otherwise howsoever obtain any judgment for any debt or pretended debt, or upon any bond, bill, note, promise or other contract whatsoever, unless such Indian shall be seized in fee simple in his own sole right of real estate in Upper Canada, the title to which shall be derived directly or through others by Letters Patent from the Crown, and shall be assessed in respect of such real estate to the amount of twenty-five pounds or upwards.

IV. And be it enacted, That no taxes shall be levied or assessed upon any Indian or any person inter-married with any Indian for or in respect of any of the said Indian lands, nor shall any taxes or assessments whatsoever be levied or imposed upon any Indian or any person inter-married with any Indian so long as he, she or they shall reside on Indian lands not ceded to the Crown, or which having been so ceded may have been again set apart by the Crown for the occupations of Indians.

V. And be it enacted, That notwithstanding any thing in this Act contained, Indians and persons inter-married with Indians, residing upon any such Indian lands and engaged in the pursuit of agriculture as their then principal means of support, shall be liable, if so directed by the Superintendent General, the Assistant Superintendent General, or by any Subordinate Superintendent of Indian Affairs, who may, for the time being, be charged with the subordinate superintendence of such Indians and persons inter-married with Indians as aforesaid, or by any such Commissioner or Commissioners, to perform labour on the public roads laid out or used in or through such Indian lands, such labour to be performed under the sole control of the said Superintendents or Commissioners, or of any or either of them, who shall have power to direct when, where, how and in what manner the said labour shall be applied, and to what extent the same shall be imposed upon Indians or persons inter-married with Indians, who shall be resident upon any of the said lands, and that the said Superintendents and Commissioners, and every of them, shall have the like power to enforce the performance of all such labor by imprisonment or otherwise as may now be done by any power or authority under any law, rule or regulation in force in this Province for the non-performance of Statute labour: Provided always, nevertheless, that the labour to be so required of any such Indian or person inter-married with an Indian, shall not exceed in amount or extent what shall or may be required of other inhabitants of Upper Canada, under the general laws requiring and regulating such labour and the performance thereof.

VI. And be it enacted, That it shall not be lawful for any person to sell, barter, exchange or give to any Indian, man, woman or child, within this Province, any kind of spirituous liquors in any manner or way, or to cause or procure the same to be done for any purpose whatsoever; and that if any person shall so sell, barter, exchange or give any such spirituous liquors to any Indian, man, woman or child as aforesaid, or shall cause the same to be done, he shall be deemed guilty of a misdemeanor, and on conviction thereof shall be fined at the discretion of the Court, not exceeding five pounds for every such offence, and shall forfeit also the sum of one pound five shillings for every such offence, to be recovered as in an action of debt with costs in any Court of competent jurisdiction, by any one who will sue for the same, one moiety of every such last mentioned pecuniary penalty or forfeiture to go to the informer or prosecutor, and the other moiety thereof to be paid to Her Majesty, Her Heirs or Successors, or to some officer acting under Her authority, to be disposed of for the use and benefit of the Indians, as the Governor of this Province for the time being may be pleased to direct: Provided always, nevertheless, that no such penalty shall be incurred by the furnishing to any Indian, in case of sickness, any spirituous liquor, either by a medical man or under the direction of any such medical man.

VII. And be it enacted, That no pawn taken of any Indian for any spirituous liquor, shall be retained by the person to whom such pawn shall be delivered, but the thing so pawned may be sued for and recovered, with costs of suit, by the Indian who may have deposited the same, before any Court of competent jurisdiction.

VIII. And whereas certain tribes of Indians in Upper Canada receive annuities and presents, which annuities, or portions thereof, are expended for and applied to the common use and benefit of the said Tribes, more especially for the encouragement of agriculture and other civilizing pursuits among them, although the articles so required or purchased out of such annuities, may be and often necessarily are, in the possession or control of some particular Indian or Indians of such Tribes, and it is important with a view to the progress and welfare of such Tribes, that the property thus acquired or purchased should be protected from seizure, distress or sale, under or by virtue of any process whatsoever: Be it therefore enacted, That none of such presents or of any property purchased or acquired with or by means of such annuities, or any part thereof, or otherwise howsoever, and in the possession of any of the Tribes or any of the Indians of such Tribes, shall be liable to be taken, seized or distrained for any matter or cause whatsoever.

IX. And be it enacted, That the Commissioner appointed under the Acts of Parliament in the next section of this Act mentioned, or either of them, and the different Superintendents of the Indian Department, either now in office or who may hereafter be appointed to either of such offices shall, by virtue of their office and appointment, be Justices of the Peace within the County, or United Counties, within which, for the time being, they or any or either of them, may be resident or employed as such Commissioners or Superintendents, without any other qualifications; any law to the contrary notwithstanding.

X. And whereas for the purpose of affording better protection to the Indians in the unmolested possession and enjoyment of their lands, it is expedient to give more summary and effectual powers to the Commissioners appointed or who may be appointed by virtue of the Act of the Province of Upper Canada, passed in the second year of Her Majesty's Reign, chaptered fifteen, and intituled, *An Act for the protection of the lands of the Crown in this Province from trespass and injury,* and also by virtue of the Act of this Province, passed in the twelfth year of Her Majesty's Reign, chaptered nine, and intituled, *An Act to explain and amend an Act of the Parliament of the late Province of Upper Canada, passed in the second year of Her Majesty's Reign, intituled, 'An Act for the protection of the lands of the Crown in this Province 'from trespass and injury, and to make further Provision for that purpose,'* to enable them more efficiently to protect the said lands from trespass and injury, and to punish all persons trespassing upon or doing damage thereto: Be it therefore enacted, That it shall not be lawful for any person or persons other than Indians, and those who may be inter-married with Indians, to settle, reside upon or occupy any lands or roads or allowances for roads running through any lands belonging to or occupied by any portion or Tribe of Indians within Upper Canada, and that all leases, contracts and agreements made or to be made, purporting to have been or to be made, by any Indians, or by any person or persons inter-married with any Indian or Indians whereby any person or persons other than Indians shall be permitted to reside upon such lands, shall be absolutely void; and if any person or persons other than Indians, or those who may be inter-married with Indians as aforesaid, shall without the license of the said Commissioners or any or either of them, (which license, however, the said Commissioners or any of them, may at any time revoke,) settle, reside upon or occupy any such lands, roads or allowances for roads, it shall be the duty of the Commissioners or any or either of them, on complaint made to them or any of them, and on due proof of the fact of such settlement, residence or occupation, to issue their or his warrant under their hands and seals, or his hand and seal, directed to the Sheriff of the County, or Union of Counties in which the said lands may lie, or if the said lands may not be situated within any County or Union of Counties, then such warrant shall be directed to any literate person who may be willing to act in the premises, commanding him forthwith to remove all such persons settling, residing upon or occupying such lands, with his, her or their families, from the said lands or roads or allowances for roads, and it shall be the duty of such Sheriff, or other person accordingly, to remove such person or persons, and for that purpose he shall have and possess the same powers as in the execution of criminal process: Provided always, nevertheless, that the provisions in this and the two following sections of the Act contained, shall extend and be construed to extend to such Indian lands only as the Governor of this Province for the time being shall from time to time, by Proclamation under the Great Seal thereof, think fit to declare and make subject to the same, and so long only as such Proclamation shall remain unrevoked and in full force.

XI. And be it enacted, That so often as any person or persons after being or having been removed as aforesaid, shall return to settle, reside upon or occupy any of the said lands or roads or allowances for roads, the said Commissioners or any or either of them, upon their or his view, or upon proof by any witness or witnesses on oath, to be made or taken before the Commissioners or any or either of them, and upon their or his being satisfied that the said person or persons has or have returned to, settled, resided upon or occupied any of the said lands or roads or allowances for roads, then and in every such case, such Commissioners or Commissioner shall direct and send their or his warrant, under their hands and seals or his hand and seal, to the Sheriff of the County or Union of Counties within which such lands may lie, or to any literate person there, or if the said lands shall not be situated within any County or Union of Counties, then to any literate person, commending him forthwith to arrest such person or persons, and to commit him, her or them to the Common Gaol of the said County or Union of Counties in which the said lands may lie, or to the Common Gaol of the nearest County or United Counties to the said lands, if the said lands shall not be within any County or United Counties, there to remain for such time as shall be ordered by the Commissioners or by any or either of them, not exceeding thirty days; and such Sheriff or other person shall accordingly arrest the said party or parties, and deliver him, her or them to the Gaoler or Sheriff of the said County or United Counties as aforesaid, who are hereby required to receive such person or persons, and the said person or persons to confine and imprison in the said Common Gaol for the term aforesaid, there to remain without bail and without being entitled to the liberties of the limits of the said Gaol; and such Commissioners or any of them shall cause the judgment or order against such person or persons to be drawn up, and no such judgment shall be liable to be removed by *Certiorari* or otherwise, or to be appealed from, but shall be deemed and taken to be final.

XII. And be it enacted, That if any person without the license in writing of the Commissioners or of any or either of them, shall hereafter trespass upon any of the said lands or roads or allowances for roads, by cutting any trees, saplings, shrubs, underwood or timber thereon, or by carrying away or removing any of the trees, saplings, shrubs, underwood or timber therefrom, or by removing any of the stone or soil of the said lands, roads or allowances for roads, each person so trespassing shall for every tree he shall cut, carry away or remove, forfeit and pay the sum of five pounds, and for cutting, carrying or removing any of the saplings, shrubs, underwood or timber, under the value of five shillings, the sum of one pound, but if over the value of five shillings, then the sum of five pounds, and for removing any of the stone or soil aforesaid, the sum of five pounds, such fine to be imposed and recovered by the said Commissioners or any or either of them, by distress and sale of the goods and chattels of the party or parties fined, or the said Commissioners may, without proceeding by distress and sale as aforesaid, upon the non-payment of the said fine, order the party or parties to be imprisoned in the Common Gaol as aforesaid, for a period not exceeding thirty days, when the fine shall not exceed five pounds, or for a period not exceeding three calendar months, when the fine shall exceed the sum of five pounds; and upon the return of any warrant for distress or sale, if the amount thereof have not been made, or if any part of it may remain unpaid, the said Commissioners or any or either of them, may commit the party or parties who may be in default upon such warrant or warrants to the Common Gaol as aforesaid, for a period not exceeding thirty days, if the sum claimed by the said Commissioners upon the said warrant do not exceed five pounds, or for a time not exceeding three calendar months, if the sum claimed do exceed five pounds; all which fines shall be paid to Her Majesty, Her Heirs or Successors, or to some officer acting under Her authority, to be disposed of for the use and benefit of the Indians, as the Governor of this Province for the time being may be pleased to direct.

XIII. And whereas great difficulty has been experienced by the said Commissioners in carrying into effect the several Acts relating to Indian lands, by reason of persons giving false names or concealing their names, and it is expedient that the Commissioners should be enabled to proceed without difficulty in this respect: Be it therefore enacted, That in all orders, writs, warrants, summonses and proceedings whatsoever to be made, issued or taken by the Commissioners or any or either of them, under this or any other Act whatsoever, it shall only be necessary for the Commissioners or such of them as may be acting, to insert or express the name or names of the person or persons summoned, arrested, distrained upon, imprisoned or otherwise proceeded against in any of such orders, writs, warrants, summonses or proceedings, when the name or names of such person or persons shall be truly given to or known by the said Commissioners, or such of them as may be acting in that behalf, and if the name or names be not truly given to or known by the Commissioners, then the Commissioners or such of them as shall be acting in that behalf, shall be at liberty to name or describe the person or persons by any part of the name or names of such person or persons which may be given to or known by them, or such of them as may be so acting; but if no part of the name or names be given to or known by the said Commissioners, or such of them as shall be so acting, they or such of them as shall be acting may describe the person or persons proceeded against in any manner by which he, she or they may be capable of being identified; And it is hereby declared that all such proceedings as aforesaid, containing the name or description, or purporting to give the name or description of any such person as aforesaid, according to this Act, shall *primâ facie* be deemed to be sufficient; any thing to the contrary notwithstanding.

XIV. And be it enacted, That all Sheriffs, Gaolers and Peace Officers, to whom any such process shall be so directed by such Commissioners or any or either of them, are hereby required to obey the same, and all other Officers upon reasonable requisition to be aiding and assisting in the execution thereof.

B11.

14 and 15 Victoria (1851) Cap. 59 (Province of Canada). An Act to Consolidate and Regulate the General Clauses Relating to Railways.
(Extract)

* * *

Twenty-secondly. If the said Rail-way shall pass through any land belonging to or in possession of any Tribe of Indians in this Province, or if any act occasioning damage to their lands shall be done under the authority of this Act or the Special Act, compensation shall be made to them therefor, in the same manner as is provided with respect to the lands or rights of other individuals; and whenever it shall be necessary that Arbitrators shall be chosen by the parties, the Chief Officer of the Indian Department within this Province, is hereby authorized and required to name an Arbitrator on behalf of the Indians, and the amount which shall be awarded in any case shall be paid, where the lands belong to the Indians, to the said Chief Officer, for the use of such Tribe or Body.

* * *

B12.

14 and 15 Victoria (1851) Cap. 59 (Province of Canada) An Act to Repeal in Part and to Amend an Jct, Intituled, An Act for the Better Protection of the Lands and Property of the Indians in Lower Canada (cf. 13 and 14 Victoria (1850) Cap. 42, No.B9. above). /passed August 30, 1851/

WHEREAS it is expedient to designate more accurately the persons who have and shall continue to have a right of property, possession or occupation in the lands and other immoveable property belonging to or appropriated to the use of the various Tribes or Bodies of Indians residing in Lower Canada: Be it therefore enacted by the Queen's Most Excellent Majesty, by and with the advice and consent of the Legislative Council and of the Legislative Assembly of the Province of Canada, constituted and assembled by virtue and under the authority of an Act passed in the Parliament of the United Kingdom of Great Britain and Ireland, and intituled, *An Act to re-unite the Provinces of Upper and Lower Canada, and for the Government of Canada*, and it is hereby enacted by the authority of the same, That the fifth section of the Act passed in the now last session of the present Parliament, chaptered forty-two, and intituled, *An Act for the better protection of the Lands and property of the Indians in Lower Canada*, shall be, and the same is hereby repealed.

II. And be it declared and enacted, That for the purpose of determining what persons are entitled to hold, use or enjoy the lands and other immoveable property belonging to or appropriated to the use of the various Tribes or Bodies of Indians in Lower Canada, the following persons and classes of persons, and none other, shall be considered as Indians belonging to the Tribe or Body of Indians interested in any such lands or immoveable property:

Firstly. All persons of Indian blood, reputed to belong to the particular Tribe or Body of Indians interested in such lands or immoveable property, and their descendants:

Secondly. All persons residing among such Indians, whose parents were or are, or either of them was or is, descended on either side from Indians, or an Indian reputed to belong to the particular Tribe or Body of Indians interested in such lands or immoveable property, and the descendants of all such persons: And

Thirdly. All women, now or hereafter to be lawfully married to any of the persons included in the several classes hereinbefore designated; the children issue of such marriages, and their descendants.

B13.

14 and 15 Victoria (1851) Cap. 106 (Province of Canada). An Act to Authorize the Setting Apart of Lands for the Use of Certain Indian Tribes in Lower Canada. /passed August 30, 1851/

WHEREAS it is expedient to set apart certain Lands for the use of certain Indian Tribes resident in Lower Canada: Be it therefore enacted by the Queen's Most Excellent Majesty, by and with the advice and consent of the Legislative Council and of the Legislative Assembly of the Province of Canada, constituted and assembled by virtue of and under the authority of an Act passed in the Parliament of the United

Kingdom of Great Britain and Ireland, and intituled, *An Act to re-unite the Provinces of Upper and Lower Canada, and for the Government of Canada,* and it is hereby enacted by the authority of the same, That tracts of Land in Lower Canada, not exceeding in the whole two hundred and thirty thousand Acres, may, under orders in Council to be made in that behalf, be described, surveyed and set out by the Commissioner of Crown Lands, and such tracts of Land shall be and are hereby respectively set apart and appropriated to and for the use of the several Indian Tribes in Lower Canada, for which they shall be respectively directed to be set apart in any order in Council, to be made as aforesaid, and the said tracts of Land shall accordingly, by virtue of this Act, and without any price or payment being required therefor, be vested in and managed by the Commissioner of Indian Lands for Lower Canada, under the Act passed in the Session held in the thirteenth and fourteenth years of Her Majesty's Reign, and intituled, *An Act for the better protection of the Lands and Property of the Indians in Lower Canada.*

II. And be it enacted, That there shall be paid yearly out of the Consolidated Revenue Fund of this Province, a sum not exceeding One Thousand Pounds currency, to be distributed amongst certain Indian Tribes in Lower Canada by the Superintendent General of Indian affairs, in such proportions amongst the said Indian Tribes, and in such manner as the Governor General in Council may from time to time direct.

B14.

16 Victoria (1853) Cap. 191 (Province of Canada). An Act to Authorize the Formation of Joint Stock Companies to Construct Works Necessary to Facilitate the Transmission of Timber down the Rivers and Streams in Upper Canada. (Extract) /passed June 10, 1853/

* * *

XVII. And be it enacted, That if any such work shall be constructed upon or otherwise interfere with any tract of land or property belonging to or in possession of any tribe of Indians in this Province, or if any property belonging to them shall be taken, or any act occasioning damage to their properties or their possessions shall be done, under authority of this Act, compensation shall be made to them therefor, in the same manner as is provided with respect to the property, possession or rights of other individuals, and that whenever it shall be necessary that Arbitrators be chosen by the parties for settling the amount of such compensation, the Chief Officer of the Indian Department within the

Province is hereby authorized and required to name an Arbitrator on behalf of the said Indians; and the amount which shall be awarded in any case shall be paid, where the said lands belong to any tribe or body of Indians, to the said Chief Officer, for the use of such tribe or body.

* * *

B15.

20 Victoria (1857) Cap. 26 (Province of Canada). An Act to Encourage the Gradual Civilization of the Indian Tribes in this Province, and to Amend the Laws Respecting Indians. /assented to June 10, 1857/

WHEREAS it is desirable to encourage the progress of Civilization among the Indian Tribes in this Province, and the gradual removal of all legal distinction between them and Her Majesty's other Canadian Subjects, and to facilitate the acquisition of property and of the rights accompanying it, by such Individual Members of the said Tribes as shall be found to desire such encouragement and to have deserved it: Therefore, Her Majesty, by and with the advice and consent of the Legislative Council and Assembly of Canada, enacts as follows:

I. The third section of the Act passed in the Session held in the thirteenth and fourteenth years of Her Majesty's Reign, chaptered seventy-four and intituled, *An Act for the protection of the Indians in Upper Canada from imposition and the properly occupied or enjoyed by them, from trespass and injury,* shall apply only to Indians or persons of Indian blood or intermarried with Indians, who shall be acknowledged as members of Indian Tribes or Bands residing upon lands which have never been surrendered to the Crown (or which having been so surrendered have been set apart or shall then be reserved for the use of any Tribe or Band of Indians in common) and who shall themselves reside upon such lands, and shall not have been exempted from the operation of the said section, under the provisions of this Act; and such persons and such persons only shall be deemed Indians within the meaning of any provision of the said Act or of any other Act or Law in force in any part of this Province by which any legal distinction is made between the rights and liabilities of Indians and those of Her Majesty's other Canadian Subjects.

II. The term "Indian" in the following enactments shall mean any person to whom under the foregoing provisions, the third section of the Act therein cited shall continue to apply; and the term "enfranchised Indian" shall mean any person to whom the said section would have been applicable, but for the operation of the provisions hereinafter made in that behalf: and the term "Tribe," shall include any Band or other recognized community of Indians.

III. The Visiting Superintendent of each Tribe of Indians, for the time being, the Missionary to such Tribe for the time being, and such other person as the Governor shall appoint from time to time for that purpose, shall be Commissioners for examining Indians, being members of such Tribe, who may desire to avail themselves of this Act, and for making due inquiries concerning them: and such Commissioners shall meet for the said purposes at such places and times as the Superintendent General of Indian affairs shall from time to time direct, and shall have full power to make such examination and inquiry: and if such Commissioners shall report in writing to the Governor that any such Indian of the male sex, and not under twenty-one years of age, is able to speak, read and write either the english or the french language readily and well, and is sufficiently advanced in the elementary branches of education and is of good moral character and free from debt, then it shall be competent to the Governor to cause notice to be given in the Official Gazette of this Province, that such Indian is enfranchised under this Act; and the provisions of the third section of the Act aforesaid, and all other enactments making any distinction between the legal rights and habilities of the Indians and those of Her Majesty's other subjects, shall cease to apply to any Indian so declared to be enfranchised, who shall no longer be deemed an Indian within the meaning thereof.

IV. The said Commissioners may also examine and inquire concerning any male Indian over twenty-one and not over forty years of age, desirous of availing himself of this Act, although he be not able to read and write or instructed in the usual branches of school education; and if they shall find him able to speak readily either the English or the French language, of sober and industrious habits, free from debt and sufficiently intelligent to be capable of managing his own affairs, they shall report accordingly in writing to the Governor; and if such report be approved by the Governor as to any Indian, he shall by virtue of such approval be in a state of probation during three years from the date of the report, and if at the end of that term the Commissioners shall again report in writing to the Governor that such Indian has during such term conducted himself to their satisfaction, then it shall be competent to the Governor to cause notice to be given in the Offical Gazette that such Indian is enfranchised under this Act, and he shall thereupon be so enfranchised.

V. Every Indian examined by the Commissioners under this Act, shall at the time of such examination declare to them the name and surname by which he wishes to be enfranchised and thereafter known, such name being his baptismal name if he have one, and such surname any one he may choose to adopt which shall be approved by the Commissioners, and the Commissioners shall enter the same in their Report; and if such Indian be thereafter enfranchised under this Act the name and surname so reported shall be those by which he shall thereafter be legally designated and known.

VI. Lists of Indians enfranchised under this Act and of any lands allotted to them under the authority thereof, shall from time to time be transmitted by the Indian Department to the Clerk of the township or other local municipality in which they reside at the time of such enfranchisement; and any Indian falsely representing himself as enfranchised under this Act when he is not so, shall be liable, on conviction before any one Justice of the Peace, to imprisonment for any period not exceeding six months.

VII. Every Indian enfranchised under this Act shall be entitled to have alloted to him by the Superintendent General of Indian affairs, a piece of land not exceeding fifty acres out of the lands reserved or set apart for the use of his Tribe, and also a sum of money equal to the principal of his share of the annuities and other yearly revenues receivable by or for the use of such tribe; such sum to be ascertained and paid to him by the said Superintendent, and due consideration being had in the allotment of such land to the quantity of land reserved for the use of the Tribe and to their means and resources; and such sum of money shall become the absolute property of such Indian, and such land shall become his property, subject to the provisions hereinafter made, but he shall by accepting the same forego all claim to any further share in the lands or moneys then belonging to or reserved for the use of his Tribe, and shall cease to have a voice in the proceedings thereof: Provided always, that if such Tribe shall thereafter surrender to the crown other lands either to be sold for their benefit, or in consideration of an annuity, such enfranchised Indian, or his personal representatives, (if any) shall be entitled to his share of the proceeds of such lands or of the annuity for which they were surrendered, such share to be ascertained and paid by the Superintendent General of Indian Affairs for the time being, and to be the absolute property of such enfranchised Indian or his said representatives.

VIII. The wife, widow, and lineal descendants of an Indian enfranchised under this Act, shall be also enfranchised by the operation thereof, and shall not be deemed members of his former tribe, unless such widow or any such lineal descendant being a female shall marry an Indian not enfranchised and a member of such tribe, in which case she shall again belong to it and shall no longer be held to be enfranchised under this Act.

IX. The wife and children of any Indian enfranchised under this Act shall be entitled to their respective shares of all annuities or annual sums payable to the tribe; subject to the provisions hereinafter made as to such shares.

X. An Indian enfranchised under this Act, to whom any of the lands reserved for the use of his Tribe shall be allotted as aforesaid, shall have a life estate only therein, but he shall have power to dispose of the same by will to any of his children or lineal descendants, and if he dies intestate as to any such lands, the same shall descend to his children or lineal descendants according to the laws of that portion of the Province in which such lands are situate, and the said children or lineal descendants to whom such land shall be so devised or shall decend, shall have the fee simple thereof; but if such Indian die without leaving any child or lineal descendant but leaving a widow, she shall, instead of Dower to which she shall not be entitled, have the said land for life or until her re-marriage, but upon her death or re-marriage it shall escheat to the Crown: and if any child or lineal descendant of such Indian shall take such land or any part thereof and die leaving no lineal descendant and without having disposed of such land or part thereof by will or otherwise, it shall escheat to the Crown.

XI. If any Indian enfranchised under this Act shall die leaving any child under the age of twenty-one years, the Superintendent General of Indians shall become *ipso facto* the tutor of such child as to property and rights in Lower Canada, and the guardian of such child as to property and rights in Upper Canada, until it shall attain the age of twenty-one years; and the widow of such Indian, being also the mother of any such child, shall receive its share of the proceeds of the estate of such Indian during the minority of the child, and shall be entitled to reside on the land left by such Indian, so long as in the opinion of the Superintendent General she shall live respectably.

XII. The capital of the annual share of the wife of any Indian enfranchised under this Act in any annuity or annual sum payable to her Tribe, shall be held in trust by the Superintendent General of Indian affairs for the purposes of this section, and the interest thereof shall be paid to her yearly while she shall be the wife or widow of such Indian, and upon her death or re-marriage one half of such capital sum shall be divided equally among her children, and the other half shall revert to the Tribe to which she belonged; but if she have no children, the whole shall revert to the said Tribe.

XIII. The capital of the share of each child of an Indian enfranchised under this Act, in any annuity or annual sum payable to his Tribe, shall be held in trust by the Superintendent General of Indian Affairs for such child, and the interest thereon shall, except in the case hereinafter mentioned, be left to accumulate until such child shall obtain the age of twenty-one; Provided always that if such child shall be put apprentice to any trade, the money so held in trust for him may be wholly or in part applied to the payment of his apprentice fee or other expenses attending such apprenticeship; and if any such child shall die before attaining the age of twenty-one, one half the money then held in trust for him shall revert to his Tribe, and the other half shall go to the other child or children of such Indian, and in equal shares if there be more than one, and if there be no other child, then the whole shall revert to the Tribe.

XIV. Lands allotted under this Act to an Indian enfranchised under it shall be liable to taxes and all other obligations and duties under the Municipal and School Laws of the section of this Province in which such land is situate, as he shall also be in respect of them and of his other property; and his estate therein shall be liable for his *boná fide* debts, but he shall not otherwise alienate or charge such land or his estate therein; and if such land be legally conveyed to any person, such person or his assigns may reside thereon, whether he be or be not of Indian blood or intermarried with any Indian; any thing in the Act first cited to the contrary notwithstanding.

XV. It shall be lawful for the Council of any Municipality in Upper Canada, or the School Commissioners of any School Municipality in Lower Canada, on application of the Superintendent General of Indian affairs, to attach the whole or any portion of any Indian Reserves in such Minicipality to a neighboring School Section or District, or to neighboring School Sections or Districts, and such land shall thereupon become a portion of the School Section or District to which it may be attached, to all intents and purposes.

B16.

23 Victoria (1860) Cap. 14 (Province of Canada). An Act Respecting Indians and Indian Lands.

HER Majesty, by and with the advice and consent of the Legislative Council and Assembly of Canada, enacts as follows:—

SELLING STRONG LIQUORS TO INDIANS.

1. No person shall sell, distribute, or otherwise dispose of, to any Indian within Lower Canada, or to any other person for their use, any rum or other strong liquors, of what kind or quality soever, or shall knowingly or willingly suffer the same, in any manner, to come to the hands of any Indian:

2. Every person offending herein shall, for the first offence, forfeit the sum of twenty dollars, and suffer imprisonment for any time not exceeding one month, and for the second and every subsequent of-

fence, shall forfeit forty dollars, and suffer an imprisonment for any time not exceeding two months;

3. If the person so offending be a publican, innkeeper, or retailer of strong liquors, he shall, over and above the said penalty and imprisonment, be rendered incapable, from the day of his conviction, of selling or retailing liquors to any person whatsoever, notwithstanding any license he has for that purpose, which license shall be null and void from the day of his conviction 17 G. 3, c. 7, s. 1—23 V. c. 38.

4. And nothing in this section shall prevent the effect of the Act twenty-third Victoria, chapter thirty-eight, applying to both Upper and Lower Canada; but an offender convicted under that Act or under this, shall not afterwards be convicted under the other Act for the same offence. 23 V. c. 38.

2. No person shall purchase, or receive in pledge or in exchange, any clothes, blankets, firearms or ammunition belonging to any Indian within this Province, under a penalty of twenty dollars, and imprisonment for any time not exceeding one month, for the first offence, and of forty dollars and imprisonment for any time not exceeding two months, for the second and every other subsequent offence. 17 G. 3, c. 7, s. 2.

SETTLING IN INDIAN VILLAGES.

3. No person shall settle in any Indian village or in any Indian country, within Lower Canada, without a license in writing from the Governor, under a penalty of forty dollars for the first offence, and eighty dollars for the second and every other subsequent offence. 17 G. 3, c. 7, s. 3.

4. The Governor may, by a written instrument, order any person who has become resident in any of the Indian villages in Lower Canada, to remove from such village; and in case of default by the said person so to remove from such Indian village, within seven days from such order being signified to him, he shall forfeit the sum of twenty dollars, for each day after the said seven days, during which he continues to remain in such Indian village, with all costs of prosecution, and shall suffer imprisonment for a period not less than one month and not exceeding two months, and further, until he has paid the said last mentioned penalty and costs. 3, 4 V c. 44, s. 2.

5. All the penalties imposed by this Act, for the offences therein specified, may be recovered by information on behalf of Her Majesty, before any two or more of Her Majesty's Justice of the Peace, for the district in which the offence is committed; and such two or more Justices of the Peace shall hear and determine such information in a summary manner, and upon the oath of one credible witness, and shall levy the said penalties, together with the costs of suing for the same by a

warrant to seize and sell the goods and chattels of the person or persons offending, and shall inflict the said imprisonment in the manner hereinbefore provided and all the said pecuniary penalties shall be paid into the hands of the Receiver General, for the public uses of this Province. 3, 4 V. c. 44, s. 3.

6. All informations under and by this Act, shall be brought within six months from the time that the offence is committed, and not afterwards. 3, 4 V. c. 44, s 4.

PROTECTION OF PROPERTY OF INDIANS

7. The Governor may appoint from time to time a Commissioner of Indian Lands for Lower Canada, in whom and in whose successors by the name aforesaid, all lands or property in Lower Canada, appropriated for the use of any tribe or body of Indians, shall be vested in trust for such tribe or body, and who shall be held in law to be in the occupation and possession of any lands in Lower Canada actually occupied or possessed by any such tribe or body in common only any chief or member thereof or other party for the use or benefit of such tribe or body, and shall be entitled to receive and recover the rents, issues and profits of such lands and property, and shall, in and by the name aforesaid, subject to the provisions hereinafter made, exercise and defend all or any of the rights lawfully appertaining to the proprietor, possessor or occupant of such lands or property:

2. This section shall extend to any lands in Lower Canada held by the Crown in trust for or for the benefit of any such tribe or body of Indians, but shall not extend to any lands vested in any corporation or community legally established and capable in law of suing and being sued, or in any person or persons of European descent, although held in trust for or for the benefit of any such tribe or body. 13, 14 V. c. 42, s. 1.

8. All suits, actions or proceedings by or against the said Commissioner shall be brought and conducted by or against him by the name aforesaid only, and shall not abate or be discontinued by his death, removal from office or resignation, but shall be continued by or against his successor in office:

2. Such Commissioner shall have in each civil district in Lower Canada, an office which shall be his legal domicile, and whereat any process, notice of like matter may be legally served upon him, and may appoint such deputy or duputies, and with such powers as he, from time to time, deems expedient, or is instructed by the governor to do. 13, 14 V. c. 42, s. 2, *except proviso*.

9. The said Commissioner may concede or lease or charge any such land or property as aforesaid, and receive or recover the rents,

issues and profits thereof as any lawful proprietor, possessor or occupant thereof might do, but shall be subject in all things to the instructions he may from time to time receive from the Governor, and shall be personally responsible to the Crown for all his acts, and more especially for any act done contrary to such instructions, and shall account for all moneys received by him, and apply and pay over the same in such manner, at such times and to such person or officer, as may be appointed by the Governor, and shall report from time to time on all matters relative to his office in such manner and form, and give such security, as the Governor shall direct and require; and all moneys and moveable property received by him or in his possession as Commissioner, if not duly accounted for, applied and paid over as aforesaid, or if not delivered by any person having been such Commissioner to his successor in office, may be recovered by the Crown or by such successor, in any Court having civil jurisdiction to the amount or value, from the person having been such Commissioner and his sureties, jointly and severally. *Ibid,* s. 3.

10. Nothing herein contained shall be construed to derogate from the rights of any individual Indian or other private party, as possessor or occupant of any lot or parcel of land forming part of or included within the limits of any land vested in the Commissioner aforesaid. *Ibid,* s. 4.

11. For the purpose of determining what persons are entitled to hold, use or enjoy the lands and other immoveable property belonging to or appropriated to the use of the various tribes or bodies of Indians in Lower Canada, the following persons and classes of persons, and none other shall be considered as Indians belonging to the tribe or body of Indians interested in any such lands or immoveable property:—

Firstly. All persons of Indian blood, reputed to belong to the particular tribe or body of Indians interested in such lands or immoveable property, and their descendants;

Secondly. All persons residing among such Indians whose parents were or are, or either one of them was or is, descended on either side from Indians, or an Indian reputed to belong to the particular tribe or body of Indians interested in such lands or immoveable property, and the descendants of all such persons; And

Thirdly. All women lawfully married to any of the persons included in the several classes hereinbefore designated the children, issue of such marriages, and their descendants 14,15 V. c. 59, s. 2.

LANDS SET APART FOR INDIANS.

12. Tracts of land in Lower Canada, not exceeding in the whole two hundred and thirty thousand acres, may, (in so far as the same has not been already done under the Act 14 15 Victoria, chapter 106,) under

Orders in Council to be made in that behalf, be described, surveyed and set out by the Commissioner of Crown Lands, and such tracts of land shall be respectively set apart and appropriated to and for the use of the several Indian tribes in Lower Canada, for which they are respectively directed to be set apart in any Order in Council, made as aforesaid, and the said tracts of land shall accordingly, by virtue of this Act, and without any price or payment being required therefor, be vested in and managed by the Commissioner of Indian lands for Lower Canada, under this Act. 14, 15 V. c. 106, s. 1.

13. There shall be paid yearly out of the Consolidated Revenue Fund of this Province, a sum not exceeding four thousand dollars. to be distributed amongst certain Indian tribes in Lower Canada by the Superintendent General of Indian affairs, in such proportions amongst the said Indian tribes, and in such manner as the Governor in Council may from time to time direct. *Ibid*, s. 2.

B17.

Laws of British Columbia after the Union of Vancouver Island and British Columbia No. 74 (1867). An Ordinance to Provide for the Taking of Oaths in Certain Cases. (Extract) /passed March 15, 1867/

WHEREAS it is expedient to provide for the taking of oaths and admission of evidence in certain cases, and to assimilate the same in all parts of the Colony of British Columbia:

Be it enacted by the Governor of British Columbia, with the advice and consent of the Legislative Council thereof, as follows:—

* * *

5. In any civil action, or upon any inquest, or upon any enquiry into any matter or offence whatsoever, or by whomsoever committed, it shall be lawful for any court, judge, coroner, gold or other commissioner, or justice of the peace, in the discretion of such court, judge, coroner, gold or other commissioner, or justice of the peace, to receive the evidence of any aboriginal native, or native of mixed blood, of the continent of North America, or the islands adjacent thereto, being an uncivilized person, destitute of the knowledge of God, and of any fixed and clear belief in religion, or in a future state of rewards and punishments, without administering the ususal form of oath to any such aboriginal native, or native of mixed blood as aforesaid, upon his solemn affirmation or declaration to tell the truth, the whole truth, and nothing but the truth, or in such other form as may be approved by such

court, judge, coroner, gold or other commissioner, or justice of the peace.

6. Provided, that in the case of any proceeding in the nature of a preliminary enquiry, the substance of the evidence or information of any such aboriginal native, or native of mixed blood as aforesaid, shall be reduced to writing, and signed by a mark by the person giving the same, and verified by the signature or mark of the person acting as interpreter, if any, and of the coroner, justice of the peace, or person before whom such information or evidence shall have been given.

7. The court, judge, coroner, gold or other commissioner, or justice of the peace shall, before taking any such evidence, information or examination, caution every such aboriginal native, or native of mixed blood as aforesaid, that he will be liable to incur punishment if he do not, so as aforesaid, tell the truth.

8. The written declaration or examination made, taken and verified in manner aforesaid, of any such aboriginal native, or native of mixed blood as aforesaid, being one of such uncivilized persons as hereinbefore described, may be lawfully read and received as evidence upon the trial of any cause, civil or criminal, in the said Colony, when under the like circumstances the written affidavit, examination, deposition or confession of any person might be lawfully read and received as evidence.

* * *

B18.

Laws of British Columbia after the Union of Vancouver Island and British Columbia No. 85 (1867). An Ordinance to Assimilate and Amend the Law Prohibiting the Sale or Gift of Intoxicating Liquor to Indians. (Extract) /passed April 2, 1867/

WHEREAS it is expedient to assimilate the law prohibiting the sale or gift of intoxicating liquor to Indians in all parts of the Colony of British Columbia, and to amend the same:

Be it enacted by the Governor of British Columbia, with the advice and consent of the Legislative Council thereof, as follows:—

* * *

10. It shall be lawful for any officer of Customs, or for any superintendent or inspector of police, or any other office specially appointed by the Governor for that purpose, or for any officer of Her

Majesty's navy on full pay, at his discretion, to rummage and search for fermented, spirituous, or intoxicating liquor, any ship, boat, canoe, or other vessel suspected of containing intoxicating liquor for the use of the Indians, and upon reasonable ground in that behalf, to detain and seize the same, and bring her for the purpose of investigation and adjudication to any convenient port or place within the said Colony; and every master of a ship, boat, canoe, or other vessel having on board his ship, boat, canoe, or other vessel, any fermented, spirituous, or intoxicating liquors not satisfactorily accounted for, shall forfeit and pay a penalty not exceeding one thousand dollars, and all such last mentioned fermented, spirituous, or intoxicating liquors shall be forfeited.

11. No ship, boat, canoe, or other vessel having fermented, spirituous, or intoxicating liquors on board shall leave any port in the Colony of British Columbia for any part of the coast of the said Colony, or for any port or place on the coast of Russian America, or to the northward thereof, without the master of such ship, boat, canoe, or other vessel, making a declaration in the form marked 1 in the schedule to this Ordinance, setting forth the quantitites, description, and destination of such liquors as aforesaid as may be on board, and obtaining from the officer of Customs, at the port of departure a permit to carry such liquors, which permit may be in the form marked 2, in the said schedule. It shall be lawful, however, for the Governor to exempt any vessel from the operation of this section of this Ordinance, whenever the circumstance shall be such as, in the opinion of such Governor, to render such exemption expedient and desirable.

* * *

B19.

Statutes of Newfoundland Chapter 80 (1916). Of the Protection of Esquimaux and Indians.

1. Without the permission of the Governor in Council first obtained, it shall be unlawful for any person to enter into any agreement with any Esquimaux, or any Nascopee, or Mountaineer Indian to leave this Colony or its Dependencies for the purpose of performing any services in any place outside this Colony or its Dependencies, or to pay or promise to pay any money, or give or promise to give any article to any Esquimaux, Nascopee, or Mountaineer Indian as a reward or inducement for leaving this Colony or its Dependencies, or to transport or furnish the means of transporting any Esquimaux, Nascopee or Moun-

taineer Indians from this Colony or its Dependencies to any place outside this Colony; provided that nothing in this section shall prevent the employment of Esquimaux, Nascopee or Mountaineer Indians by any person for the purpose of fishing, hunting or exploring upon any part of the coast or territories of Canadian Labrador.

2. Any person violating any of the provisions of the first section of this Chapter shall be liable to a penalty not exceeding six months, to be recovered or imposed upon the complaint of any person in a summary manner before a Stipendiary Magistrate.

3. In this Chapter "Esquimaux" shall mean native residents of the Coast of Labrador who are commonly known as Esquimaux.

Section C

The British North America Act, The Indian Acts, and Allied Documents

C1.

30 Victoria (1867) Cap. 3 (United Kingdom). An Act for the Union of Canada, Nova Scotia, and New Brunswick, and the Government thereof; and for Purposes Connected therewith (The British North America Act, 1867). /assented to March 29, 1867/(Extract)

* * *

VI. DISTRIBUTION OF LEGISLATIVE POWERS

Powers of the Parliament

91. It shall be lawful for the Queen, by and with the Advice and Consent of the Senate and House of Commons, to make Laws for the Peace, Order, and good Government of Canada, in relation to all Matters not coming within the Classes of Subjects by this Act assigned exclusively to the Legislatures of the Provinces; and for greater Certainty, but not so as to restrict the Generality of the foregoing Terms of this Section, it is hereby declared that (notwithstanding anything in this Act) the exclusive Legislative Authority of the Parliament of Canada extends to all Matters coming within the Classes of Subjects next hereinafter enumerated; that is to say,—

   1. The amendment from time to time of the Constitution of Canada, except as regards matters coming within the classes of subjects by this Act assigned exclusively to the Legislatures of the provinces or as regards rights or privileges by this or any other Constitutional Act granted or secured to the Legislature or the Government of a province, or to any class of persons with respect to schools or as regards the use of the

English or the French language or as regards the requirements that there shall be a session of the Parliament of Canada at least once each year, and that no House of Commons shall continue for more than five years from the day of the return of the Writs for choosing the House: provided, however, that a House of Commons may in time of real or apprehended war, invasion or insurrection be continued by the Parliament of Canada if such continuation is not opposed by the votes of more than one-third of the members of such House.

2. The Regulation of Trade and Commerce.
3. The raising of Money by any Mode or System of Taxation.
4. The borrowing of Money on the Public Credit.
5. Postal Service.
6. The Census and Statistics.
7. Militia, Military and Naval Service, and Defence.
8. The fixing of and providing for the Salaries and Allowances of Civil and other Officers of the Government of Canada.
9. Beacons, Buoys, Lighthouses, and Sable Island.
10. Navigation and Shipping.
11. Quarantine and the Establishment and Maintenance of Marine Hospitals.
12. Sea Coast and Inland Fisheries.
13. Ferries between a Province and any British or Foreign Country or between Two Provinces.
14. Currency and Coinage.
15. Banking, Incorporation of Banks, and the Issue of Paper Money.
16. Savings Banks.
17. Weights and Measures.
18. Bills of Exchange and Promissory Notes.
19. Interest.
20. Legal Tender.
21. Bankruptcy and Insolvency.
22. Patents of Invention and Discovery.
23. Copyrights.
24. Indians and Lands reserved for the Indians.
25. Naturalization and Aliens.
26. Marriage and Divorce.
27. The Criminal Law, except the Constitution of Courts of Criminal Jurisdiction, but including the Procedure in Criminal Matters.
28. The Establishment, Maintenance, and Management of Penitentiaries.

29.   Such Classes of Subjects as are expressly excepted in the Enumeration of the Classes of Subjects by this Act assigned exclusively to the Legislatures of the Provinces.

And any Matter coming within any of the Classes of Subjects enumerated in this Section shall not be deemed to come within the Class of Matters of a local or private Nature comprised in the Enumeration of the Classes of Subjects by this Act assigned exclusively to the Legislatures of the Provinces.

C2.

31 Victoria (1868) Cap. 42 (Canada). An Act Providing for the Organisation of the Department of Secretary of State of Canada, and for the Management of Indian and Ordnance Lands. /assented to May 22, 1868/

HER Majesty, by and with the advice and consent of the Senate and House of Commons of Canada, enacts as follows:

1.   There shall be a department to be called "The Department of the Secretary of State of Canada," over which the Secretary of State of Canada for the time being, appointed by the Governor General by commission under the Great Seal, shall preside; and the said Secretary of State shall hold office during pleasure.

2.   The Governor General may also appoint an "Under Secretary of State," and such other officers as may be necessary for the proper conduct of the business of the said Department, all of whom shall hold office during pleasure.

3.   It shall be the duty of the Secretary of State to have charge of the State correspondence, to keep all State records and papers not specially transferred to other Departments, and to perform such other duties as shall from time to time be assigned to him by the Governor General in Council.

4.   The Secretary of State shall be the Registrar General of Canada, and shall as such register all Instruments of Summons, Commissions, Letters Patent, Writs, and other Instruments and Documents issued under the Great Seal.

5.   The Secretary of State shall be the Superintendent General of Indian affairs, and shall as such have the control and management of the lands and property of the Indians in Canada.

6.   All lands reserved for Indians or for any tribe, band or body of Indians, or held in trust for their benefit, shall be deemed to be reserved

and held for the same purposes as before the passing of this Act, but subject to its provisions; and no such lands shall be sold, alienated or leased until they have been released or surrendered to the Crown for the purposes of this Act.

7. All moneys or securities of any kind applicable to the support or benefit of the Indians or any tribe, band or body of Indians, and all moneys accrued or hereafter to accrue from the sale of any lands or of any timber on any lands reserved or held in trust as aforesaid, shall, subject to the provisions of this Act, be applicable to the same purposes, and be dealt with in the same manner as they might have been applied to or dealt with before the passing of this Act.

8. No release or surrender of lands reserved for the use of the Indians or of any tribe, band or body of Indians, or of any individual Indian, shall be valid or binding, except on the following conditions:

1. Such release or surrender shall be assented to by the chief, or if there be more than one chief, by a majority of the chiefs of the tribe, band or body of Indians, assembled at a meeting or council of the tribe, band or body summoned for that purpose according to their rules and entitled under this Act to vote thereat, and held in the presence of the Secretary of State or of an officer duly authorized to attend such council by the Governor in Council or by the Secretary of State; provided that no Chief or Indian shall be entitled to vote or be present at such council, unless he habitually resides on or near the lands in question;

2. The fact that such release or surrender has been assented to by the Chief of such tribe, or if more than one, by a majority of the chiefs entitled to vote at such council or meeting, shall be certified on oath before some Judge of a Superior, County or District Court, by the officer authorized by the Secretary of State to attend such council or meeting, and by some one of the chiefs present thereat and entitled to vote, and when so certified as aforesaid shall be transmitted to the Secretary of State by such officer, and shall be submitted to the Governor in Council for acceptance or refusal.

9. It shall not be lawful to introduce at any council or meeting of Indians held for the purpose of discussing or of assenting to a release or surrender of lands, any strong or intoxicating liquors of any kind; and any person who shall introduce at such meeting, and any agent or officer employed by the Secretary of State, or by the Governor in Council, who shall introduce, allow or countenance by his presence the use of such liquors a week before, at, or a week after, any such council or meeting, shall forfeit two hundred dollars, recoverable by action in any of the Superior Courts of Law, one half of which penalty shall go to the informer.

10. Nothing in this Act shall confirm any release or surrender which would have been invalid if this Act had not been passed; and no

release or surrender of any such lands to any party other than the Crown, shall be valid.

11. The Governor in Council may, subject to the provisions of this Act, direct how, and in what manner, and by whom the moneys arising from sales of Indian Lands, and from the property held or to be held in trust for the Indians, or from any timber thereon, or from any other source for the benefit of Indians, shall be invested from time to time, and how the payments or assistance to which the Indians may be entitled shall be made or given, and may provide for the general management of such lands, moneys and property, and direct what percentage or proportion thereof shall be set apart from time to time, to cover the cost of and attendant upon such management under the provisions of this Act, and for the construction or repair of roads passing through such lands, and by way of contribution to schools frequented by such Indians.

12. No person shall sell, barter, exchange or give to any Indian man, woman or child in Canada, any kind of spirituous liquors, in any manner or way, or cause or procure the same to be done for any purpose whatsoever;—and if any person so sells, barters, exchanges or gives any such spirituous liquors to any Indian man, woman or child as aforesaid, or causes the same to be done, he shall on conviction thereof, before any Justice of the Peace upon the evidence of one credible witness, other than the informer or prosecutor, be fined not exceeding twenty dollars for each such offence, one moiety to Her Majesty to form part of the fund for the benefit of that tribe, band or body of Indians with respect to one or more members of which the offence was committed; but no such penalty shall be incurred by furnishing to any Indian in case of sickness, any spirituous liquor, either by a medical man or under the direction of a medical man or clergyman.

13. No pawn taken of any Indian for any spirituous liquor, shall be retained by the person to whom such pawn is delivered, but the thing so pawned may be sued for and recovered, with costs of suit, by the Indian who has deposited the same, before any Court of competent jurisdiction.

14. No presents given to Indians nor any property purchased or acquired with or by means of any annuities granted to Indians, or any part thereof, or otherwise howsoever, and in the possession of any Tribe, band or body of Indians or of any Indian of any such Tribe, band or body, shall be liable to be taken, seized or distrained for any debt, matter or cause whatsoever.

15. For the purpose of determining what persons are entitled to hold, use or enjoy the lands and other immoveable property belonging to or appropriated to the use of the various tribes, bands or bodies of Indians in Canada, the following persons and classes of persons, and

none other, shall be considered as Indians belonging to the tribe, band or body of Indians interested in any such lands or immoveable property:

Firstly. All persons of Indian blood, reputed to belong to the particular tribe, band or body of Indians interested in such lands or immoveable property, and their descendants;

Secondly. All persons residing among such Indians, whose parents were or are, or either of them was or is, descended on either side from Indians or an Indian reputed to belong to the particular tribe, band or body of Indians interested in such lands or immoveable property, and the descendants of all such persons; And

Thirdly. All women lawfully married to any of the persons included in the several classes hereinbefore designated; the children issue of such marriages, and their descendants.

16. Indians and persons intermarried with Indians, residing upon any Indian Lands, and engaged in the pursuit of agriculture as their then principal means of support, shall be liable, if so directed by the Secretary of State, or any officer or person by him thereunto authorized, to perform labor on the public roads laid out or used in or through or abutting upon such Indian lands, such labor to be performed under the sole control of the said Secretary of State, officer or person, who may direct when, where and how and in what manner, the said labor shall be applied, and to what extent the same shall be imposed upon Indians or persons intermarried with Indians, who may be resident upon any of the said lands; and the said Secretary of State, officer or person shall have the like power or authority under law, rule or regulation in force in that one of the Provinces of Canada in which such lands lie, for the non-performance of statute law; But the labor to be so required of any such Indian or person intermarried with an Indian, shall not exceed in amount or extent what may be required of other inhabitants of the same province, county or other local division, under the laws requiring and regulating such labor and the performance thereof.

17. No persons other than Indians and those intermarried with Indians, shall settle, reside upon or occupy any land or road, or allowance for roads running through any lands belonging to or occupied by any tribe, band or body of Indians; and all mortgages or hypotheces given or consented to by any Indians or any persons intermarried with Indians, and all leases, contracts and agreements made or purporting to be made, by any Indians or any person intermarried with Indians, whereby persons other than Indians are permitted to reside upon such lands, shall be absolutely void.

18. If any persons other than Indians or those intermarried with Indians do, without the license of the Secretary of State, (which license, however, he may at any time revoke,) settle, reside upon or occupy any such lands, roads or allowances for roads, the Secretary of

State, or such officer or person as he may thereunto depute and authorize, shall, on complaint made to him, and on proof of the fact to his satisfaction, issue his warrant signed and sealed, directed to the sheriff of the proper county or district, then directed to any literate person willing to act in the premises, commanding him forthwith to remove from the said lands or roads, or allowances for roads, all such persons and their families, so settled, residing upon or occupying the same; and such sheriff or other person shall, accordingly, remove such persons, and for that purpose shall have the same powers as in the execution of criminal process; but the provisions in this and the four next following sections shall extend to such Indian lands only, as the Governor, from time to time, by Proclamation published in the *Canada Gazette,* declares and makes subject to the same, and so long only as such proclamation remains in force.

19. If any person after having been removed as aforesaid returns to, settles upon, resides upon, or occupies, any of the said lands or roads or allowances for roads, the Secretary of State or any officer or person deputed and authorized, as aforesaid, upon view, or upon proof on oath made before him or to his satisfaction, that the said person has returned to, settled or resided upon or occupied any of the said lands or roads or allowances for roads, shall direct and send his warrant signed and sealed, to the Sheriff of the proper County or District, or to any literate person therein, and if the said lands be not situated within any County, then to any literate person, commanding him forthwith to arrest such person and commit him to the Common Gaol of the said County or District or to the Common Gaol of the nearest County or District to the said lands, if the lands be not within any County or District, there to remain for the time ordered by such warrant, but which shall not exceed thirty days.

20. Such Sheriff or other person shall accordingly arrest the said party, and deliver him to the Gaoler or Sheriff of the proper County or District who shall receive such person, and imprison him in the said Common Gaol for the term aforesaid, there to remain without bail and without being entitled to the liberties or limits of the said Gaol.

21. The said Secretary of State, or such officer or person as aforesaid, shall cause the judgment or order against the offender to be drawn up, and such judgment shall not be removed by *Certiorari* or otherwise, or be appealed from, but shall be final.

22. If any person without the license in writing of the Secretary of State, or of some officer or person deputed by him for that purpose, trespasses upon any of the said lands or roads or allowances for roads, by cutting, carrying away or removing therefrom, any of the trees, saplings, shrubs, underwood or timber thereon, or by removing any of the stone or soil of the said lands, roads or allowances for roads, the

person so trespassing shall for every tree he cuts, carries away or removes, forfeit and pay the sum of twenty dollars, and for cutting, carrying or removing any of the saplings, shrubs, underwood or timber, if under the value of one dollar, the sum of four dollars, but if over the value of one dollar, then the sum of twenty dollars, and for removing any of the stone or soil aforesaid, the sum of twenty dollars, such fine to be recovered by the said Secretary of State, or any officer or person by him deputed, by distress and sale of the goods and chattels of the party or parties fined, or the said Secretary of State, officer or person without proceeding by distress and sale as aforesaid, may, upon the non-payment of the said fine, order the party or parties to be imprisoned in the Common Gaol as aforesaid, for a period not exceeding thirty days, when the fine does not exceed twenty dollars, or for a period not exceeding three months, where the fine does exceed twenty dollars; and upon the return of any warrant for distress or sale, if the amount thereof has not been made, or if any part of it remains unpaid, the said Secretary of State, officer or person, may commit the party in default upon such warrant, to the Common Gaol as aforesaid, for a period not exceeding thirty days if the sum claimed by the Secretary of State, upon the said warrant, does not exceed twenty dollars, or for a time not exceeding three months if the sum claimed does exceed twenty dollars; all such fines shall be paid to the Receiver General, to be disposed of for the use and benefit of the Tribe, band or body of Indians for whose benefit the lands are held, in such manner as the Governor may direct.

23. In all orders, writs, warrants, summonses and proceedings whatsoever made, issued or taken by the Secretary of State, or any officer or person by him deputed as aforesaid, it shall not be necessary for him or such officer or person, to insert or express the name of the person summoned, arrested, distrained upon, imprisoned or otherwise proceeded against therein, except when the name of such person is truly given to or known by the Secretary of State, officer or person, and if the name be not truly given to or known by him, he may name or describe the person by any part of the name of such person given to or known by him; and if no part of the name be given to or known by him he may describe the person proceeded against in any manner by which he may be identified; and all such proceedings containing or purporting to give the name or description of any such person as aforesaid shall *primâ facie* be sufficient.

24. All Sheriffs, Gaolers or Peace Officers to whom any such process is directed by the said Secretary of State, or by any officer or person by him deputed as aforesaid, shall obey the same, and all other officers upon reasonable requisition shall assist in the execution thereof.

25. If any Railway, road or public work passes through or causes

injury to any land belonging to or in possession of any tribe, band or body of Indians, compensation shall be made to them therefor, in the same manner as is provided with respect to the lands or rights of other persons; the Secretary of State shall act for them in any matter relating to the settlement of such compensation, and the amount awarded in any case shall be paid to the Receiver General for the use of the tribe, band or body of Indians for whose benefit the lands are held.

26.   The Secretary of State is hereby substituted for the Commissioner of Indian Lands for Lower Canada, under the fourteenth chapter of the Consolidated Statutes for Lower Canada, respecting Indians and Indian lands, which shall continue to apply to Indians and Indian lands, in the Province of Quebec, in so far as it is not inconsistent with this Act, and shall have all the powers and duties assigned to such Commissioner by the said Act, except that the lands and property heretofore vested in the said Commissioner shall henceforth be vested in the Crown, and shall be under management of the Secretary of State, who shall manage the same on behalf of the Crown, and the suits respecting them shall be brought in the name of the Crown, and the said Secretary of State shall not be bound to have any domicile in the Province of Quebec or to give security; and so much of the said Act as in inconsistent with the Act is repealed.

27.   The period limited by the sixth section of the Act last cited, as that within which informations may be brought under that Act, shall be one year instead of six months.

28.   In all cases of encroachment upon any lands set apart for Indian reservations or for the use of the Indians, not hereinbefore provided for, it shall be lawful to proceed by information in the name of Her Majesty in the Superior Courts of Law or Equity, notwithstanding the legal title may not be vested in the Crown.

29.   The Governor may authorize surveys, plans and reports to be made of any lands reserved for Indians shewing and distinguishing the improved lands, the forests and lands fit for settlement, and such other information as may be required.

30.   The proceeds arising from the sale or lease of any Indian lands or from the timber thereon shall be paid to the Receiver General to the credit of Indian Fund.

31.   The fifty-seventh chapter of the Revised Statutes of Nova Scotia, Third Series, is hereby repealed, and the chief Commissioner and Deputy Commissioners under the said chapter, shall forthwith pay over all monies in their hands arising from the selling or leasing of Indian lands, or otherwise under the said chapter, to the Receiver General of Canada by whom they shall be credited to the Indian Fund of Nova Scotia; and all such monies in the hands of the Treasurer of Nova Scotia, shall be paid over by him to the Receiver General of Canada, by

whom they shall be credited to the said Indian Fund. And all Indian lands and property now vested in the said Chief Commissioner, Deputy Commissioner, or other person whomsoever, for the use of Indians, shall henceforth be vested in the Crown and shall be under the management of the Secretary of State.

32. The eighty-fifth chapter of the Revised Statutes of New Brunswick respecting Indian Reserves is hereby repealed, and the Commissioners under the said chapter, shall forthwith pay over all monies in their hands arising from the selling or leasing of Indian Lands or otherwise under the said chapter, to the Receiver General of Canada, by whom they shall be credited to the Indians of New Brunswick, and all such monies now in the hands of the Treasurer of New Brunswick shall be paid over to the Receiver General of Canada, to be credited to the said Indians. And all Indian lands and property now vested in the said Commissioner, or other person whomsoever, for the use of Indians, shall henceforth be vested in the Crown and shall be under the management of the Secretary of State.

33. Nothing in this Act contained shall affect the provisions of the ninth chapter of the Consolidated Statutes of Canada, intituled: *An Act respecting the civilization and enfranchisement of certain Indians,* in so far as respects Indians in the Provinces of Quebec and Ontario, nor of any other Act when the same is not inconsistent with this Act.

34. The Secretary of State is hereby substituted for the Commissioner of Crown Lands as regards the Ordnance and Admiralty lands transferred to the late Province of Canada and lying in the Provinces of Quebec and Ontario.

35. All powers and duties vested in the Commissioner of Crown Lands with respect to the said Ordnance or Admiralty Lands, in the Provinces of Quebec and Ontario, by the Act of the Parliament of the late Province of Canada, passed in the twenty-third year of Her Majesty's reign, and chaptered two, intituled: *An Act respecting the sale and management of the Public Lands,* or by the twenty-third chapter of the Consolidated Statutes of the said late Province, intitutled: *An Act respecting the sale and management of Timber on Public Lands,* (both which Acts shall continue to apply to the said lands;)—or by any other Act or law in force in any of the Provinces now composing the Dominion of Canada, at the time of the Union of the said Provinces, are hereby transferred to and vested in the said Secretary of State, and shall be exercised and performed by him: Provided that in construing the two Acts cited in this Section, with reference to the said lands, the words "Secretary of State" shall be substituted for the words "Commissioner of Crown Lands," and for the words "Registrar of the Province,"—the words "Governor General" shall be substituted for the word "Governor" and the words "Governor General in Council" for

the words "Governor in Council,"—and the Governor General in Council may direct that the said two Acts or either of them, or any part or parts of either or both of them shall apply to the Indian Lands in the Provinces of Quebec and Ontario, or to any of the said lands, and may from time to time repeal any such Order in Council and make another or others instead thereof; and provided further, that all the powers and duties by this section vested in the Secretary of State, shall be deemed to have been so vested from and after the first day of July now last past, and may be by him exercised with reference to any act or thing done or performed since that date, in connection with Ordnance or Indian Lands.

36. The Secretary of State shall also have the control and management of all Crown Lands being the property of the Dominion, that are not specially under the control of the Public Works Department.

37. The Governor in Council may, from time to time, make such Regulations as he deems expedient for the protection and management of the Indian lands in Canada or any part thereof, and of the timber thereon or cut from off the said lands, whether surrendered for sale or reserved or set apart for the Indians, and for ensuring and enforcing the collection of all moneys payable in respect of the said lands or timber, and for the direction and government of the officers and persons employed in the management thereof or otherwise with reference thereto, and generally for carrying out and giving effect to the provisions of this Act;—and by such Regulations the Governor in Council may impose such fines not exceeding in any case two hundred dollars, as he deems necessary for ensuring the due observance of such Regulations, the payment of all such moneys as aforesaid, and the enforcing of due obedience to the provisions of this Act,—and may by such Regulations provide for the forfeiture, or the seizure and detention of any timber in respect of which the said Regulations have been infringed, or on which any sum payable in respect thereof has not been paid, and for the sale of such timber (if not forfeited,) in case the dues, damages and fine be not paid within the time limited by such regulations, and the payment thereof out of the proceeds of the sale; and if forfeited such timber shall be dealt with as the regulation may direct:—and may appropriate any such fines in such manner he may see fit; and the Governor in Council may by such regulations provide for the forfeiture of any lease, licence of occupation, licence to cut timber, or other licence or permission of any kind with respect to such lands, if the conditions on which such licence or permission is granted are not observed; but no such provision imposing any penalty or forfeiture shall impair or diminish any right or remedy of the Crown to recover any money or enforce the performance of the conditions of any such

sale, lease, contract, obligation, licence, or permission in the ordinary course of law.

38. All Regulations or Orders in Council made under the next preceding section shall be published in the *Canada Gazette,* and being so published shall have the force of law, from the date of their publication or from such later date as may be therein appointed for their coming into force: and any such regulation may be repealed, amended or re-enacted by any subsequent regulation, and shall be in force until so repealed or amended unless an earlier period be therein appointed for their ceasing to be in force; and a copy of any such Regulations purporting to be printed by the Queen's Printer shall be *primâ facie* evidence thereof.

39. The Governor may, from time to time, appoint officers and agents to carry out this Act, and any Orders in Council made under it, which officers and agents shall be paid in such manner and at such rates as the Governor in Council may direct.

40. The Governor in Council may at any time assign any of the duties and powers hereby assigned to and vested in the Secretary of State, to any other member of the Queen's Privy Council for Canada, and his department, and from the period appointed for that purpose by any order in Council such duties and powers shall be transferred to, and vested in such other member of Her Majesty's Privy Council for Canada and his department.

41. The Secretary of State shall annually lay before Parliament, within ten days after the meeting thereof, a report of the proceedings, transactions and affairs of the department during the year then next preceding.

42. So much of any Act or law as may be inconsistent with this Act, or as makes any provision in any matter provided for by this Act, other than such as is hereby made, is repealed, except only as to things done, obligations contracted, or penalties incurred before the coming into force of this Act.

C3.

32 and 33 Victoria (1869) Cap. 6 (Canada). An Act for the Gradual Enfranchisement of Indians, the Better Management of Indian Affairs, and to Extend the Provisions of the Act 31 Victoria Cap. 42. |assented to June 22, 1869|

HER Majesty, by and with the advice and consent of the Senate and House of Commons of Canada, enacts as follows:

1. In Townships or other tracts of land set apart or reserved for Indians in Canada, and subdivided by survey into lots, no Indian or person claiming to be of Indian blood, or intermarried with an Indian family, shall be deemed to be lawfully in possession of any land in such Townships or tracts, unless he or she has been or shall be located for the same by the order of the Superintendent General of Indian affairs; and any such person or persons, assuming possession of any lands of that description, shall be dealt with as illegally in possession, and be liable to be summarily ejected therefrom, unless that within six months from the passing of this Act, a location title be granted to such person or persons by the said Superintendent General of Indian affairs or such officer or person as he may thereunto depute and authorize; but the conferring of any such location title shall not have the effect of rendering the land covered thereby transferable or subject to seizure under legal process.

2. Any person liable to be summarily ejected, under the next preceding section, may be removed from the land of which he may have assumed possession, in the manner provided by the eighteenth section of the Act passed in the thirty-first year of Her Majesty's reign, chapter forty-two, with respect to persons other than Indians or those intermarried with Indians settling on the lands therein referred to without license of the Secretary of State; and the said section and the nineteenth, twentieth and twenty-first sections of the said Act, are hereby extended to and shall apply to persons liable to be summarily ejected under this Act, as fully in all respects as to persons liable to be removed from lands under the said Act.

3. Any person who shall sell, barter, exchange or give to any Indian man, woman, or child, any kind of spirituous or other intoxicating liquors, or cause or procure the same to be done, or open and keep or cause to be opened and kept, on any land set apart or reserved for Indians a tavern, house or building where spirituous or intoxicating liquors are sold or disposed of, shall, upon conviction in the manner provided by section twelve of the said Act thirty-first Victoria, chapter forty-two, be subject to the fine therein mentioned; and in default of payment of such fine, or of any fine imposed by the above mentioned twelfth section of the said Act, any person so offending may be committed to prison by the Justice of the Peace before whom the conviction shall take place, for a period not more than three months, or until such fine be paid; and the commander of any steamer or other vessel, or boat, from on board or on board of which, any spirituous or other intoxicating liquor shall have been, or may be sold or disposed of to any Indian man, woman, or child, shall be liable to a similar penalty.

4. In the division among the members of any tribe, band, or body of Indians, of any annuity money, interest money or rents, no person of

less than one-fourth Indian blood, born after the passing of this Act, shall be deemed entitled to share in any annuity, interest or rents, after a certificate to that effect is given by the Chief or Chiefs of the band or tribe in Council, and sanctioned by the Superintendent General of Indian affairs.

5. Any Indian or person of Indian blood who shall be convicted of any crime punishable by imprisonment in any Penitentiary or other place of confinement, shall, during such imprisonment, be excluded from participating in the annuities, interest money, or rents payable to the Indian tribe, band or body, of which he or she is a member; and whenever any Indian shall be convicted of any crime punishable by imprisonment in a Penitentiary, or other place of confinement, the legal costs incurred in procuring such conviction, and in carrying out the various sentences recorded, may be defrayed by the Superintendent General of Indian Affairs, and paid out of any annuity or interests coming to such Indian, or to the band or tribe, as the case may be.

6. The fifteenth section of the thirty-first Victoria, Chapter: forty-two, is amended by adding to it the following proviso:

"Provided always that any Indian woman marrying any other than an Indian, shall cease to be an Indian within the meaning of this Act, nor shall the children issue of such marriage be considered as Indians within the meaning of this Act; Provided also, that any Indian woman marrying an Indian of any other tribe, band or body shall cease to be a member of the tribe, band or body to which she formerly belonged, and become a member of the tribe, band or body of which her husband is a member, and the children, issue of this marriage, shall belong to their father's tribe only."

7. The Superintendent General of Indian affairs shall have power to stop the payment of the annuity and interest money of any person of Indian blood who may be proved to the satisfaction of the Superintendent General of Indian affairs to have been guilty of deserting his wife or child, and the said Superintendent may apply the same towards the support of any woman or child so deserted.

8. The Superintendent General of Indian Affairs in cases where sick or disabled, or aged and destitute persons are not provided for by the tribe, band or body of Indians of which they are members, may furnish sufficient aid from the funds of each tribe, band or body, for the relief of such sick, disabled, aged or destitute persons.

9. Upon the death of any Indian holding under location title any lot or parcel of land, the right and interest therein of such deceased Indian shall, together with his goods and chattels, devolve upon his children on condition of their providing for the maintenance of their mother, if living; and such children shall have a life estate only in such land which shall not be transferable or subject to seizure under legal

process, but should such Indian die without issue, such lot or parcel of land and goods and chattels shall be vested in the Crown for the benefit of the tribe, band or body of Indians, after providing for the support of the widow (if any) of such deceased Indian.

10. The Governor may order that the Chiefs of any tribe, band or body of Indians shall be elected by the male members of each Indian Settlement of the full age of twenty-one years at such time and place, and in such manner, as the Superintendent General of Indian Affairs may direct, and they shall in such case be elected for a period of three years, unless deposed by the Governor for dishonesty, intemperance, or immorality, and they shall be in the proportion of one Chief and two Second Chiefs for every two hundred people; but any such band composed of thirty people may have one Chief; Provided always that all life Chiefs now living shall continue as such until death or resignation, or until their removal by the Governor for dishonesty, intemperance or immorality.

11. The Chief or Chiefs of any tribe, band or body of Indians shall be bound to cause the roads, bridges, ditches and fences within their Reserve to be put and maintained in proper order, in accordance with the instructions received from time to time from the Superintendent General of Indian Affairs; and whenever in the opinion of the Superintendent General of Indian Affairs the same are not so put or maintained in order, he may cause the work to be performed at the cost of the said tribe, band or body of Indians, or of the particular Indian in default, as the case may be either out of their annual allowances, or otherwise.

12. The Chief or Chiefs of any Tribe in Council may frame, subject to confirmation by the Governor in Council, rules and regulations for the following subjects, viz:

1. The care of the public health.
2. The observance of order and decorum at assemblies of the people in General Council, or on other occasions.
3. The repression of intemperance and profligacy.
4. The prevention of trespass by cattle.
5. The maintenance of roads, bridges, ditches and fences.
6. The construction of and maintaining in repair of school houses, council houses and other Indian public buildings.
7. The establishment of pounds and the appointment of pound-keepers.

13. The Governor General in Council may on the report of the Superintendent General of Indian Affairs order the issue of Letters Patent granting to any Indian who from the degree of civilization to

which he has attained, and the character for integrity and sobriety which he bears, appears to be a safe and suitable person for becoming a proprietor of land, a life estate in the land which has been or may be allotted to him within the Reserve belonging to the tribe band or body of which he is a member; and in such case such Indian shall have power to dispose of the same by will, to any of his children, and if he dies intestate as to any such lands, the same shall descend to his children according to the laws of that portion of the Dominion of Canada in which such lands are situate, and the said children to whom such land is so devised or descends shall have the fee simple thereof.

14. If any enfranchised Indian owning land by virtue of the thirteenth and sixteenth sections of this Act, dies without leaving any children, such land shall escheat to the Crown for the benefit of the tribe, band, or body of Indians to which he, or his father, or mother (as the case may be) belonged; but if he leaves a widow, she shall, instead of Dower to which she shall not be entitled, have the said land for life or until her re-marriage, and upon her death or re-marriage it shall escheat to the Crown for the benefit of the tribe, band or body of Indians to which he, or his father, or mother (as the case may be) belonged.

15. The wife or unmarried daughters of any deceased Indian who may, in consequence of the operation of the thirteenth and sixteenth sections of this Act be deprived of all benefit from their husband's or father's land, shall in the periodical division of the annuity and interest money or other revenues of their husband's or father's tribe or band, and so long as she or they continue to reside upon the reserve belonging to the tribe or band, and remain in widowhood or unmarried, be entitled to and receive two shares instead of one share of such annuity and interest money.

16. Every such Indian shall, before the issue of the letters patent mentioned in the thirteenth section of this Act, declare to the Superintendent General of Indian Affairs, the name and surname by which he wishes to be enfranchised and thereafter known, and on his receiving such letters patent, in such name and surname, he shall be held to be also enfranchised, and he shall thereafter be known by such name and surname, and his wife and minor unmarried children, shall be held to be enfranchised; and from the date of such letters patent, the provisions of any Act or law making any distinction between the legal rights and liabilities of Indians and those of Her Majesty's other subjects shall cease to apply to any Indian, his wife or minor children as aforesaid, so declared to be enfranchised, who shall no longer be deemed Indians within the meaning of the laws relating to Indians, except in so far as their right to participate in the annuities and interest money and rents, of the tribe, band, or body of Indians to which they belonged is concerned;

except that the twelfth, thirteenth, and fourteenth sections of the Act thirty-first Victoria, chapter forty-two, and the eleventh section of this Act, shall apply to such Indian, his wife and children.

17. In the allotting of locations, and in the issue of Letters Patent to Indians for land, the quantity of land located or to be located or passed into Patent, shall, except in special cases to be reported upon to the Governor in Council, bear (as nearly as may be) the same proportion to the total quantity of land in the Reserve, as the number of persons to whom such lands are located or patented bears to the total number of heads of families of the tribe, band or body of Indians and male members thereof not being heads of families, but being above the age of fourteen years, in such reserve.

18. If any Indian enfranchised under this Act dies leaving any child under the age of twenty-one years, the Superintendent General of Indian Affairs shall appoint some person to be the tutor or guardian as the case may be of such child as to property and rights until it attains the age of twenty-one years; and the widow of such Indian, being also the mother of any such child, shall receive its share of the proceeds of the estate of such Indian during the minority of the child, and shall be entitled to reside on the land left by such Indian, so long as in the opinion of the Superintendent General she lives respectably.

19. Any Indian falsely representing himself as enfranchised under this Act when he is not so, shall be liable on conviction before any one Justice of the Peace, to imprisonment for any period not exceeding three months.

20. Such lands in any Indian Reserve as may be conveyed to any enfranchised Indian by Letters Patent, shall not, as long as the life estate of such Indian continues, be subject to seizure under legal process, or be mortgaged, hypothecated, sold, exchanged, transferred, leased, or otherwise disposed of.

21. Indians not enfranchised shall have the right to sue for debt due to them, or for any wrong inflicted upon them, or to compel the performance of obligations made with them.

22. The Under Secretary of State shall be charged, under the Secretary of State of Canada, with the performance of the Departmental duties of the Secretary of State under the said Act, and with the control and management of the officers, clerks, and servants of the Department, and with such other powers and duties as may be assigned to him by the Governor in Council.

23. Chapter nine of the Consolidated Statutes of Canada is hereby repealed.

24. This Act shall be construed as one Act with the Act thirty-first Victoria, chapter forty-two.

C4.

*33 Victoria (1870) Cap. 3 (Canada). An Act to Amend and Continue the
Act 32 and 33 Victoria Cap. 3; and to Establish and Provide for the
Government of the Province of Manitoba (The Manitoba Act, 1870).
/assented to May 12, 1870/ (Extract)*

* * *

31. And whereas, it is expedient, towards the extinguishment of
the Indian Title to the lands in the Province, to appropriate a portion of
such ungranted lands, to the extent of one million four hundred
thousand acres thereof, for the benefit of the families of the half-breed
residents, it is hereby enacted, that, under regulations to be from time to
time made by the Governor General in Council, the Lieutenant-
Governor shall select such lots or tracts in such parts of the Province as
he may deem expedient, to the extent aforesaid, and divide the same
among the children of the half-breed heads of families residing in the
Province at the time of the said transfer to Canada, and the same shall be
granted to the said children respectively, in such mode and on such
conditions as to settlement and otherwise, as the Governor General in
Council may from time to time determine.

32. For the quieting of titles, and assuring the settlers in the
Province the peaceable possession of the lands now held by them, it is
enacted as follows:—

1. All grants of land in freehold made by the Hudson's Bay
Company up to the eighth day of March, in the year 1869, shall, if
required by the owner, be confirmed by grant from the Crown.

2. All grants of estates less than freehold in land made by the
Hudson's Bay Company up to the eighth day of March aforesaid, shall,
if required by the owner, be converted into an estate in freehold by grant
from the Crown.

3. All titles by occupancy with the sanction and under the license
and authority of the Hudson's Bay Company up to the eighth day of
March aforesaid, of land in that part of the Province in which the Indian
Title has been extinguished, shall, if required by the owner, be converted into an estate in freehold by grant from the Crown.

4. All persons in peaceable possession of tracts of land at the time
of the transfer to Canada, in those parts of the Province in which the
Indian Title has not been extinguished, shall have the right of pre-
emption of the same, on such terms and conditions as may be determined by the Governor in Council.

5. The Lieutenant-Governor is hereby authorized, under regula-

tions to be made from time to time by the Governor General in Council, to make all such provisions for ascertaining and adjusting, on fair and equitable terms, the rights of Common, and rights of cutting Hay held and enjoyed by the settlers in the Province, and for the commutation of the same by grants of land from the Crown.

33. The Governor General in Council shall from time to time settle and appoint the mode and form of Grants of Land from the Crown, and any Order in Council for that purpose when published in the *Canada Gazette*, shall have the same force and effect as if it were a portion of this Act.

34. Nothing in this Act shall in any way prejudice or affect the rights or properties of the Hudson's Bay Company, as contained in the conditions under which that Company surrendered Rupert's Land to Her Majesty.

35. And with respect to such portion of Rupert's Land and the North-Western Territory, as is not included in the Province of Manitoba, it is hereby enacted, that the Lieutenant-Governor of the said Province shall be appointed, by Commission under the Great Seal of Canada, to be the Lieutenant-Governor of the same, under the name of the North-West Territories, and subject to the provisions of the Act in the next section mentioned.

36. Except as hereinbefore is enacted and provided, the Act of the Parliament of Canada, passed in the now last Session thereof, and entitled ''An Act for the Temporary Government of Rupert's Land, and the North-Western Territory when united with Canada,'' is hereby re-enacted, extended and continued in force until the first day of January, 1871, and until the end of the Session of Parliament then next succeeding.

* * *

C5.

Order of Her Majesty in Council Admitting Rupert's Land and the North-Western Territory into the Union. At the Court at Windsor, June 23, 1870. (Extract)

* * *

14. Any claims of Indians to compensation for lands required for purposes of settlement shall be disposed of by the Canadian Government in communication with the Imperial Government; and the Company[1] shall be relieved of all responsibility in respect of them.

* * *

[1] i.e. The Hudson's Bay Company.

C6.

Order of Her Majesty in Council Admitting British Columbia into the Union. At the Court at Windsor, May 16, 1871. (Extract)

* * *

13. The charge of the Indians, and the trusteeship and management of the lands reserved for their use and benefit, shall be assumed by the Dominion Government, and a policy as liberal as that hitherto pursued by the British Columbia Government shall be continued by the Dominion Government after the Union.

To carry out such policy, tracts of land of such extent as it has hitherto been the practice of the British Columbia Government to appropriate for that purpose , shall from time to time be conveyed by the Local Government to the Dominion Government in trust for the use and benefit of the Indians on application of the Dominion Government; and in case of disagreement between the two Governments respecting the quantity of such tracts of land, to be so granted, the matter shall be referred for the decision of the Secretary of State for the Colonies.

* * *

C7.

37 Victoria (1874) Cap. 21 (Canada). An Act to Amend Certain Laws Respecting Indians, and to Extend Certain Laws Relating to Matters Connected with Indians to the Provinces of Manitoba and British Columbia. /assented to May 26, 1874/

HER Majesty, by and with the advice and consent of the Senate and House of Commons of Canada, enacts as follows:—

1. The twelfth section of the Act thirty-first Victoria, chapter forty-two, intiutled *"An Act providing for the organization of the Department of the Secretary of State of Canada, and for the management of Indian and Ordnance Lands,"* and the third section of the Act thirty-second and thirty-third Victoria, chapter six, intituled *"An Act for the gradual enfranchisement of Indians, the better management of Indian affairs, and to extend the provisions of the Act thirty-first Victoria, chapter forty-two,"* are hereby repealed, and the following shall be read in lieu of the last mentioned section:—

"3. 1. Whoever sells, exchanges with, barters, supplies, or gives to any Indian man, woman or child in Canada, any kind of intoxicating liquor, or causes or procures the same to be done, or connives or attempts threat or opens or keeps, or causes to be opened or kept on any land set apart or reserved for Indians, a tavern, house, or building where intoxicating liquor is sold, bartered, exchanged, or given, or is found in possession of intoxicating liquor in the house, or building where intoxicating liquor is sold, bartered, exchanged, or given, or is found in possesion of intoxicating liquor in the house, tent, wigwam, or place of abode of any Indian, shall, on conviction thereof before any Justice of the Peace upon the evidence on one credible witness other than the informer or prosecutor, be liable to imprisonment for a period not exceeding two years, and be fined not more than five hundred dollars, one moiety to go to the informer or prosecutor, and the other moiety to Her Majesty, to form part of the fund for the benefit of that tribe or body of Indians with respect to one or more members of which the offence was committed; and the commander or person in charge of any steamer or other vessel, or boat, from or on board of which any intoxicating liquor shall have been sold, bartered, exchanged, supplied or given to any Indian man, woman or child, shall be liable, on conviction thereof before any Justice of the Peace, upon the evidence of one credible witness other than the informer or prosecutor, to be fined not exceeding five hundred dollars for each such offence, the moieties thereof to be applicable as hereinbefore mentioned, and in default of immediate payment of such fine any person so fined may be committed to any common gaol, house of correction, lock-up, or other place of confinement by the Justice of the Peace before whom the conviction shall take place, for a period of not more than twelve months, or until such fine shall be paid; and in all cases arising under this section, Indians shall be competent witnesses: but no penalty shall be incurred in case of sickness where any intoxicating liquor is made use of under the sanction of any medical man or under the directions of a minister of religion.''

"2. The keg, barrel, case, box, package or receptacle whence intoxicating liquor has been sold, exchanged, bartered, supplied or given, and as well that in which the original supply was contained as the vessel wherein any portion of such original supply was supplied as aforesaid, and the balance of the contents thereof, if such barrel, keg, case, box, package, receptacle or vessel aforesaid respectively, can be identified and any intoxicating liquor imported or manufactured or brought into and upon any land set apart or reserved for Indians, or into the house, tent, wigwam or place of abode of any Indian, may be seized by any constable wheresoever found on such land; and on complaint before any Judge, Stipendiary Magistrate or Justice of the Peace, he may, on the evidence of any credible witness that this Act has been contravened in respect thereof, declare the same forfeited, and cause the same to be forthwith destroyed; and the person in whose possession they were found may be condemned to pay a penalty not exceeding one hundred dollars, nor less than fifty dollars, and the costs of prosecution; and one-half of such penalty shall belong to the prosecutor, and the other half to Her Majesty for the purposes hereinbefore mentioned, and in default of immediate payment the offender may be committed to any common gaol, house of correction, lock-up or other place of confinement for any time not exceeding six months unless such fine and costs are sooner paid.''

"3. When it shall be proved before any Judge, Stipendiary Magistrate or Justice of the Peace that any vessel, boat, canoe, or conveyance of any description upon the sea or sea-coast, or upon any river, lake or stream in Canada, is employed in carrying intoxicating liquor, to be supplied to any Indian or Indians, such vessel, boat, canoe, or conveyance so employed may be seized and declared forfeited as in the last sub-section mentioned, and sold, and the proceeds thereof paid to Her Majesty for the purposes hereinbefore mentioned.''

"4. It shall be lawful for any constable, without process of law, to arrest any Indian whom he may find in a state of intoxication, and to convey him to any common gaol, house of correction, lock-up or other place of confinement, there to be kept until he shall have become sober; and such Indian shall, when sober, be brought before any Judge, Stipendiary Magistrate, or Justice of the Peace, and if convicted of being so found in a state of intoxication, shall be liable to imprisonment in any common gaol, house of correction, lock-up or other place of confinement, for any period not exceeding one month. And if any Indian having been so convicted as aforesaid, shall refuse, upon examination, to state or give information of the person, place and time, from whom, where and when he procured intoxicating liquor, and if from any other Indian, then, if within his knowledge, from whom, where and when such intoxicating liquor was originally procured or received, he shall be liable to imprisonment as aforesaid for a further period not exceeding fourteen days.''

"5. The words 'intoxicating liquor' shall mean and include all spirits, strong waters, spirituous liquors, wines, or fermented or compounded liquors or intoxicating drink of any kind whatsoever, and intoxicating liquor or fluid; as also opium and any preparation thereof, whether liquid or solid; and any other intoxicating drug or substance, and tobacco or tea mixed or compounded or impregnated with opium or with other intoxicating drug or substance, and whether the same, or any of them, be liquid or solid.''

"6. No prosecution, conviction or commitment under this Act shall be invalid on account of want of form so long as the same is according to the true meaning of the Act.''

2. The following shall be taken and read as part of the fourteenth section of the thirty-first Victoria, chapter forty-two, that is to say:—

"Nor shall the same be sold, bartered, exchanged or given by any tribe, band or body of Indians or any Indian of any such tribe, band or body to any person or persons other than a tribe, band or body of Indians or any Indian of any tribe; and any such sale, barter, exchange or gift, shall be abolutely null or void, unless any such sale, barter, exchange or gift be made with the written assent of the Indian agent; and any person who may buy or otherwise acquire any presents or property purchased as aforesaid without the written consent of the Indian agent as aforesaid shall be guilty of a misdemeanor, and be punishable by fine not exceeding two hundred dollars, or by imprisonment not exceeding six months in any place of confinement other than a Penitentiary."

3. Upon any inquest, or upon any enquiry into any matter involving a criminal charge, or upon the trial of any crime or offence whatsoever, or by whomsoever committed, it shall be lawful for any Court, Judge, Stipendiary Magistrate, Coroner or Justice of the Peace to receive evidence of any Indian or aboriginal native or native of mixed blood, who is destitute of the knowledge of God, and of any fixed and clear belief in religion or in a future state of rewards and punishments, without administering the usual form of oath to any such Indian, aboriginal native or native of mixed blood as aforesaid, upon his solemn affirmation or declaration to tell the truth, the whole truth and nothing but the truth, or in such form as may be approved by such Court, Judge, Stipendiary Magistrate, Coroner or Justice of the Peace, as most binding in his conscience.

4. Provided that in the case of any inquest, or upon any inquiry into any matter involving a criminal charge, or upon the trial of any crime or offence whatsoever, the substance of the evidence or information of any such Indian, aboriginal native or native of mixed blood as aforesaid, shall be reduced to writing, and signed by a mark of the person giving the same, and verified by the signature or mark of the person acting as interpreter (if any) and of the judge, Stipendiary Magistrate, Coroner or Justice of the Peace or person before whom such information shall have been given.

5. The court, judge, Stipendiary Magistrate, or Justice of the Peace shall, before taking any such evidence, information or examination, caution every such Indian, aboriginal native or native of mixed blood as aforesaid that he will be liable to incur punishment if he do not so as aforesaid tell the truth.

6. The written declaration or examination made, taken and verified in manner aforesaid, of any such Indian, aboriginal native or native of mixed blood as aforesaid, may be lawfully read and received

as evidence upon the trial of any criminal suit or proceedings when, under the like circumstances, the written affidavit, examination, deposition or confession of any person, might be lawfully read and received as evidence.

7. Every solemn affirmation or declaration in whatever form made or taken by any person as aforesaid shall be on the same force and effect, as if such person had taken an oath in the usual form, and shall, in like manner, incur the penalty of perjury in case of falsehood.

8. An Indian is hereby defined to be a person within the definition contained in the fifteenth section of the thirty-first Victoria, chapter forty-two, as amended by the sixth section of the thirty-second and thirty-third Victoria, chapter six, and who shall participate in the annuities and interest moneys and rents of any tribe, band or body of Indians.

9. Upon, from and after the passing of this Act, the Acts and portions of Acts hereinafter mentioned of the Parliament of Canada shall be and are hereby extended to and shall be in force in the Provinces of Manitoba and of British Columbia; and all enactments and laws theretofore in force in the said Provinces, inconsistent with the said Acts, or making any provision in any matter provided for by the said Acts, other than such as is made by the said Acts, shall be repealed on and after the passing of this Act.

10. The Acts and portions of Acts hereinbefore mentioned and hereby extended to and to be in force in the Provinces of Manitoba and of British Columbia, are as follows:—

1. Sections six to twenty-five both inclusive, and sections twenty-eight, twenty-nine, thirty, thirty-seven, thirty-eight, thirty-nine and forty-two, of the Act passed in the thirty-first year of Her Majesty's reign, and intituled: *"An Act providing for the organization of the Department of the Secretary of State of Canada, and for the management of Indian and Ordnance Lands;"*

2. Sections one to twenty-one, both inclusive, and section twenty-four of the Act passed in the thirty-second and thirty-third years of Her Majesty's reign, intituled: *"An Act for the gradual enfranchisement of Indians, the better management of Indian affairs, and to extend the provisons of the Act thirty-first Victoria, chapter forty-two;"*

3. Sections one, three, six, seven, eight, nine and sixteen, of the Act passed in the thirty-sixth year of Her Majesty's reign, and intituled: *"An Act to provide for the establishment of the Department of the Interior."*

11. The Governor in Council may, by proclamation from time to time, exempt from the operation of the Act passed in the thirty-first year of Her Majesty's reign, and intituled: *"An Act providing for the organization of the Department of the Secretary of State of Canada,*

and for the management of Indian and Ordnance Lands,'' or from the operation of an Act passed in the thirty-second and thirty-third years of Her Majesty's reign, intituled *"An Act for the gradual enfranchisement of Indians, the better management of Indian affairs, and to extend the provisions of the Act thirty-first Victoria chapter forty-two,''* or from the operation of the Act passed in the thirty-first year of Her Majesty's reign, and intitutled: *"An Act to provide for the establishment of the Department of the Interior,''* or from the operation of this Act, or from the operation of any one or more of the clauses of any one or more of the said Acts, the Indians or any of them, or any tribe of them or the Indian lands or any portions of them in the Province of Manitoba, or in the Province of British Columbia, or in either of them, and may again, by proclamation, from time to time, remove such exemption.

12. The Governor in Council may, by proclamation from time to time, direct the application of the Act passed in the thirty-first year of Her Majesty's reign, and intituled *"An Act providing for the organization of the Department of the Secretary of State of Canada, and for the management of Indian and Ordnance Lands;''* and of an Act passed in the thirty-second and thirty-third years of Her Majesty's reign, intituled *"An Act for the gradual enfranchisement of Indians, the better management of Indian affairs, and to extend the provisions of the Act thirty-first Victoria, chapter forty-two;''* and an Act passed in the thirty-sixth year of Her Majesty's reign, and intituled *"An Act to provide for the establishment of the Department of the Interior;''* or of any one or more of the clauses of any one or more of the said Acts to the Indians or any of them or any tribe of them or the Indian lands or any portions of them, or that the same be in force generally in the North West Territories.

13. The second, third, and seventh sections of the Ordinance, No. 85, of the Revised Statutes of British Columbia are hereby repealed.

14. This Act shall be construed as one Act with the Acts thirty-first Victoria, chapter forty-two, and thirty-second and thirty-third Victoria, chapter six.

C8.

39 Victoria (1876) Cap. 18 (Canada). An Act to Amend and Consolidate the Laws Respecting Indians (The Indian Act, 1876). /assented to April 12, 1876/

WHEREAS it is expedient to amend and consolidate the laws respecting Indians: Therefore Her Majesty, by and with the advice and consent of the Senate and House of Commons of Canada, enacts as follows:—

1. This Act shall be known and may be cited as *"The Indian Act, 1876;"* and shall apply to all the Provinces, and to the North West Territories, including the Territory of Keewatin.

2. The Minister of the Interior shall be Superintendent-General of Indian Affairs, and shall be governed in the supervision of the said affairs, and in the control and management of the reserves, lands, moneys, and property of Indians in Canada by the provisions of this Act.

TERMS

3. The following terms contained in this Act shall be held to have the meaning hereinafter assigned to them, unless such meaning be repugnant to the subject or inconsistent with the context:—

1. The term "band" means any tribe, band or body of Indians who own or are interested in a reserve or in Indian lands in common, of which the legal title is vested in the Crown, or who share alike in the distribution of any annuities or interest moneys for which the Government of Canada is responsible; the term "the band" means the band to which the context relates; and the term "band," when action is being taken by the band as such, means the band in council.

2. The term "irregular band" means any tribe, band or body of persons of Indian blood who own no interest in any reserve or lands of which the legal title is vested in the Crown, who possess no common fund managed by the Government of Canada, or who have not had any treaty relations with the Crown.

3. The term "Indian" means

First. Any male person of Indian blood reputed to belong to a particular band;

Secondly. Any child of such person;

Thirdly. Any woman who is or was lawfully married to such person:

(*a*) Provided that any illegitimate child, unless having shared with the consent of the band in the distribution moneys of such band for a period exceeding two years, may, at any time, be excluded from the membership thereof by the band, if such proceeding be sanctioned by the Superintendent-General:

(*b*) Provided that any Indian having for five years continuously resided in a foreign country shall with the sanction of the Superintendent-General, cease to be a member thereof and shall not be permitted to become again a member thereof, or of any other band, unless the consent of the band with the approval of the Superintendent-General or his agent, be first had and obtained; but this provision shall not apply to any professional man, mechanic, missionary, teacher or interpreter, while discharging his or her duty as such:

(c) Provided that any Indian woman marrying any other than an Indian or a non-treaty Indian shall cease to be an Indian in any respect within the meaning of this Act, except that she shall be entitled to share equally with the members of the band to which she formerly belonged, in the annual or semi-annual distribution of their annuities, interest moneys and rents; but this income may be commuted to her at any time at ten years' purchase with the consent of the band:

(d) Provided that any Indian woman marrying an Indian of any other band, or a non-treaty Indian shall cease to be a member of the band to which she formerly belonged, and become a member of the band or irregular band of which her husband is a member:

(e) Provided also that no half-breed in Manitoba who has shared in the distribution of half-breed lands shall be accounted an Indian; and that no half-breed head of a family (except the widow of an Indian, or a half-breed who has already been admitted into a treaty), shall, unless under very special circumstances, to be determined by the Superintendent-General or his agent, be accounted an Indian, or entitled to be admitted into any Indian treaty.

4. The term "non-treaty Indian" means any person of Indian blood who is reputed to belong to an irregular band, or who follows the Indian mode of life, even though such person be only a temporary resident in Canada.

5. The term "enfranchised Indian" means any Indian, his wife or minor unmarried child, who has received letters patent granting him in fee simple any portion of the reserve which may have been allotted to him, his wife and minor children, by the band to which he belongs, or any unmarried Indian who may have received letters patent for an allotment of the reserve.

6. The term "reserve" means any tract or tracts of land set apart by treaty or otherwise for the use or benefit of or granted to a particular band of Indians, of which the legal title is in the Crown, but which is unsurrendered, and includes all the trees, wood, timber, soil, stone, minerals, metals, or other valuables thereon or therein.

7. The term "special reserve" means any tract or tracts of land and everything belonging thereto set apart for the use or benefit of any band or irregualr band of Indians, the title of which is vested in a society, corporation or community legally established, and capable of suing and being sued, or in a person or persons of European descent but which land is held in trust for, or benevolently allowed to be used by, such band or irregualr band of Indians.

8. The term "Indian lands" means any reserve or portion of a reserve which has been surrendered to the Crown.

9. The term "intoxicants" means and includes all spirits, strong waters, spirituous liquors, wines or fermented or compounded liquors or intoxicating drink of any kind whatsoever, and any intoxicating liquor or fluid, as also opium and any preparation thereof, whether liquid or solid, and any other intoxicating drug or substance, and tobacco or tea mixed or compounded or impregnated with opium or with other intoxicating drugs, spirits or substances, and whether the same or any of them be liquid or solid.

10. The term "Superintendent-General" means the Super-intendent-General of Indian Affairs.

11. The term "agent" means a commissioner, superintendent, agent, or other officer acting under the instructions of the Superintendent-General.

12. The term "person" means an individual other than an Indian, unless the context clearly requires another construction.

RESERVES.

4. All reserves for Indians or for any band of Indians, or held in trust for their benefit, shall be deemed to be reserved and held for the same purposes as before the passing of this Act, but subject to its provisions.

5. The Superintendent-General may authorize surveys, plans and reports to be made of any reserve for Indians, shewing and distinguishing the improved lands, the forests and lands fit for settlement, and such other information as may be required; and may authorize that the whole or any portion of a reserve be subdivided into lots.

6. In a reserve, or portion of a reserve, subdivided by survey into lots, no Indian shall be deemed to be lawfully in possession of one or more of such lots, or part of a lot, unless he or she has been or shall be located for the same by the band, with the approval of the Superintendent-General:

Provided that no Indian shall be dispossessed of any lot or part of a lot, on which he or she has improvements, without receiving compensation therefor, (at a valuation to be approved by the Superintendent-General) from the Indian who obtains the lot or part of a lot, or from the funds of the band, as may be determined by the Superintendent-General.

7. On the Superintendent-General approving of any location as aforesaid, he shall issue in triplicate a ticket granting a location title to such Indian, one triplicate of which he shall retain in a book to be kept

for the purpose; the other two he shall forward to the local agent, one to be delivered to the Indian in whose favor it was issued, the other to be filed by the agent, who shall permit it to be copied into the register of the band, if such register has been established:

8. The conferring of any such location title as aforesaid shall not have the effect of rendering the land covered thereby subject to seizure under legal process, or transferable except to an Indian of the same band, and in such case, only with the consent of the council thereof and the approval of the Superintendent-General, when the transfer shall be confirmed by the issue of a ticket in the manner prescribed in the next preceding section.

9. Upon the death of any Indian holding under location or other duly recognized title any lot or parcel of land, the right and interest therein of such deceased Indian shall, together with his goods and chattels, devolve one-third upon his widow, and the remainder upon his children equally; and such children shall have a like estate in such land as their father; but should such Indian die without issue but leaving a widow, such lot or parcel of land and his goods and chattels shall be vested in her, and if he leaves no widow, then in the Indian nearest akin to the deceased, but if he have no heir nearer than a cousin, then the same shall be vested in the Crown for the benefit of the band: But whatever may be the final disposition of the land, the claimant or claimants shall not be held to be legally in possession until they obtain a location ticket from the Superintendent-General in the manner prescribed in the case of new locations.

10. Any Indian or non-treaty Indian in the Province of British Columbia, the Province of Manitoba, in the North-West Territories, or in the Territory of Keewatin, who has, or shall have, previously to the selection of a reserve, possession of and made permanent improvements on a plot of land which has been or shall be included in or surrounded by a reserve, shall have the same privileges, neither more nor less, in repect of such plot, as an Indian enjoys who holds under a location title.

PROTECTION OF RESERVES.

11. No person, or Indian other than an Indian of the band, shall settle, reside or hunt upon, occupy or use any land or marsh, or shall settle, reside upon or occupy any road, or allowance for roads running through any reserve belonging to or occupied by such band; and all mortgages or hypothecs given or consented to by any Indian, and all leases, contracts and agreements made or purporting to be made by any Indian, whereby persons or Indians other than Indians of the band are permitted to reside or hunt upon such reserve, shall be absolutely void.

12. If any person or Indian other than an Indian of the band, without the license of the Superintendent-General (which license, however, he may at any time revoke), settles, resides or hunts upon or occupies or uses any such land or marsh; or settles, resides upon or occupies any such roads or allowances for roads, on such reserve, or if any Indian is illegally in possession of any lot or part of a lot in a subdivided reserve, the Superintendent-General or such officer or person as he may thereunto depute and authorize, shall, on complaint made to him, and on proof of the fact to his satisfaction, issue his warrant signed and sealed, directed to the sheriff of the proper county or district, or if the said reserve be not situated within any county or district, then directed to any literate person willing to act in the premises, commanding him forthwith to remove from the said land or marsh or roads or allowances for roads, or lots or parts of lots, every such person or Indian and his family so settled, residing or hunting upon or occupying, or being illegally in possession of the same, or to notify such person or Indian to cease using as aforesaid the said lands, marshes, roads or allowances for roads; and such sheriff or other person shall accordingly remove or notify such person or Indian, and for that purpose shall have the same powers as in the execution of criminal process; and the expenses incurred in any such removal or notification shall be borne by the party removed or notified, and may be recovered from him as the costs in any ordinary suit:

Provided that nothing contained in this Act shall prevent an Indian or non-treaty Indian, if five years a resident in Canada, not a member of the band, with the consent of the band and the approval of the Superintendent-General, from residing upon the reserve, or receiving a location thereon.

13. If any person or Indian, after having been removed or notified as aforesaid, returns to, settles upon, resides or hunts upon or occupies, or uses as aforesaid, any of the said land, marsh or lots, or parts of lots; or settles, resides upon or occupies any of the said roads, allowances for roads, or lots or parts of lots, the Superintendent-General, or any officer or person deputed and authorized as aforesaid, upon view, or upon proof on oath made before him, or to his satisfaction, that the said person or Indian has returned to, settled, resided or hunted upon or occupied or used as aforesaid any of the said lands, marshes, lots or parts of lots, or has returned to, settled or resided upon or occupied any of the said roads or allowances for roads, or lots or parts of lots, shall direct and send his warrant signed and sealed to the sheriff of the proper county or district, or to any literate person therein, and if the said reserve be not situated within any county or district, then to any literate person, commanding him forthwith to arrest such person or Indian, and commit him to the common gaol of the said county or district, or if there

be no gaol in the said county or district, then to the gaol nearest to the said reserve in the Province or Territory there to remain for the time ordered by such warrant, but which shall not exceed thirty days.

14. Such sheriff or other person shall accordingly arrest the said party, and deliver him to the gaoler or sheriff of the proper county, district, Province or Territory, who shall receive such person or Indian and imprison him in the said gaol for the term aforesaid.

15. The Superintendent-General, or such officer or person as aforesaid, shall cause the judgment or order against the offender to be drawn up and filed in his office, and such judgment shall not be removed by *certiorari* or otherwise, or be appealed from, but shall be final.

16. If any person or Indian other than an Indian of the band to which the reserve belongs, without the license in writing of the Superintendent-General or of some officer or person deputed by him for that purpose, trespasses upon any of the said land, roads or allowances for roads in the said reserve, by cutting, carrying away or removing therefrom any of thr trees, saplings, shrubs, underwood, timber or hay thereon, or by removing any of the stone, soil, minerals, metals or other valuables off the said land, roads or allowances for roads, the person or Indian so trespassing shall, for every tree he cuts, carries away or removes, forfeit and pay the sum of twenty dollars; and for cutting, carrying away or removing any of the saplings, shrubs, underwood, timber or hay, if under the value of one dollar, the sum of four dollars, but if over the value of one dollar, then the sum of twenty dollars; and for removing any of the stone, soil, minerals, metals or other valuables aforesaid, the sum of twenty dollars, such fine to be recovered by the Superintendent-General, or any officer or person by him deputed, by distress and sale of the goods and chattels of the party or parties fined: or the Superintendent-General, or such officer or person, without proceeding by distress and sale as aforesaid, may, upon the non-payment of the said line, order the party or parties to be imprisoned in the common goal as aforesaid, for a period not exceeding thirty days, when the fine does not exceed twenty dollars, or for a period not exceeding three months when the fine does exceed twenty dollars; and upon the return of any warrant for distress or sale, if the amount thereof has not been made, or if any part of it remains unpaid, the said Superintendent-General, officer or person, may commit the party in default upon such warrant, to the common gaol as aforesaid for a period not exceeding thirty days if the sum claimed by the Superintendent-General, upon the said warrant does not exceed twenty dollars, or for a time not exceeding three months if the sum claimed does exceed twenty dollars:. all such fines shall be paid to the Receiver-General, to be disposed of for the use and benefit of the band

of Indians for whose benefit the reserve is held, in such manner as the Governor in Council may direct.

17. If any Indian, without the license in writing of the Superintendent-General, or of some officer or person deputed by him for that purpose, trespasses upon the land of an Indian who holds a location title, or who is otherwise recognized by the department as the occupant of such land, by cutting, carrying away, or removing therefrom, any of the trees, saplings, shrubs, underwood, timber or hay thereon, or be removing any of the stone, soil, minerals, metals or other valuables off the said land; or if any Indian, without license as aforesaid, cuts, carries away or removes from any portion of the reserve of his band for sale (and not for the immediate use of himself and his family) any trees, timber or hay thereon, or removes any of the stone, soil, minerals, metals, or other valuables therefrom for sale as aforesaid, he shall be liable to all the fines and penalties provided in the next preceding section in respect to Indians of other bands and other persons.

18. In all orders, writs, warrants, summonses and proceedings whatsoever made, issued or taken by the Superintendent-General, or any officer or person by him deputed as aforesaid, it shall not be necessary for him or such officer or person to insert or express the name of the person or Indian summoned, arrested, distrained upon, imprisoned, or otherwise proceeded against therein, except when the name of such person or Indian is truly given to or known by the Superintendent-General, or such officer or person, and if the name be not truly given to or known by him, he may name or describe the person or Indian by any part of the name of such person or Indian given to or known by him; and if no part of the name be given to or known by him he may describe the person or Indian proceeded against in any manner by which he may be identified; and all such proceedings containing or purporting to give the name or description of any such person or Indian as aforesaid shall *primâ facie* be sufficient.

19. All sheriffs, gaolers or peace officers to whom any such process is directed by the Superintendent-General. or by any officer or person by him deputed as aforesaid, shall obey the same, and all other officers upon reasonable requisition shall assist in the execution thereof.

20. If any railway, road, or public work passes through or causes injury to any reserve belonging to or in possession of any band of Indians, or if any act occasioning damage to any reserve be done under the authority of any Act of Parliament, or of the legislature of any province, compensation shall be made to them therefor in the same manner as is provided with respect to the lands or rights of other persons; the Superintendent-General shall in any case in which an arbitration may be had, name the arbitrator on behalf of the Indians, and

shall act for them in any matter relating to the settlement of such compensation; and the amount awarded in any case shall be paid to the Receiver General for the use of the band of Indians for whose benefit the reserve is held, and for the benefit of any Indian having improvements thereon.

SPECIAL RESERVES.

21. In all cases of encroachment upon, or of violation of trust respecting any special reserve, it shall be lawful to proceed by information in the name of Her Majesty, in the superior courts of law or equity, notwithstanding the legal title may not be vested in the Crown.

22. If by the violation of the conditions of any such trust as aforesaid, or by the breaking up of any society, corporation, or community, or if by the death of any person or persons without a legal succession of trusteeship in whom the title to a special reserve is held in trust, the said title lapses or becomes void in law, then the legal title shall become vested in the Crown in trust, and the property shall be managed for the band or irregular band previously interested therein, as an ordinary reserve.

REPAIR OF ROADS.

23. Indians residing upon any reserve, and engaged in the pursuit of agriculture as their then principal means of support, shall be liable, if so directed by the Superintendent-General, or any officer or person by him thereunto authorized, to perform labor on the public roads laid out or used in or through, or abutting upon such reserve, such labor to be performed under the sole control of the said Superintendent-General, officer or person, who may direct when, where and how and in what manner the said labor shall be applied, and to what extent the same shall be imposed upon Indians who may be resident upon any of the said lands; and the said Superintendent-General, officer or person shall have the like power to enforce the performance of all such labor by imprisonment or otherwise, as may be done by any power or authority under any law, rule or regulation in force in the province or territory in which such reserve lies, for the non-performance of statute labor; but the labor to be so required of any such Indian shall not exceed in amount or extent what may be required of other inhabitants of the same province, territory, county, or other local division, under the laws requiring and regulating such labor and the performance thereof.

24. Every band of Indians shall be bound to cause the roads, bridges, ditches and fences within their reserve to be put and maintained in proper order, in accordance with the instructions received

from time to time from the Superintendent-General, or from the agent of the Superintendent-General; and whenever in the opinion of the Superintendent-General the same are not so put or maintained in order, he may cause the work to be performed at the cost of such band, or of the particular Indian in default, as the case may be, either out of their or his annual allowances, or otherwise.

SURRENDERS.

25. No reserve or portion of a reserve shall be sold, alienated or leased until it has been released or surrendered to the Crown for the purposes of this Act.

26. No release or surrender of a reserve, or portion of a reserve, held for the use of the Indians of any band or of any individual Indian, shall be valid or binding, except on the following conditions:—

1. The release or surrender shall be assented to by a majority of the male members of the band of the full age of twenty-one years, at a meeting or council thereof summoned for that purpose according to their rules, and held in the presence of the Superintendent-General, or of an officer duly authorized to attend such council by the Governor in Council or by the Superintendent-General; Provided, that no Indian shall be entitled to vote or be present at such council, unless he habitually resides on or near and is interested in the reserve in question;

2. The fact that such release or surrender has been assented to by the band at such council or meeting, shall be certified on oath before some judge of a superior, county, or district court, or stipendiary magistrate, by the Superintendent-General or by the officer authorized by him to attend such council or meeting, and by some one of the chiefs or principal men present thereat and entitled to vote, and when so certified as aforesaid shall be submitted to the Governor in Council for acceptance or refusal;

3. But nothing herein contained shall be construed to prevent the Superintendent-General from issuing a license to any person or Indian to cut and remove trees, wood, timber and hay, or to quarry and remove stone and gravel on and from the reserve; Provided he, or his agent acting by his instructions, first obtain the consent of the band thereto in the ordinary manner as aforesaid provided.

27. It shall not be lawful to introduce at any council or meeting of Indians held for the purpose of discussing or of assenting to a release or surrender of a reserve or portion thereof, or of assenting to the issuing of a timber or other license, any intoxicant; and any person introducing at such meeting, and any agent or officer employed by the Superintendent-General or by the Governor in Council, introducing, allowing or countenancing by his presence the use of such intoxicant

among such Indians a week before, at , or a week after, any such council or meeting, shall forfeit two hundred dollars, recoverable by action in any of the superior courts of law, one half of which penalty shall go to the informer.

28. Nothing in this Act shall confirm any release or surrender which would have been invalid if this Act had not been passed; and no release or surrender of any reserve to any party other than the Crown, shall be valid.

MANAGEMENT AND SALE OF INDIAN LANDS.

29. All Indian lands, being reserves or portions of reserves surrendered or to be surrendered to the Crown, shall be deemed to be held for the same purposes as before the passing of this Act; and shall be managed, leased and sold as the Governor in Council may direct, subject to the conditions of surrender, and to the provisions of this Act.

30. No agent for the sale of Indian lands shall, within his division, directly or indirectly, unless under an order of the Governor in Council, purchase any land which he is appointed to sell, or become proprietor of or interested in any such land, during the time of his agency; and any such purchase or interest shall be void; and if any such agent offends in the premises, he shall forfeit his office and the sum of four hundred dollars for every such offence, which may be recovered in action of debt by any person who may sue for the same.

31. Every certificate of sale or receipt for money received on the sale of Indian lands, heretofore granted or made or to be granted or made by the Superintendent-General or any agent of his, so long as the sale to which such receipt or certificate relates is in force and not rescinded, shall entitle the party to whom the same was or shall be made or granted, or his assignee, by instrument registered under this or any former Act providing for registration in such cases, to take possession of and occupy the land therein comprised, subject to the conditions of such sale, and thereunder, unless the same shall have been revoked or cancelled, to maintain suits in law or equity against any wrongdoer or trespasser, as effectually as he could do under a patent from the Crown;—and such receipt of certificate shall be *primâ facie* evidence for the purpose of possession by such person, or the assignee under an instrument registered as aforesaid, in any such suit; but the same shall have no force against a license to cut timber existing at the time of the making or granting thereof.

32. The Superintendent-General shall keep a book for registering (at the option of the parties interested) the particulars of any assignment made, as well by the original purchaser or lessee of Indian lands or his heir or legal representative, as by an subsequent assignee of any such

lands, or the heir or legal representative of such assignee;—and upon any such assignment being produced to the Superintendent-General, and, except in cases where such assignment is made under a corporate seal, with an affidavit of due execution thereof, and of the time and place of such execution, and the names, residences and occupations of the witnesses, or, as regards lands in the province of Quebec, upon the production of such assignment executed in notarial form, or of a notarial copy thereof, the Superintendent-General shall cause the material parts of every such assignment to be registered in such book of registry, and shall cause to be endorsed on every such assignment a certificate of such registration, to be signed by himself or his deputy, or any other officer of the department by him authorized to sign such certificates;—And every such assignment so registered shall be valid against any one previously executed, but subsequently registered, or unregistered; but all the conditions of the sale, grant or location must have been complied with, or dispensed with by the Superintendent-General before such registration is made.

33. If any subscribing witness to any such assignment is deceased or has left the province, the Superintendent-General may register such assignment upon the production of an affidavit proving the death or absence of such witness and his handwriting or the handwriting of the party making such assignment.

34. On any application for a patent by the heir, assignee or devisee of the original purchaser from the Crown, the Superintendent-General may receive proof in such manner as he may direct and require in support of any claim for a patent when the original purchaser is dead, and upon being satisfied that, the claim has been equitably and justly established, may allow the same and cause a patent to issue accordingly; but nothing in this section shall limit the right of a party claiming a patent to land in the province of Ontario to make application at any time to the commissioner, under the "*Act respecting claims to lands in Upper Canada for which no patents have issued.*"

35. If the Superintendent-General is satisfied that any purchaser or lessee of any Indian lands, or any assignee claiming under or through him has been guilty of any fraud or imposition, or has violated any of the conditions of sale or lease, or if any such sale or lease has been or is made or issued in error or mistake, he may cancel such sale or lease, and resume the land therein mentioned, or dispose of it as if no sale or lease thereof had ever been made; and all such cancellations heretofore made by the Governor in Council or the Superintendent-General shall continue valid until altered.

36. When any purchaser, lessee or other person refuses or neglects to deliver up possession of any land after revocation or cancellation of the sale or lease as aforesaid, or when any person is wrongfully in

possession of any Indian lands and refuses to vacate or abandon possession of the same, the Superintendent-General may apply to the county judge of the county, or to a judge of the superior court in the circuit in which the land lies in Ontario or Quebec, or to any judge of a superior court of law or any county judge of the county in which the land lies in any other province, or to any stipendiary magistrate in any territory in which the land lies, for an order in the nature of a writ of *habere facias possessionem,* or writ of possession, and the said judge or magistrate, upon proof to his satisfaction that the right or title of the party to hold such land has been revoked or cancelled as aforesaid, or that such person is wrongfully in possession of Indian lands, shall grant an order upon the purchaser, lessee or person in possession, to deliver up the same to the Superintendent-General, or person by him authorized to receive the same; and such order shall have the same force as a writ of *habere facias possessionem,* or writ of possession; and the sheriff, or any bailiff or person to whom it may have been trusted for execution by the Superintendent-General, shall execute the same in like manner as he would execute such writ in an action of ejectment or possessory action.

37. Whenever any rent payable to the Crown on any lease of Indian lands is in arrears, the Superintendent-General, or any agent or officer appointed under this Act and authorized by the Superintendent-General to act in such cases, may issue a warrant, directed to any person or persons by him named therein, in the shape of a distress warrant as in ordinary cases of landlord and tenant, or as in the case of distress and warrant of a justice of the peace for non-payment of a pecuniary penalty; and the same proceedings may be had thereon for the collection of such arrears as in either of the said last mentioned cases; or an action of debt as in ordinary cases or rent in arrear may be brought therefor in the name of the Superintendent-General; but demand of rent shall not be necessary in any case.

38. When by law or by any deed, lease or agreement relating to any of the lands herein referred to, any notice is required to be given, or any act to be done, by or on behalf of the Crown, such notice may be given and done by or by the authority of the Superintendent-General.

39. Whenever letters patent have been issued to or in the name of the wrong party, through mistake, or contain any clerical error or misnomer, or wrong description of any material fact therein, or of the land thereby intended to be granted, the Superintendent-General (there being no adverse claim,) may direct the defective letters patent to be cancelled and a minute of such cancellation to be entered in the margin of the registry of the original letters patent, and correct letters patent to be issued in their stead, which corrected letters patent shall relate back

to the date of those so cancelled, and have the same effect as if issued at the date of such cancelled letters patent.

40. In all cases in which grants or letters patent have issued for the same land inconsistent with each other through error, and in all cases of sales or appropriations of the same land inconsistent with each other, the Superintendent-General may, in cases of sale, cause a repayment of the purchase money, with interest, or when the land has passed from the original purchaser or has been improved before a discovery of the error, he may in substitution assign land or grant a certificate entitling the party to purchase Indian lands, of such value and to such extent as to him, the Superintendent-General, may seem just and equitable under the circumstances; but no such claim shall be entertained unless it be preferred within five years from the discovery of the error.

41. Whenever by reason of false survey or error in the books or plans in the Indian Branch of the Department of the Interior, any grant, sale or appropriation of land is found to be deficient, or any parcel of land contains less than the quantity of land mentioned in the patent therefor, the Superintendent-General may order the purchase money of so much land as is deficient, with the interest thereon from the time of the application therefor, or, if the land has passed from the original purchaser, then the purchase money which the claimant (provided he was ignorant of a deficiency at the time of his purchase) has paid for so much of the land as is deficient, with interest thereon from the time of the application therefor, to be paid to him in land or in money, as he, the Superintendent-General, may direct;—But no such claim shall be entertained unless application has been made within five years from the date of the patent, nor unless the deficiency is equal to one-tenth of the whole quantity described as being contained in the particular lot or parcel of land granted.

42. In all cases wherein patents for Indian lands have issued through fraud or in error or improvidence, the Exchequer Court of Canada, or a superior court of law or equity in any province may, upon action, bill or plaint, respecting such lands situate within their jurisdiction, and upon hearing of the parties interested, or upon default of the said parties after such notice of proceeding as the said courts shall respectively order, decree such patents to be void; and upon a registry of such decree in the office of the Registrar General of Canada, such patents shall be void to all intents. The practice in court, in such cases, shall be regulated by orders to be from time to time made by the said courts respectively; and any action or proceeding commenced under any former Act may be continued under this section, which, for the purpose of any such action or proceeding shall be construed as merely continuing the provisions of such former Act.

43. If any agent appointed or continued in office under this Act knowingly and falsely informs, or causes to be informed, any person applying to him to purchase any land within his division and agency, that the same has already been purchased, or refuses to permit the person so applying to purchase the same according to existing regulations, such agent shall be liable therefor to the person so applying in the sum of five dollars for each acre of land which the person so applying offered to purchase, to be recovered by action of debt in any court, having jurisdiction in civil cases to the amount.

44. If any person, before or at the time of the public sale of any Indian lands, by intimidation, combination, or unfair management, hinders or prevents, or attempts to hinder or prevent, any person from bidding upon or purchasing any lands so offered for sale, every such offender, his, her, or their aiders and abettors, shall, for every such offence, be guilty of a misdemeanor, and on conviction thereof shall be liable to a fine not exceeding four hundred dollars, or imprisonment for a term not exceeding two years, or both, in the discretion of the court.

MANAGEMENT AND SALE OF TIMBER.

45. The Superintendent-General, or any officer or agent authorized by him to that effect, may grant licenses to cut timber on reserves and ungranted Indian lands at such rates, and subject to such conditions, regulations and restrictions, as may from time to time be established by the Governor in Council, such conditions, regulations and restrictions to be adapted to the locality in which such reserves or lands are situated.

46. No license shall be so granted for a longer period than twelve months from the date thereof; and if in consequence of any incorrectness of survey or other error, or cause whatsoever, a license is found to comprise land included in a license of a prior date, or land not being reserves or ungranted Indian lands, the license granted shall be void in so far as it comprises such land, and the holder or proprietor of the license so rendered void shall have no claim upon the Government for indemnity or compensation by reason of such avoidance.

47. Every license shall describe the lands upon which the timber may be cut, and shall confer for the time being on the nominee, the right to take and keep exclusive possession of the land so described, subject to such regulations and restrictions as may be established;—And every license shall vest in the holder thereof all rights of property whatsoever in all trees, timber and lumber cut within the limits of the license during the term thereof, whether such trees, timber and lumber are cut by authority of the holder of such license or by any other person, with or without his consent;—And every license shall entitle the holder thereof to seize in revendication or otherwise, such trees, timber or lumber

where the same are found in the possession of any unauthorized person, and also to institute any action or suit at law or in equity against any wrongful possessor or trespasser, and to persecute all trespassers and other offenders to punishment, and to recover damages, if any:—And all proceedings pending at the expiration of any license may be continued to final termination as if the license had not expired.

48. Every person obtaining a license shall, at the expiration thereof, make to the officer or agent granting the same, or to the Superintendent-General a return of the number and kinds of trees cut and of the quantity and description of sawlogs, or of the number and description of sticks of square timber, manufactured and carried away under such license; and such statement shall be sworn to by the holder of the license, or his agent, or by his foreman; And any person refusing or neglecting to furnish such statement, or evading or attempting to evade any regulation made by Order in Council, shall be held to have cut without authority, and the timber made shall be dealt with accordingly.

49. All timber cut under license shall be liable for the payment of the dues thereon, so long as and wheresoever the said timber or any part of it may be found, whether in the original logs or manufactured into deals, boards or other stuff,—and all officers or agents entrusted with the collection of such dues may follow all such timber and seize and detain the same wherever it is found, until the dues are paid or secured.

50. Bonds or promissory notes taken for the dues, either before or after the cutting of the timber, as collateral security or to facilitate collection, shall not in any way affect the lien of the Crown on the timber, but the lien shall subsist until the said dues are actually discharged.

51. If any timber so seized and detained for non-payment of dues remains more than twelve months in the custody of the agent or person appointed to guard the same, without the dues and expenses being paid,—then the Superintendent-General, with the previous sanction of the Governor in Council, may order a sale of the said timber to be made after sufficient notice,—and the balance of the proceeds of such sale, after retaining the amount of dues and costs incurred, shall be handed over to the owner or claimant of such timber.

52. If any person without authority cuts or employs or induces any other person to cut, or assists in cutting any timber of any kind on Indian lands, or removes or carries away or employs or induces or assists any other person to remove or carry away any merchantable timber of any kind so cut from Indian lands aforesaid, he shall not acquire any right to the timber so cut, or any claim to any remuneration for cutting, preparing the same for market, or conveying the same to or towards market,—and when the timber or saw-logs made, has or have been

removed out of the reach of the officers of the Indian Branch of the Department of the Interior, or it is otherwise found impossible to seize the same, he shall in addition to the loss of his labour and disbursements, forfeit a sum of three dollars for each tree (rafting stuff excepted), which he is proved to have cut or caused to be cut or carried away,—and such sum shall be recoverable with costs, at the suit and in the name of the Superintendent-General or resident agent, in any court having jurisdiction in civil matters to the amount of the penalty;—And in all such cases it shall be incumbent on the party charged to prove his authority to cut; and the averment of the party seizing or prosecuting, that he is duly employed under the authority of this Act, shall be sufficient proof thereof, unless the defendant proves the contrary.

53. Whenever satisfactory information, supported by affidavit made before a justice of the peace or before any other competent authority, is received by the Superintendent-General, or any other officer or agent acting under him, that any timber or quantity of timber has been cut without authority on Indian lands, and describing where the said timber can be found, the said Superintendent-General, officer, or agent, or any one of them, may seize or cause to be seized, in Her Majesty's name, the timber so reported to have been cut without authority, wherever it is found, and place the same under proper custody, until a decision can be had in the matter from competent authority;

2. And where the timber so reported to have been cut without authority on Indian lands, has been made up with other timber into a crib, dram or raft, or in any other manner has been so mixed up at the mills or elsewhere, as to render it impossible or very difficult to distinguish the timber so cut on reserves or Indian lands without license, from other timber with which it is mixed up, the whole of the timber so mixed shall be held to have been cut without authority on Indian lands, and shall be liable to seizure and forfeiture accordingly, until satisfactorily separated by the holder.

54. Any officer or person seizing timber, in the discharge of his duty under this Act, may in the name of the Crown call in any assistance necessary for securing and protecting the timber so seized; and whosoever under any pretence, either by assault, force or violence, or by threat of such assault, force or violence, in any way resists or obstructs any officer or person acting in his aid, in the discharge of his duty under this Act, is guilty of felony, and liable to punishment accordingly.

55. Whosoever, whether pretending to be the owner or not, either secretly or openly, and whether with or without force or violence, takes or carries away, or causes to be taken or carried away, without permis-

sion of the officer or person who seized the same, or of some competent authority, any timber seized and detained as subject to forfeiture under this Act, before the same has been declared by competent authority to have been seized without due cause, shall be deemed to have stolen such timber being the property of the Crown, and guilty of felony, and is liable to punishment accordingly;

2. And whenever any timber is seized for non-payment of Crown dues or for any other cause of forfeiture, or any prosecution is brought for any penalty or forfeiture under this Act, and any question arises whether the said dues have been paid on such timber, or whether the said timber was cut on other than any of the lands aforesaid, the burden of proving payment, or on what land the said timber was cut, shall lie on the owner or claimant of such timber, and not on the officer who seizes the same, or the party bringing such prosecution.

56. All timber seized under this Act shall be deemed to be condemned, unless the person from whom it was seized, or the owner thereof, within one month from the day of the seizure, gives notice to the seizing officer, or nearest officer or agent of the Superintendent-General, that he claims or intends to claim the same; failing such notice, the officer or agent seizing shall report the circumstances to the Superintendent-General, who may order the sale of the said timber by the said officer or agent, after a notice on the spot, of at least thirty days:

2. And any Judge having competent jurisdiction, may, whenever he deems it proper, try and determine such seizures, and may order the delivery of the timber to the alleged owner, on receiving security by bond with two good and sufficient sureties to be first approved by the said agent, to pay double the value in case of condemnation,—and such bond shall be taken in the name of the Superintendent-General, to Her Majesty's use, and shall be delivered up to and kept by the Superintendent-General,—and if such seized timber is condemned, the value thereof shall be paid forthwith to the Superintendent-General, or agent, and the bond cancelled, otherwise the penalty of such bond shall be enforced and recovered.

57. Every person availing himself of any false statement or oath to evade the payment of dues under this Act, shall forfeit the timber on which dues are attempted to be evaded.

MONEYS.

58. All moneys or securities of any kind applicable to the support or benefit of Indians, or any band of Indians, and all moneys accrued or hereafter to accrue from the sale of any Indian lands or of any timber on any reserves or Indian lands shall, subject to the provisions of this Act,

be applicable to the same purposes, and be dealt with in the same manner as they might have been applied to or dealt with before the passing of this Act.

59. The Governor in Council may, subject to the provisions of this Act, direct how, and in what manner, and by whom the moneys arising from sales of Indian lands, and from the property held or to be held in trust for the Indians, or from any timber on Indian lands or reserves, or from any other source for the benefit of Indians (with the exception of any small sum not exceeding ten per cent. of the proceeds of any lands, timber or property, which may be agreed at the time of the surrender to be paid to the members of the band interested therein), shall be invested from time to time, and how the payments or assistance to which the Indians may be entitled shall be made or given, and may provide for the general management of such moneys, and direct what percentage or proportion thereof shall be set apart from time to time, to cover the cost of and attendant upon the management of reserves, lands, property and moneys under the provisions of this Act, and for the construction or repair of roads passing through such reserves or lands, and by way of contribution to schools frequented by such Indians.

60. The proceeds arising from the sale or lease of any Indian lands, or from the timber, hay, stone, minerals or other valuables thereon, or on a reserve, shall be paid to the Receiver General to the credit of the Indian fund.

COUNCILS AND CHIEFS.

61. At the election of a chief or chiefs, or the granting of any ordinary consent required of a band of Indians under this Act, those entitled to vote at the council or meeting thereof shall be the male members of the band of the full age of twenty-one years; and the vote of a majority of such members at a council or meeting of the band summoned according to their rules, and held in the presence of the Superintendent-General, or an agent acting under his instructions, shall be sufficient to determine such election, or grant such consent;

Provided that in the case of any band having a council of chiefs or councillors, any ordinary consent required of the band may be granted by a vote of a majority of such chiefs or councillors at a council summoned according to their rules, and held in the presence of the Superintendent-General or his agent.

62. The Governor in Council may order that the chiefs of any band of Indians shall be elected, as hereinbefore provided, at such time and place, as the Superintendent-General may direct, and they shall in such case be elected for a period of three years, unless deposed by the

Governor for dishonesty, intemperance, immorality, or incompetency; and they may be in the proportion of one head chief and two second chiefs or councillors for every two hundred Indians; but any such band composed of thirty Indians may have one chief: Provided always, that all life chiefs now living shall continue as such until death or resignation, or until their removal by the Governor for dishonesty, intemperance, immorality, or incompetency.

63. The chief or chiefs of any band in council may frame, subject to confirmation by the Governor in Council, rules and regulations for the following subjects, viz:

1. The care of the public health;

2. The observance of order and decorum at assemblies of the Indians in general council, or on other occasions;

3. The repression of intemperance and profligacy;

4. The prevention of trespass by cattle;

5. The maintenance of roads, bridges, ditches and fences;

6. The construction and repair of school houses, council houses and other Indian public builings;

7. The establishment of pounds and the appointment of pound-keepers;

8. The locating of the land in their reserves, and the establishment of a register of such locations.

PRIVILEGES OF INDIANS.

64. No Indian or non-treaty Indian shall be liable to be taxed for any real or personal property, unless he holds real estate under lease or in fee simple, or personal property, outside of the reserve or special reserve in which case he shall be liable to be taxed for such real or personal property at the same rate as other persons in the locality in which it is situate.

65. All land vested in the Crown, or in any person or body corporate, in trust for or for the use of any Indian or non-treaty Indian, or any band or irregular band of Indians or non-treaty Indians shall be exempt from taxation.

66. No person shall take any security or otherwise obtain any lien

or charge, whether by mortgage, judgment or otherwise, upon real or personal property of any Indian or non-treaty Indian within Canada, except on real or personal property subject to taxation under section sixty-four of this Act: Provided always, that any person selling any article to an Indian or non-treaty Indian may, notwithstanding this section, take security on such article for any part of the price thereof which may be unpaid.

67. Indians and non-treaty Indians shall have the right to sue for debts due to them or in respect of any tort or wrong inflicted upon them, or to compel the performance of obligations contracted with them.

68. No pawn taken of any Indian or non-treaty Indian for any intoxicant shall be retained by the person to whom such pawn is delivered, but the thing so pawned may be sued for and recovered, with costs of suit, by the Indian or non-treaty Indian who has deposited the same, before any court of competent jurisdiction.

69. No presents given to Indians or non-treaty Indians, nor any property purchased, or acquired with or by means of any annuities granted to Indians or any part thereof or otherwise howsoever, and in the possession of any band of such Indians or of any Indian of any band or irregular band, shall be liable to be taken, sezied or distrained for any debt, matter or cause whatsoever. Nor in the province of British Columbia, the province of Manitoba, the North-West Territories or in the territory of Keewatin, shall the same be sold, bartered, exchanged or given by any band or irregular band of Indians or any Indian of any such band to any person or Indian other than an Indian of such band; and any such sale, barter, exchange or gift shall be absolutely null and void, unless such sale, barter, exchange or gift be made with the written assent of the Superintendent-General or his agent; and whosoever buys or otherwise acquires any presents or property purchased as aforesaid, without the written consent of the Superintendent-General, or his agent as aforesaid, is guilty of a misdemeanor, and is punishable by fine not exceeding two hundred dollars, or by imprisonment not exceeding six months, in any place of confinement other than a penitentiary.

DISABILITIES AND PENALTIES.

70. No Indian or non-treaty Indian, resident in the province of Manitoba, the North-West Territories or the territory of Keewatin, shall be held capable of having acquired or acquiring a homestead or pre-emption right to a quarter section, or any portion of land in any surveyed or unsurveyed lands in the said province of Manitoba, the North-West Territories or the territory of Keewatin, or the right to share in the distribution of any lands allotted to half-breeds, subject to the following exceptions:

(*a*) He shall not be disturbed in the occupation of any plot on which he has or may have permanent improvements prior to his becoming a party to any treaty with the Crown:

(*b*) Nothing in this section shall prevent the Government of Canada, if found desirable, from compensating any Indian for his improvements on such a plot of land without obtaining a formal surrender therefor from the band:

(*c*) Nothing in this section shall apply to any person who withdrew from any Indian treaty prior to the first day of October, in the year one thousand eight hundred and seventy-four.

71. Any Indian convicted of any crime punishable by imprisonment in any penitentiary or other place of confinement, shall during such imprisonment, be excluded from participating in the annuities, interest money, or rents payable to the band of which he or she is a member; and whenever any Indian shall be convicted of any crime punishable by imprisonment in a penitentiary or other place of confinement, the legal costs incurred in procuring such conviction, and in carrying out the various sentences recorded, may be defrayed by the Superintendent-General, and paid out of any annuity or interest coming to such Indian, or to the band, as the case may be.

72. The Superintendent-General shall have power to stop the payment of the annuity and interest money of any Indian who may be proved, to the satisfaction of the Superintendent-general, to have been guilty of deserting his or her family, and the said Superintendent-General may apply the same towards the support of any family, woman or child so deserted; also to stop the payment of the annuity and interest money of any woman having no children, who deserts her husband and lives immorally with another man.

73. The Superintendent-General in cases where sick, or disabled, or aged and destitute persons are not provided for by the band of Indians of which they are members, may furnish sufficient aid from the funds of the band for the relief of such sick, disabled, aged or destitute persons.

EVIDENCE OF NON-CHRISTIAN INDIANS.

74. Upon any inquest, or upon any enquiry into any matter involving a criminal charge, or upon the trial of any crime or offence whatsoever or by whomsoever committed, it shall be lawful for any court, judge, stipendiary magistrate, coroner or justice of the peace to receive the evidence of any Indian or non-treaty Indian, who is destitute of the knowledge of God and of any fixed and clear belief in religion or in a future state of rewards and punishments, without administering the usual form of oath to any such Indian, or non-treaty Indian, as aforesaid, upon his solemn affirmation or declaration to tell the truth,

the whole truth and nothing but the truth, or in such form as may be approved by such court, judge, stipendiary magistrate, coroner or justice of the peace as most binding on the conscience of such Indian or non-treaty Indian.

75. Provided that in the case of any inquest, or upon any inquiry into any matter involving a criminal charge, or upon the trial of any crime or offence whatsoever, the substance of the evidence or information of any such Indian, or non-treaty Indian, as aforesaid, shall be reduced to writing, and signed by the person (by mark if necessary) giving the same, and verified by the signature or mark of the person acting as interpreter (if any) and by the signature of the judge, stipendiary magistrate or coroner, or justice of the peace or person before whom such evidence or information has been given.

76. The court, judge, stipendiary magistrate, or justice of the peace shall, before taking any such evidence, information or examination, caution every such Indian, or non-treaty Indian, as aforesaid, that he will be liable to incur punishment if he do not so as aforesaid tell the truth.

77. The written declaration or examination, made, taken and verified in manner aforesaid, of any such Indian or non-treaty Indian as aforesaid, may be lawfully read and received as evidence upon the trial of any criminal suit or proceedings, when under the like circumstances the written affidavit, examination, deposition or confession of any other person, might be lawfully read and received as evidence.

78. Every solemn affirmation or declaration in whatever form made or taken by any Indian or non-treaty Indian as aforesaid shall be of the same force and effect as if such Indian or non-treaty Indian had taken an oath in the usual form, and he or she shall in like manner incur the penalty of perjury in case of falsehood.

INTOXICANTS.

79. Whoever sells, exchanges with, barters, supplies or gives to any Indian, or non-treaty Indian in Canada, any kind of intoxicant, or causes or procures the same to be done, or connives or attempts thereat or opens or keeps, or causes to be opened or kept, on any reserve or special reserve, a tavern, house or building where any intoxicant is sold, bartered, exchanged or given, or is found in possession of any intoxicant in the house, tent, wigwam or place of abode of any Indian or non-treaty Indian, shall, on conviction thereof before any judge, stipendiary magistrate or two justices of the peace, upon the evidence of one credible witness other than the informer or prosecutor, be liable to imprisonment for a period not less than one month nor exceeding six months, with or without hard labor, and be fined not less than fifty nor

more than three hundred dollars, with costs of prosecution,—one moiety of the fine to go to the informer or prosecutor, and the other moiety to Her Majesty, to form part of the fund for the benefit of that body of Indians or non-treaty Indians, with respect to one or more members of which the offence was committed: and the commander or person in charge of any steamer or other vessel, or boat, from or on board of which any intoxicant has been sold, bartered, exchanged, supplied or given to any Indian or non-treaty Indian, shall be liable, on conviction thereof before any judge, stipendiary magistrate or two justices of the peace, upon the evidence of one credible witness other than the informer or prosecutor, to be fined not less than fifty nor exceeding three hundred dollars for each such offence, with costs of prosecution,—the moieties of the fine to be applicable as hereinbefore mentioned; and in default of immediate payment of such fine and costs any person so fined shall be committed to any common gaol, house of correction, lock-up, or other place of confinement by the judge, stipendiary magistrate or two justices of the peace before whom the conviction has taken place, for a period of not less than one nor more than six months, with or without hard labor, or until such fine and costs are paid: and any Indian or non-treaty Indian who makes or manufactures any intoxicant, or who has in his possession, or concealed, or who sells, exchanges with, barters, supplies or gives to any other Indian or non-treaty Indian in Canada any kind of intoxicant shall, on conviction thereof, before any judge, stipendiary magistrate or two justices of the peace, upon the evidence of one credible witness other than the informer or prosecutor, be liable to imprisonment for a period of not less than one month nor more than six months, with or without hard labor; and in all cases arising under this section, Indians or non-treaty Indians, shall be competent witnesses: but no penalty shall be incurred in case of sickness where the intoxicant is made use of under the sanction of a medical man or under the directions of a minister of religion.

80. The keg, barrel, case, box, package or receptacle whence any intoxicant has been sold, exchanged, bartered, supplied or given, and as well that in which the original supply was contained as the vessel wherein any portion of such original supply was supplied as aforesaid, and the remainder of the contents thereof, if such barrel, keg, case, box, package, receptacle or vessel aforesaid respectively, can be identified, and any intoxicant imported or manufactured or brought into and upon any reserve or special reserve, or into the house, tent, wigwam or place of abode of any Indian or non-treaty Indian, may be seized by any constable wheresoever found on such land or in such place; and on complaint before any judge, stipendiary magistrate or justice of the peace, he may, on the evidence of any credible witness that this Act has been contravened in respect thereof, declare the same forfeited, and

cause the same to be forthwith destroyed; and may condemn the Indian or other person in whose possession they were found to pay a penalty not exceeding one hundred dollars nor less than fifty dollars, and the costs of prosecution; and one-half of such penalty shall belong to the prosecutor and the other half to Her Majesty, for the purposes hereinbefore mentioned; and in default of immediate payment, the offender may be committed to any common gaol, house of correction, lock-up or other place of confinement with or without hard labor, for any time not exceeding six nor less than two months unless such fine and costs are sooner paid.

81. When it is proved before any judge, stipendiary magistrate or two justices of the peace that any vessel, boat, canoe or conveyance of any description upon the sea or sea coast, or upon any river, lake or stream in Canada, is employed in carrying any intoxicant, to be supplied to Indians or non-treaty Indians, such vessel, boat, canoe or conveyance so employed may be seized and declared forfeited, as in the next preceding section, and sold, and the proceeds thereof paid to Her Majesty for the purposes hereinbefore mentioned.

82. Every article, chattel, commodity or thing in the purchase, acquisition, exchange, trade or barter of which in contravention of this Act the consideration, either wholly or in part, may be any intoxicant, shall be forfeited to Her Majesty and shall be seized as in the eightieth section in respect to any receptacle of any intoxicant, and may be sold and the proceeds thereof paid to Her Majesty for the purposes hereinbefore mentioned.

83. It shall be lawful for any constable, without process of law, to arrest any Indian or non-treaty Indian whom he may find in a state of intoxication, and to convey him to any common gaol, house of correction, lock-up or other place of confinement, there to be kept until he shall have become sober; and such Indian or non-treaty Indian shall, when sober, be brought before any judge, stipendiary magistrate, or justice of the peace, and if convicted of being so found in a state of intoxication shall be liable to imprisonment in any common gaol, house of correction, lock-up or other place of confinement, for any period not exceeding one month. And if any Indian or non-treaty Indian, having been so convicted as aforesaid, refuses upon examination to state or give information of the person, place and time from whom, where and when, he procured such intoxicant, and if from any other Indian or non-treaty Indian, then, if within his knowledge, from whom, where and when such intoxicant was originally procured or received, he shall be liable to imprisonment as aforesaid for a further period not exceeding fourteen days.

84. No appeal shall lie from any conviction under the five next preceding sections of this Act, except to a Judge of any superior court of

law, country, or circuit, or district court, or to the Chairman or Judge of the Court of the Sessions of the Peace, having jurisdiction where the conviction was had, and such appeal shall be heard, tried, and adjudicated upon by such judge without the intervention of a jury; and no such appeal shall be brought after the expiration of thirty days from the conviction.

85. No prosecution, conviction or commitment under this Act shall be invalid on account of want of form, so long as the same is according to the true meaning of this Act.

ENFRANCHISEMENT.

86. Whenever any Indian man, or unmarried woman, of the full age of twenty-one years, obtains the consent of the band of which he or she is a member to become enfranchised, and whenever such Indian has been assigned by the band a suitable allotment of land for that purpose, the local agent shall report such action of the band, and the name of the applicant to the Superintendent-General; whereupon the said Superintendent-General, if satisfied that the proposed allotment of land is equitable, shall authorize some competent person to report whether the applicant is an Indian who, from the degree of civilization to which he or she has attained, and the character for integrity, morality and sobriety which he or she bears, appears to be qualified to become a proprietor of land in fee simple; and upon the favorable report of such person, the Superintendent-General may grant such Indian a location ticket as a probationary Indian, for the land allotted to him or her by the band.

(1.) Any Indian who may be admitted to the degree of Doctor of Medicine, or to any other degree by any University of Learning, or who may be admitted in any Province of the Dominion to practice law either as an Advocate or as a Barrister or Counsellor or Solicitor or Attorney or to be a Notary Public, or who may enter Holy Orders or who may be licensed by any denomination of Christians as a Minister of the Gospel, shall *ipso facto* become and be enfranchised under this Act.

87. After the expiration of three years (or such longer period as the Superintendent-General may deem necessary in the event of such Indian's conduct not being satisfactory). the Governor may, on the report of the Superintendent-General, order the issue of letters patent, granting to such Indian in fee simple the land which had, with this object in view, been allotted to him or her by location ticket.

88. Every such Indian shall, before the issue of the letters patent mentioned in · the next preceding section, declare to the Superintendent-General the name and surname by which he or she wishes to be enfranchised and thereafter known, and on his or her

receiving such letters patent, in such name and surname, he or she shall be held to be also enfranchised, and he or she shall thereafter be known by such name or surname, and if such Indian be a married man his wife and minor unmarried children also shall be held to be enfranchised; and from the date of such letters patent the provisions of this Act and of any Act or law making any distinction between the legal rights, privileges, disabilities and liabilities of Indians and those of Her Majesty's other subjects shall cease to apply to any Indian, or to the wife or minor unmarried children of any Indian as aforesaid, so declared to be enfranchised, who shall no longer be deemed Indians within the meaning of the laws relating to Indians, except in so far as their right to participate in the annuities and interest moneys, and rents and councils of the band of Indians to which they belonged is concerned: Provided always, that any children of a probationary Indian, who being minors and unmarried when the probationary ticket was granted to such Indian, arrive at the full age of twenty-one years before the letters patent are issued to such Indian, may, at the discretion of the Governor in Council, receive letters patent in their own names for their respective shares of the land allotted under the said ticket, at the same time that letters patent are granted to their parent: and provided, that if any Indian child having arrived at the full age of twenty-one years, during his or her parents' probationary period, be unqualified for enfranchisement, or if any child of such parent, having been a minor at the commencement of such period, be married during such period, then a quantity of land equal to the share of such child shall be deducted in such manner as may be directed by the Superintendent-General, from the allotment made to such Indian parent on receiving his probationary ticket.

89. If any probationary Indian should fail in qualifying to become enfranchised, or should die before the expiration of the required probation, his or her claim, or the claim of his or her heirs to the land, for which a probationary ticket was granted, or the claim of any unqualified Indian, or of any Indian who may marry during his or her parents' probationary period, to the land deducted under the operation of the next preceding section from his or her parents' probationary allotment, shall in all respects be the same as that conferred by an ordinary location ticket, as provided in the sixth, seventh, eighth and ninth sections of this Act.

90. The children of any widow who becomes either a probationary or enfranchised Indian shall be entitled to the same privileges as those of a male head of a family in like circumstances.

91. In allotting land to probationary Indians, the quantity to be located to the head of a family shall be in proportion to the number of such family compared with the total quantity of land in the reserve, and the whole number of the band, but any band may determine what

quantity shall be allotted to each member for enfranchisement purposes, provided each female of any age, and each male member under fourteen years of age receive not less than one-half the quantity allotted to each male member of fourteen years of age and over.

92. Any Indian, not a member of the band, or any non-treaty Indian, who, with the consent of the band and the approval of the Superintendent-General, has been permitted to reside upon the reserve, or obtain a location thereon, may, on being assigned a suitable allotment of land by the band for enfranchisement, become enfranchised on the same terms and conditions as a member of the band; and such enfranchisement shall confer upon such Indian the same legal rights and privileges, and make such Indian subject to such disabilities and liabilities as affect Her Majesty's other subjects; but such enfranchisement shall not confer upon such Indian any right to participate in the annuities, interest moneys, rents and councils of the band.

93. Whenever any band of Indians, at a council summoned for the purpose according to their rules, and held in the presence of the Superintendent-General or of an agent duly authorized by him to attend such council, decides to allow every member of the band who chooses, and who may be found qualified, to become enfranchised, and to receive his or her share of the principal moneys of the band, and sets apart for such member a suitable allotment of land for the purpose, any applicant of such band after such a decision may be dealt with as provided in the seven next preceding sections until his or her enfranchisement is attained; and whenever any member of the band, who for the three years immediately succeeding the date on which he or she was granted letters patent, or for any longer period that the Superintendent-General may deem necessary, by his or her exemplary good conduct and management of property, proves that he or she is qualified to receive his or her share of such moneys, the Governor may, on the report of the Superintendent-General to that effect, order that the said Indian be paid his or her share of the capital funds at the credit of the band, or his or her share of the principal of the annuities of the band, estimated as yielding five per cent. out of such moneys as may be provided for the purpose by Parliament; and if such Indian be a married man then he shall also be paid his wife and minor unmarried children's share of such funds and other principal moneys, and if such Indian be a widow, she shall also be paid her minor unmarried children's share: and the unmarried children of such married Indians, who become of age during either the probationary period for enfranchisement for for payment of such moneys, if qualified by the character for integrity, morality and sobriety which they bear, shall receive their own share of such moneys when their parents are paid, and if not so qualified, before they can become enfranchised or receive payment of such moneys they

must themselves pass through the probationary periods; and all such Indians and their unmarried minor children who are paid their share of the principal moneys of their band as aforesaid, shall thenceforward cease in every respect to be Indians of any class within the meaning of this Act, or Indians within the meaning of any other Act or law.

94. Sections eighty-six to ninety-three, both inclusive, of this Act, shall not apply to any band of Indians in the Province of British Columbia, the Province of Manitoba, the North-West Territories, or the Territory of Keewatin, save in so far as the said sections may, by proclamation of the Governor-General, be from time to time extended, as they may be, to any band of Indians in any of the said provinces or territories.

MISCELLANEOUS PROVISIONS.

95. All affidavits required under this Act, or intended to be used in reference to any claim, business or transaction in the Indian Branch of the Department of the Interior, may be taken before the judge or clerk of any county or circuit court, or any justice of the peace, or any commissioner for taking affidavits in any of the courts, or the Superintendent-General, or any Indian agent, or any surveyor duly licensed and sworn, appointed by the Superintendent-General to enquire into or take evidence or report in any matter submitted or pending before such Superintendent-General, or if made out of Canada, before the mayor or chief magistrate of, or the British consul in, any city, town or other municipality: and any wilful false swearing in any such affidavit shall be perjury.

96. Copies of any records, documents, books or papers belonging to or deposited in the Department of the Interior, attested under the signature of the Superintendent-General or of his deputy shall be competent evidence in all cases in which the original records, documents, books or papers, could be evidence.

97. The Governor in Council may, by proclamation from time to time, exempt from the operation of this Act, or from the operation of any one or more of the sections of this Act. Indians or non-treaty Indians, or any of them, or any band or irregular band of them, or the reserves or special reserves, or Indian lands or any portions of them, in any province, in the North-West Territories, or in the territory of Keewatin, or in either of them, and may again, by proclamation from time to time, remove such exemption.

98. The Governor may, from time to time, appoint officers and agents to carry out this Act, and any Orders in Council made under it, which officers and agents shall be paid in such manner and at such rates

as the Governor in Council may direct out of any fund that may be appropriated by law for that purpose.

99. Section fifty-six of chapter sixty-one and section fifty of chapter sixty-eight of the Consolidated Statutes of Canada, section twenty-nine of chapter forty-nine of the Consolidated Statues for Upper Canada, and so much of chapter eighty-one of the said Consolidated Statutes for Upper Canada as relates to Indians or Indian lands, sections five to thirty-three, inclusive, and sections thirty-seven and thirty-eight of the Act passed in the session held in the thirty-first year of Her Majesty's reign, chaptered forty-two, and the Act passed in the session held in the thirty-second and thirty-third years of Her Majesty's reign, chaptered six, and the Act passed in the thirty-seventh year of Her Majesty's reign, chaptered twenty-one, are hereby repealed, with so much of any Act or law as may be inconsistent with this Act, or as makes any provision in any matter provided for by this Act, except only as to things done, rights acquired, obligations contracted, or penalties incurred before the coming into force of this Act; and this Act shall be construed not as a new law but as a consolidation of those hereby repealed into far as they make the same provision that is made by this Act in any matter hereby provided for.

100. No Act or enactment repealed by any Act hereby repealed shall revive by reason of such repeal.

C9.

42 Victoria (1879) Cap. 34 (Canada). An Act to Amend the Indian Act, 1876. |assented to May 15, 1879|

HER Majesty, by and with the advice and consent of the Senate and House of Commons of Canada, enacts as follows:—

1. Paragragh (*e*) of sub-section three, of section three of *"The Indian Act 1876,"* is hereby amended by adding at the end thereof the words "And any half-breed who may have been admitted into a treaty shall be allowed to withdraw therefrom on refunding all annuity money received by him or her under the said treaty, or suffering a corresponding reduction in the quantity of any land, or scrip, which such half-breed as such may be entitled to receive from the Government."

2. Section sixteen of the Act aforesaid is hereby repealed, and the following section substituted in lieu thereof:—

"16. If any person or Indian, other than an Indian of the band to which the reserve belongs, without the license in writing of the Superintendent-General, or of some officer or person deputed by him

for that purpose, trespasses upon any of the said land, roads or allowances for roads in the said reserve, by cutting, carrying away, or
removing therefrom any of the trees, saplings, shrubs, underwood,
timber or hay thereon, or by removing any of the stone, soil, minerals,
metals or other valuables, off the said land, roads or allowances for
roads, the person or Indian so trespassing shall, on conviction thereof
before any Stipendiary Magistrate, Police Magistrate or Justice of the
Peace, for every tree he cuts, carries away or removes, forfeit and pay
the sum of twenty dollars; and for cutting, carrying away, or removing
any of the saplings, shrubs, underwood, timber or hay, if under the
value of one dollar, the sum of four dollars; but if over the value of one
dollar, then the sum of twenty dollars; and for removing any of the
stone, soil, minerals, metals or other valuables aforesaid, the sum of
twenty dollars, with costs of prosecution in all cases; and in default of
immediate payment of the said penalties and costs, the Superintendent-General, or such other person as he may have authorized in
that behalf, may issue a warrant, directed to any person or persons by
him named therein, to levy the amount of the said penalties and costs by
distress and sale of the goods and chattels of the person liable to pay the
same; and similar proceedings may be had upon such warrant as if it
had been issued by the magistrate or Justice of the Peace before whom
the person was convicted; or the Superintendent-General, or such other
person as aforesaid, without proceeding by distress or sale, may, upon
non-payment of the said penalties and costs, order the person liable
therefor to be imprisoned in the common gaol of the county or district in
which the said reserve or any part thereof lies, for a period not exceeding thirty days when the penalty does not exceed twenty dollars, or for a
period not exceeding three months when the penalty does exceed
twenty dollars; and upon the return of any warrant for distress or sale, if
the amount thereof has not been made, or if any part of it remains
unpaid, the said Superintendent-General, or such other person as
aforesaid, may commit the person in default to the common gaol, as
aforesaid, for a period not exceeding thirty days, if the sum claimed
upon the said warrant does not exceed twenty dollars, or for a time not
exceeding three months if the sum does exceed twenty dollars: all such
penalties shall be paid to the Receiver-General to be disposed of for the
use and benefit of the band of Indians for whose benefit the reserve is
held, in such manner as the Governor in Council may direct.''

3. Section seventeen of the said Act is hereby amended by adding
thereto the words ''and similar proceedings may be had for the recovery
thereof as are provided for in the next preceding section.''

4. Section sixty-three of the said Act is hereby amended by adding

to the fourth subsection thereof the words "also for the protection of sheep;"

And by substituting for the words "maintenance of" in the fifth subsection thereof, the words "construction and maintenance of water courses;"

And by adding to the said section the two following subsections:—

"9. The repression of noxious weeds;

"10. The imposition of punishment, by fine or penalty, or by imprisonment, or both, for infraction of any of such rules or regulations,—the fine or penalty in no case to exceed thirty dollars, and the imprisonment in no case to exceed thirty days."

5. Section sixty-nine of the said Act is hereby amended by striking out the words "or otherwise, howsoever," in the fourth line thereof, and by adding at the end of the said section the words "If any presents given to Indians or non-treaty Indians, or any property purchased or acquired with or by means of any annuities granted to Indians be unlawfully in the possession of any person, within the true intent and meaning of this section, any person acting under the authority (either general or special) of the Superintendent-General, may, with such assistance in that behalf as he may think necessary, seize and take possession of the same, and he shall deal therewith as the Superintendent-General may direct."

6. Section eighty-seven is hereby amended by adding thereto the words "and in such cases compliance with the provisions of sections twenty-five and twenty-six and the sub-sections thereof shall not be necessary."

7. If any person, being the keeper of any house, allows or suffers any Indian woman to be or remain in such house, knowing, or having probable cause for believing, that such Indian woman is in or remains in such house with the intention of prostituting herself therein, such person shall be deemed guilty of an offence against this Act, and shall, on conviction thereof, in a summary way, before any Stipendiary Magistrate, Police Magistrate or Justice of the Peace, be liable to a fine of not less than ten dollars, or more than one hundred dollars, or to imprisonment in any gaol or place of confinement other than a penitentiary, for a term not exceeding six months.

8. Any person who appears, acts or behaves as master or mistress, or as the person having the care, government or management of any house in which any Indian woman is or remains for the purpose of prostituting herself therein, shall be deemed and taken to be the keeper thereof, notwithstanding he or she may not in fact be the real keeper thereof.

C10.

43 Victoria (1880) Cap. 28 (Canada). An Act to Amend and Consolidate the Laws Respecting Indians (The Indian Act, 1880). /assented to May 7, 1880/

WHEREAS it is expedient to amend and consolidate the laws respecting Indians: Therefore Her Majesty, by and with the advice and consent of the Senate and House of Commons of Canada, enacts as follows:—

1. This Act shall be known and may be cited as *"The Indian Act, 1880;"* and shall, subject to the exceptions herein contained, apply to all the Provinces, and to the North-West Territories, including the District of Keewatin.

2. The following terms contained in this Act shall be held to have the meaning hereinafter assigned to them, unless such meaning be repugnant to the subject or inconsistent with the context:—

1. The term "band" means any tribe, band or body of Indians who own or are interested in a reserve or in Indian lands in common, of which the legal title is vested in the Crown, or who share alike in the distribution of any annuities or interest moneys for which the Government of Canada is responsible; the term "the band" means the band to which the context relates; and the term "band," when action is being taken by the band as such, means the band in council.

2. The term "irregular band" means any tribe, band or body of persons of Indian blood who own no interest in any reserve or lands of which the legal title is vested in the Crown, who possess no common fund managed by the Government of Canada, or who have not had any treaty relations with the Crown.

3. The term "Indian" means—

First. Any male person of Indian blood reputed to belong to a particular band;

Secondly. Any child of such person;

Thirdly. Any woman who is or was lawfully married to such person.

4. The term "non-treaty Indian" means any person of Indian blood who is reputed to belong to an irregular band, or who follows the Indian mode of life, even though such person be only a temporary resident in Canada.

5. The term "enfranchised Indian" means any Indian, his wife or minor unmarried child, who has received letters patent granting him in fee simple any portion of the reserve which may have been allotted to him, his wife and minor children, by the band to which he belongs, or any unmarried Indian who may have received letters patent for an allotment of the reserve.

6. The term "reserve" means any tract or tracts of land set apart by

treaty or otherwise for the use or benefit of or granted to a particular band of Indians, of which the legal title is in the Crown, but which is unsurrendered, and includes all the trees, wood, timber, soil, stone, minerals, metals and other valuables thereon or therein.

7. The term "special reserve" means any tract or tracts of land and everything belonging thereto set apart for the use or benefit of any band or irregular band of Indians, the title of which is vested in a society, corporation or community legally established, and capable of suing and being sued, or in a person or persons of European descent, but which land is held in trust for such band or irregular band of Indians.

8. The term "Indian lands" means any reserve or portion of a reserve which has been surrendered to the Crown.

9. The term "intoxicants" means and includes all spirits, strong waters, spirituous liquors, wines, or fermented or compounded liquors or intoxicating drink of any kind whatsoever, and any intoxicating liquor or fluid, as also opium and any preparation thereof, whether liquid or solid, and any other intoxicating drug or substance, and tobacco or tea mixed or compounded or impregnated with opium or with other intoxicating drugs, spirits or substances, and whether the same or any of them be liquid or solid.

10. The term "Superintendent-General" means the Superintendent-General of Indian Affairs.

11. The term "agent" includes a commissioner, superintendent, agent, or other officer acting under the instructions of the Superintendent-General.

12. The term "person" means an individual other than an Indian, unless the context clearly requires another construction.

3. The Minister of the Interior shall be the Superintendent-General of Indian Affairs.

4. There shall be a Department of the Civil Service of Canada to be called the Department of Indian Affairs, over which the Superintendent-General of Indian Affairs shall preside.

5. The Governor General in Council may, by commission under the Great Seal, appoint a Deputy of the Superintendent-General of Indian Affairs, who shall be charged under the Superintendent-General with the performance of his Departmental duties, and with the control and management of the officers, clerks and servants of the Department, and with such other powers and duties as may be assigned to him by the Governor in Council.

6. Schedule A of the "*Canada Civil Service Act, 1868*," is hereby amended by adding thereto the words "Deputy of the Superintendent-General of Indian Affairs."

7. Upon the passing of this Act, so much of the business of the

Department of the Interior as relates to Indian Affairs, and which has hitherto been conducted in what is usually known as the "Indian Branch" of that Department, shall fall under the management, charge and direction of the Department of Indian Affairs; and the Governor in Council may from time to time assign to the Department of Indian Affairs any of the present officers and employees of the Department of the Interior, or may direct any one or more of the officers and employees of the last-named Department to act as an officer of both Departments.

8. The Governor in Council may also appoint, subject to "*The Canada Civil Service Act, 1868*," such officers, clerks and servants as may be requisite for the proper conduct of the business of the Department of Indian Affairs.

9. The Governor in Council may appoint an Indian Commissioner for Manitoba, Keewatin and the North-West Territories, with such powers and duties as may be provided by Order in Council. The Governor in Council may also appoint an Indian Superintendent for the Province of British Columbia, with such powers and duties as may be provided by Order in Council.

10. Any illegitimate child, unless having shared with the consent of the band whereof the father or mother of such child is a member in the distribution moneys of such band for a period exceeding two years, may, at any time, be excluded from the membership thereof by the Superintendent-General.

11. Any Indian having for five years continuously resided in a foreign country without the consent in writing of the Superintendent-General or his agent, shall cease to be a member of the band of which he or she was formerly a member, nor shall he or she become again a member of that band, or become a member of any other band, unless the consent of the band with the approval of the Superintendent-General or his agent, be first had and obtained.

12. Any Indian woman marrying any other than an Indian or a non-treaty Indian shall cease to be an Indian in any respect within the meaning of this Act, except that she shall be entitled to share equally with the members of the band to which she formerly belonged, in the annual or semi-annual distribution of their annuities, interest moneys and rents; but this income may be commuted to her at any time at ten years' purchase with the consent of the band.

13. Any Indian woman marrying an Indian of any other band, or a non-treaty Indian, shall cease to be a member of the band to which she formerly belonged, and become a member of the band or irregular band of which her husband is a member; but should she marry a non-treaty Indian, while becoming a member of the irregular band of which her

husband is a member, she shall be entitled to share equally with the members of the band of which she was formerly a member in the distribution of their moneys; but this income may be commuted to her at any time at ten years' purchase with the consent of the band.

14. No half-breed in Manitoba who has shared in the distribution of half-breed lands shall be accounted an Indian; and no half-breed head of a family (except the widow of an Indian or a half-breed who has already been admitted into a treaty) shall, unless under very special circumstances, to be determined by the Superintendent-General or his agent, be accounted an Indian, or entitled to be admitted into any Indian treaty; and any half-breed who may have been admitted into a treaty shall be allowed to withdraw therefrom on refunding all annuity money received by him or her under the said treaty, or suffering a corresponding reduction in the quantity of any land, or scrip, which such half-breed, as such, may be entitled to receive from the Government.

2. The Half-breeds who are by the father's side either wholly or partly of Indian blood now settled in the Seigniory of Caughnawaga, and who have inhabited the said Seigniory for the last twenty years, are hereby confirmed in their possession and right of residence and property, but not beyond the tribal rights and usages which others of the band enjoy.

15. All reserves for Indians or for any band of Indians, or held in trust for their benefit, shall be deemed to be reserved and held for the same purposes as before the passing of this Act, but subject to its provisions.

16. The Superintendent-General may authorize surveys, plans and reports to be made of any reserve for Indians, shewing and distinguishing the improved lands, the forests and lands fit for settlement, and such other information as may be required; and may authorize that the whole or any portion of a reserve be subdivded into lots.

17. No Indian shall be deemed to be lawfully in possession of any land in a reserve, unless he or she has been or shall be located for the same by the band or council of the band, with the approval of the Superintendent-General: Provided that no Indian shall be dispossessed of any land on which he or she has improvements, without receiving compensation therefor (at a valuation to be approved by the Superintendent-General) from the Indian who obtains the land, or from the funds of the band, as may be determined by the Superintendent-General.

18. On the Superintendent-General approving of any location as aforesaid, he shall issue in triplicate a ticket granting a location title to such Indian, one triplicate of which he shall retain in a book to be kept for the purpose; the other two he shall forward to the local agent,—one

to be delivered to the Indian in whose favor it was issued, the other to be filed by the agent, who shall also cause the same to be copied into a register of the band to be provided for the purpose.

19. The conferring of any such location title as aforesaid shall not have the effect of rendering the land covered thereby subject to seizure under legal process, and such title shall be transferable only to an Indian of the same band, and then only with the consent and approval of the Superintendent-General, whose consent and approval shall be given only by the issue of a ticket in the manner prescribed in the next preceding section.

20. Upon the death of any Indian holding under location or other duly recognized title any parcel of land, the right and interest therein of such deceased Indian shall, together with his goods and chattels, devolve one-third upon his widow (if any), and the remainder upon his children in equal shares; and such children shall have a like estate in such land as their father had. During the minority of such children the administration and charge of such land and goods and chattels as they may be entitled to under this clause, shall devolve upon the widow (if any) of such deceased Indian. As each male child attains the age of twenty-one, and as each female child attains that age, or marries before that age with the consent of the said widow, his or her share is to be handed to him or her: Provided always, that the Superintendent-General may, at any time, remove the widow from such administration and charge, and confer the same upon some other person, and in like manner remove such other person and appoint another, and so on as occasion may require. Should such Indian die without issue but leaving a widow, such lot or parcel of land and his goods and chattels shall be vested in her, and if he leaves no widow, then in the Indian nearest akin to the deceased; but if he have no heir nearer than a cousin then the same shall be vested in the Crown for the benefit of the band; but whatever may be the final disposition of the land, the claimant or claimants shall not be held to be legally in possession until he, she or they obtains or obtain a location ticket from the Superintendent-General in the manner prescribed in the case of new locations: Provided always, that the Superintendent-General may, whenever there are minor children, appoint a fit and proper person to take charge of such children and their property, and remove such person and appoint another, and so on as occasion may require. Provided also, that the Superintendent-General shall have power to decide all questions which may arise respecting the distribution, among those entitled, of the land and goods and chattels of a deceased Indian; also to do whatever he may, under the circumstances, think will best give to each claimant his or her share, according to the true meaning and spirit of this Act, whether such share be a part of the lands or goods and chattels them-

selves, or be part of the proceeds thereof, in case it be thought best to dispose thereof,—regard always being had any such disposition to the restrictions upon the disposition of property in a reserve.

21. Any Indian or non-treaty Indian in the Province of British Columbia, in the Province of Manitoba, in the North-West Territories, or in the District of Keewatin, who has, or shall have, previously to the selection of a reserve, possession of and made permanent improvements on a plot of land which has been or shall be included in or surrounded by a reserve, shall have the same privileges, neither more nor less, in respect of such plot, as an Indian enjoys who holds under a location title.

22. No person, or Indian other than an Indian of the band, shall settle, reside or hunt upon, occupy or use any land or marsh, or shall settle, reside upon or occupy any road, or allowance for roads running through any reserve belonging to or occupied by such band; and all mortgages or hypothecs given or consented to by any Indian, and all leases, contracts and agreements made or purporting to be made by any Indian, whereby persons or Indians other than Indians of the band are permitted to reside or hunt upon such reserve, shall be absolutely void.

23. If any person or Indian other than an Indian of the band, without the license of the Superintendent-General (which license, however, he may at any time revoke), settles, resides or hunts upon or occupies or uses any such land or marsh; or settles, resides upon or occupies any such roads or allowances for roads, on such reserve, or if any Indian is illegally in possession of any land in a reserve, the Superintendent-General, or such officer or person as he may thereunto depute and authorize, shall, on complaint made to him, and on proof of the fact to his satisfaction, issue his warrant signed and sealed, directed to the sheriff of the proper county or district, or if the said reserve be not situated within any country or district, then directed to any literate person willing to act in the premises, commanding him forthwith to remove from the said land or marsh, or roads or allowances for roads, or land, every such person or Indian and his family, so settled, residing or hunting upon or occupying, or being illegally in possession of the same, or to notify such person or Indian to cease using as aforesaid the said lands, marshes, roads or allowances for roads; and such sheriff or other person shall accordingly remove or notify such person or Indian, and for that purpose shall have the same powers as in the execution of criminal process; and the expenses incurred in any such removal or notification shall be borne by the party removed or notified, and may be recovered from him as the costs in any ordinary suit:

Provided that nothing contained in this Act shall prevent an Indian or non-treaty Indian, if five years a resident in Canada, not a member of the band, with the consent of the band and the approval of the

Superintendent-General, from residing on the reserve or receiving a location thereon.

24. If any person or Indian, after having been removed or notified as aforesaid, returns to, settles, resides or hunts upon or occupies, or uses as aforesaid, any of the said land, marsh or lots or parts of lots; or settles or resides upon or occupies any of the said roads, allowances for roads, or lots or parts of lots, the Superintendent-General, or any officer or person deputed and authorized as aforesaid, upon view, or upon proof on oath made before him, or to his satisfaction, that the said person or Indian has returned to, settled, resided or hunted upon or occupied or used as aforesaid any of the said lands, marshes, lots or parts of lots, or has returned to, settled or resided upon or occupied any of the said roads or allowances for roads, or lots or parts of lots, shall direct and send his warrant signed and sealed to the sheriff of the proper county or district, or to any literate person therein, and if the said reserve be not situated within any county or district, then to any literate person, commanding him forthwith to arrest such person or Indian, and bring him before any Stipendiary Magistrate, Police Magistrate or Justice of the Peace, who may, on conviction, commit him to the common gaol of the said county or district, or if there be no gaol in the said county or district, then to the gaol nearest to the said reserve in the Province or Territory, there to remain for the time ordered by such warrant, but which shall not exceed thirty days for the first offence, and thirty days additional for each subsequent offence.

25. Such sheriff or other person shall accordingly arrest the said party, and deliver him to the gaoler or sheriff of the proper county, district, Province or Territory, who shall receive such person or Indian and imprison him in the said gaol for the term aforesaid.

26. The Superintendent-General, or such officer or person aforesaid, shall cause the judgment or order against the offender to be drawn up and filed in his office; and such judgment shall not be removed by *certiorari* or otherwise, or be appealed from, but shall be final.

27. If any person or Indian, other than an Indian of the band to which the reserve belongs, without the license in writing of the Superintendent-General, or of some officer or person deputed by him for that purpose, trespasses upon any of the said land, roads, or allowances for roads in the said reserve, by cutting, carrying away, or removing therefrom any of the trees, saplings, shrubs, underwood, timber, or hay thereon, or by removing any of the stone, soil, minerals, metals, or other valuables, off the said land, roads, or allowances for roads, the person or Indian so trespassing shall, on conviction thereof before any Stipendiary Magistrate, Police Magistrate or Justice of the Peace, for every tree he cuts, carries away, or removes, forfeit and pay

the sum of twenty dollars; and for cutting, carrying away, or removing any of the saplings, shrubs, underwood, timber or hay, if under the value of one dollar, the sum of four dollars; but if over the value of one dollar, then the sum of twenty dollars; and for removing any of the stone, soil, minerals, metals, or other valuables aforesaid, the sum of twenty dollars, with costs of prosecution in all cases. And in default of immediate payment of the said penalties and costs, the Super-intendent-General, or such other person as he may have authorized in that behalf, may issue a warrant, directed to any person or persons by him named therein, to levy the amount of the said penalties and costs by distress and sale of the goods and chattels of the person liable to pay the same; and similar proceedings may be had upon such warrant as if it had been issued by the Magistrate or Justice of the Peace before whom the person was convicted; or the Superintendent-General, or such other person as aforesaid, without proceeding by distress or sale, may, upon non-payment of the said penalties and costs, order the person liable therefor to be imprisoned in the common gaol of the county or district in which the said reserve or any part thereof lies, for a period not exceed-ing thirty days when the penalty does not exceed twenty dollars, or for a period not exceeding three months when the penalty does exceed twenty dollars; and upon the return of any warrant for distress or sale, if the amount thereof has not been made, or if any part of it remains unpaid, the said Superintendent-General, or such other person as aforesaid, may commit the person in default to the common gaol, as aforesaid, for a period not exceeding thirty days, if the sum claimed upon the said warrant does not exceed twenty dollars, or for a time not exceeding three months if the sum does exceed twenty dollars. All such penalties shall be paid to the Receiver-General to be disposed of for the use and benefit of the band of Indians for whose benefit the reserve is held, in such manner as the Governor in Council may direct.

2. But nothing herein contained shall be construed to prevent the Superintendent-General from issuing a license to any person or Indian to cut and remove trees, wood, timber and hay, or to quarry and remove stone and gravel on and from the reserve. Provided he, or his agent acting by his instructions, first obtain the consent of the band thereto in the ordinary manner as hereinafter provided.

28. If any Indian, without the license in writing of the Superintendent-General, or of some officer or person deputed by him for that purpose, trespasses upon the land of an Indian who holds a location title, or who is otherwise recognized by the Department as the occupant of such land, by cutting, carrying away, or removing there-from, any of the trees, saplings, shrubs, underwood, timber or hay thereon, or by removing any of the stone, soil, minerals, metals or other valuables off the said land: or if any Indian, without license as

aforesaid, cuts, carries away or removes from any portion of the reserve of his band, for sale (and not for the immediate use of himself and his family), any trees, timber or hay thereon, or removes any of the stone, soil, minerals, metals, or other valuables therefrom for sale as aforesaid, he shall be liable to all the fines and penalties provided in the next preceding section in respect to Indians of other bands and other persons, and similar proceedings may be had for the recovery thereof as are provided for in the next preceding section.

29. In all orders, writs, warrants, summonses and proceedings whatsoever made, issued or taken by the Superintendent-General, or any officer or person by him deputed as aforesaid, it shall not be necessary for him or such officer or person to insert or express the name of the person or Indian summoned, arrested, distrained upon, imprisoned, or otherwise proceeded against therein, except when the name of such person or Indian is truly given to or known by the Superintendent-General, or such officer or person; and if the name be not truly given to or known by him, he may name or describe the person or Indian by any part of the name of such person or Indian given to or known by him; and if no part of the name be given to or known by him he may describe the person or Indian proceeded against in any manner by which he may be identified; and all such proceedings containing or purporting to give the name or description of any such person or Indian as aforesaid shall *prima facie* be sufficient.

30. All sheriffs, gaolers or peace officers to whom any such process is directed by the Superintendent-General, or by any officer or person by him deputed as aforesaid, shall obey the same; and all other officers upon reasonable requisition shall assist in the execution thereof.

31. If any railway, road or public work passes through or causes injury to any reserve belonging to or in possession of any band of Indians, or if any act occasioning damage to any reserve be done under the authority of any Act of Parliament, or of the Legislature of any Province, compensation shall be made to them therefor in the same manner as is provided with respect to the lands or rights of other persons; the Superintendent-General shall, in any case in which an arbitration may be had, name the arbitrator on behalf of the Indians, and shall act for them on any matter relating to the settlement of such compensation; and the amount warded in any case shall be paid to the Receiver-General for the use of the band of Indians for whose benefit the reserve is held, and for the benefit of any Indian having improvements thereon.

32. In all cases of encroachment upon, or of violation of trust respecting any special reserve, it shall be lawful to proceed by informa-

tion in the name of Her Majesty, in the superior courts of law or equity, notwithstanding the legal title may not be vested in the Crown.

33. If by the violation of the conditons of any such trust as aforesaid, or by the breaking up of any society, corporation, or community, or if by the death of any person or persons without a legal succession of trusteeship, in whom the title to a special reserve is held in trust, the said title lapses or becomes void in law, then the legal title shall become vested in the Crown in trust, and the property shall be managed for the band or irregular band previously interested therein, as an ordinary reserve. The trustees of any special reserve may at any time surrender the same to Her Majesty in trust, whereupon the property shall be managed for the band or irregular band previously interested therein as an ordinary reserve.

34. Indians residing upon any reserve, and engaged in the pursuit of agriculture as their then principal means of support, shall be liable, if so directed by the Superintendent-General, or any officer or person by him thereunto authorized, to perform labour on the public roads laid out or used in or through, or abutting upon such reserve,—such labour to be performed under the sole control of the said Superintendent-General, officer or person, who may direct when, where and how and in what manner the said labour shall be applied, and to what extent the same shall be imposed upon Indians who may be resident upon any of the said lands; and the said Superintendent-General, officer or person shall have the like power to enforce the performance of all such labour by imprisonment or otherwise, as may be done by any power or authority under any law, rule or regulation in force in the Province or territory in which such reserve lies, for the non-performance of statue labour; but the labour to be so required of any such Indian shall not exceed in amount or extent what may be required of other inhabitants of the same Province, territory, county, or other local division, under the laws requiring and regulating such labour and the performance thereof.

35. Every band of Indians shall be bound to cause the roads, bridges, ditches and fences within their reserve to be put and maintained in proper order, in accordance with the instructions received from time to time from the Superintendent-General, or from the agent of the Superintendent-General; and whenever in the opinion of the Superintendent-General the same are not so put or maintained in order, he may cause the work to be performed at the cost of such band, or of the particular Indian in default, as the case may be, either out of their or his annual allowances, or otherwise.

36. No reserve or portion of a reserve shall be sold, alienated or leased until it has been released or surrendered to the Crown for the purposes of this Act, excepting that in cases of aged, sick and infirm

Indians and widows or children left without a guardian, the Superintendent-General shall have the power to lease the lands to which they may be entitled for their support or benefit.

37. No release or surrender of a reserve, or portion of a reserve, held for the use of the Indians of any band or of any individual Indian, shall be valid or binding, except on the following conditions:—

1. The release or surrender shall be assented to by a majority of the male members of the band of the full age of twenty-one years, at a meeting or council thereof summoned for that purpose accroding to their rules, and held in the presence of the Superintendent-General, or of an officer duly authorized to attend such council by the Governor in Council or by the Superintendent-General: Provided, that no Indian shall be entitled to vote or be present at such council, unless he habitually resides on or near and is interested in the reserve in question:

2. The fact that such release or surrender has been assented to by the band at such council or meeting, shall be certified on oath before some judge of a superior, county or district court, or Stipendiary Magistrate, by the Superintendent-General, or by the officer authorized by him to attend such council or meeting, and by some one of the chiefs or principal men present thereat and entitled to vote, and when so certified as aforesaid shall be submitted to the Governor in Council for acceptance or refusal.

38. It shall not be lawful to introduce, at any council or meeting of Indians held for the purpose of discussing or of assenting to a release or surrender of a reserve or portion thereof, or of assenting to the issuing of a timber or other license, any intoxicant; and any person introducing at such meeting, and any agent or officer employed by the Superintendent-General, or by the Governor in Council, introducing, allowing or countenancing by his presence the use of such intoxicant among such Indians a week before, at, or a week after, any such council or meeting, shall forfeit two hundred dollars, recoverable by action in any of the superior courts of law, one-half of which penalty shall go to the informer.

39. Nothing in this Act shall confirm any release or surrender which would have been invalid if this Act had not been passed; and no release or surrender of any reserve or portion of a reserve to any party other than the Crown, shall be valid.

40. All Indian lands, being reserves or portions of reserves surrendered or to be surrendered to the Crown, shall be deemed to be held for the same purposes as before the passing of this Act; and shall be managed, leased and sold as the Governor in Council may direct, subject to the conditions of surrender and the provisions of this Act.

41. No agent for the sale of Indian lands shall, within his division, directly or indirectly, unless under an order of the Governor in Council,

purchase any land which he is appointed to sell, or become proprietor of or interested in any such land, during the time of his agency; and any such purchase or interest shall be void; and if any such agent offends in the premises, he shall forfeit his office and the sum of four hundred dollars for every such offence, which may be recovered in action of debt by any person who may sue for the same.

42. Every certificate of sale or receipt for money received on the sale of Indian lands, heretofore granted or made or to be granted or made by the Superintendent-General or any agent of his, so long as the sale to which such receipt or certificate relates is in force and not rescinded, shall entitle the party to whom the same was or shall be made or granted, or his assignee, by instrument registered under this or any former Act providing for registration in such cases, to take possession of and occupy the land therein comprised, subject to the conditions of such sale, and thereunder, unless the same shall have been revoked or cancelled, to maintain suits in law or equity against any wrongdoer or trespasser, as effectually as he could do under a patent from the Crown;—and such receipt or certificate shall be *prima facie* evidence for the purpose of possession by such person, or the assignee under an instrument registered as aforesaid, in any such suit; but the same shall have no force against a license to cut timber existing at the time of the making or granting thereof.

43. The Superintendent-General shall keep a book for registering (at the option of the parties interested) the particulars of any assignment made, as well by the original purchaser or lessee of Indian lands or his heir or legal representative, as by any subsequent assignee of any such lands, or the heir or legal representative of such assignee:—and upon any such assignment being produced to the Superintendent-General, and, (except in cases where such assignment is made under a corporate seal), with an affidavit of due execution thereof, and of the time and place of such execution, and the names, residences and occupations of the witnesses, or, as regards lands in the Province of Quebec, upon the production of such assignment executed in notarial form, or of a notarial copy thereof, the Superintendent-General shall cause the material parts of every such assignment to be registered in such book of registry, and shall cause to be endorsed on every such assignment a certificate of such registration, to be signed by himself or his deputy, or any other officer of the department by him authorized to sign such certificates: And every such assignment so registered shall be valid against any one previously executed, but subsequently registered, or unregistered; but all the conditions of the sale, grant or location must have been complied with, or dispensed with by the Superintendent-General, before such registration is made. But any assignment to be registered as aforesaid must be unconditional in its terms.

44. If any subscribing witness to any such assignment is deceased, or has left the province, the Superintendent-General may register such assignment upon the production of an affidavit proving the death or absence of such witness and his handwriting, or the handwriting of the party making such assignment.

45. On any application for a patent by the heir, assignee or devisee of the original purchaser from the Crown, the Superintendent-General may receive proof in such manner as he may direct and require in support of any claim for a patent when the original purchaser is dead, and upon being satisfied that the claim has been equitably and justly established, may allow the same, and cause a patent to issue accordingly; but nothing in this section shall limit the right of a party claiming a patent to land in the Province of Ontario to make application at any time to the Commissioner, under the *"Act respecting the Heir, Devisee and Assignee Commission,"* being chapter twenty-five of the Revised Statutes of Ontario.

46. If the Superintendent-General is satisfied that any purchaser or lessee of any Indian lands, or any assignee claiming under or through him, has been guilty of any fraud or imposition, or has violated any of the condtions of sale or lease, or if any such sale or lease has been or is made or issued in error or mistake, he may cancel such sale or lease, and resume the land therein mentioned, or dispose of it as if no sale or lease thereof had ever been made; and all such cancellations heretofore made by the Governor in Council or the Superintendent-General shall continue valid until altered.

47. When any purchaser, lessee or other person refuses or neglects to deliver up possession of any land after revocation or cancellation of the sale or lease as aforesaid, or when any person is wrongfully in possession of any Indian lands and refuses to vacate or abandon possession of the same, the Superintendent-General may apply to the county judge of the county, or to a judge of the Superior Court in the circuit, in which the land lies in Ontario or Quebec, or to any judge of a superior court of law or any county judge of the county in which the land lies in any other province, or to any Stipendiary Magistrate in any territory in which the land lies, for an order in the nature of a writ of *habere facias possessionem* or writ of possession, and the said judge or magistrate, upon proof to his satisfaction that the right or title of the party to hold such land has been revoked or cancelled as aforesaid, or that such person is wrongfully in possession of Indian lands, shall grant an order upon the purchaser, lessee or person in possession, to deliver up the same to the Superintendent-General, or person by him authorized to receive the same; and such order shall have the same force as a writ of *habere facias possessionem*, or writ of possession; and the sheriff, or any bailiff or person to whom it may have been trusted for

execution by the Superintendent-General, shall execute the same in like manner as he would execute such writ in an action of ejectment or possessory action.

48. Whenver any rent payable to the Crown on any lease of Indian lands is in arrear, the Superintendent-General, or any agent or officer appointed under this Act and authorized by the Superintendent-General to act in such cases, may issue a warrant, directed to any person or persons by him named therein, in the shape of a distress warrant as in ordinary cases of landlord and tenant, or as in the case of distress and warrant of a justice of the peace for non-payment of a pecuniary penalty; and the same proceedings may be had thereon for the collection of such arrears as in either of the said last-mentioned cases; or an action of debt as in ordinary cases of rent in arrear may be brought therefor in the name of the Superintendent-General; but demand of rent shall not be necessary in any case.

49. When by law or by any deed, lease or agreement relating to any of the lands herein referred to, any notice is required to be given, or any act to be done, by or on behalf of the Crown, such notice may be given and act done by or by the authority of the Superintendent-General.

50. Whenever letters patent have been issued to or in the name of the wrong party, through mistake, or contain any clerical error or misnomer, or wrong description of any material fact therein, or of the land thereby intended to be granted, the Superintendent-General (there being no adverse claim) may direct the defective letters patent to be cancelled and a minute of such cancellation to be entered in the margin of the registry of the original letters patent, and correct letters patent to be issued in their stead,—which corrected letters patent shall relate back to the date of those so cancelled, and have the same effect as if issued at the date of such cancelled letters patent.

51. In all cases in which grants or letters patent have issued for the same land inconsistent with each other through error, and in all cases of sales or appropriations of the same land inconsistent with each other, the Superintendent-General may, in cases of sale, cause a repayment of the purchase money, with interest, or when the land has passed from the original purchaser or has been improved before a discovery of the error, he may in substitution assign land or grant a certificate entitling the party to purchase Indian lands, of such value and to such extent as to him, the Superintendent-General, may seem just and equitable under the circumstances; but no such claim shall be entertained unless it be preferred within five years from the discovery of the error.

52. Whenever by reason of false survey or error in the books or plans in the Department of Indian Affairs, or in the late Indian Branch of the Department of the Interior, any grant, sale or appropriation of land is found to be deficient, or any parcel of land contains less than the

quantity of land mentioned in the patent therefor, the Superintendent-General may order the purchase money of so much land as is deficient, with the interest thereon from the time of the application therefor, or, if the land has passed from the original purchaser, then the purchase money which the claimant (provided he was ignorant of a deficiency at the time of his purchase) has paid for so much of the land as is deficient, with interest thereon from the time of the application therefor, to be paid to him in land or in money, as he, the Superintendent-General, may direct;—But no such claim shall be entertained unless application has been made within five years from the date of the patent, nor unless the deficiency is equal to one-tenth of the whole quantity described as being contained in the particular lot or parcel of land granted.

53. In all cases wherein patents for Indian lands have issued through fraud or in error or improvidence, the Exchequer Court of Canada, or a superior court of law or equity in any Province may, upon action, bill or plaint, respecting such lands situate within their jurisdiction, and upon hearing of the parties interested, or upon default of the said parties after such notice of proceeding as the said courts shall respectively order, decree such patents to be void; and upon a registry of such decree in the office of the Registrar-General of Canada, such patents shall be void to all intents. The practice in court, in such cases, shall be regulated by orders to be, from time to time, made by the said courts respectively; and any action or proceeding commenced under any former Act may be continued under this section,—which, for the purpose of any such action or proceeding shall be construed as merely continuing the provisions of such former Act.

54. If any agent appointed or continued in office under this Act knowingly and falsely informs, or causes to be informed, any person applying to him to purchase any land within his division and agency, that the same has already been purchased, or refuses to permit the person so applying to purchase the same according to existing regulations, such agent shall be liable therefor to the person so applying in the sum of five dollars for each acre of land which the person so applying offered to purchase, to be recovered by action of debt in any court having jurisdiction in civil cases to the amount.

55. If any person, before or at the time of the public sale of any Indian lands, by intimidation, combination or unfair management, hinders or prevents, or attempts to hinder or prevent any person from bidding upon or purchasing any lands so offered for sale, every such offender, his, her or their aiders and abettors, shall, for every such offence, be guilty of a misdemeanor, and on conviction thereof shall be liable to a fine not exceeding four hundred dollars, or imprisonment for a term not exceeding two years, or both, in the discretion of the court.

56. The Superintendent-General, or any officer or agent au-

thorized by him to that effect, may grant licenses to cut trees on reserves and ungranted Indian lands at such rates, and subject to such conditions, regulations and restrictions, as may, from time to time, be established by the Governor in Council,—such conditions, regulations and restrictions to be adapted to the locality in which such reserves or lands are situated.

57. No license shall be so granted for a longer period than twelve months from the date thereof: and if, in consequence of any incorrectness of survey or other error, or cause whatsoever, a license is found to comprise land included in a license of a prior date, or land not being reserves or ungranted Indian lands, the license granted shall be void in so far as it comprises such land, and the holder or proprietor of the license so rendered void shall have no claim upon the Government for indemnity or compensation by reason of such avoidance.

58. Every license shall describe the lands upon which the trees may be cut and the kind of trees to be cut, and shall confer for the time being on the nominee, the right to take and keep exclusive possession of the land so described, subject to such regulations and restrictions as may be established; and every license shall vest in the holder thereof all rights of property whatsoever in all trees of the kind specified cut within the limits of the license during the term thereof, whether such trees are cut by authority of the holder of such license or by any other person, with or without his consent; and every license shall entitle the holder thereof to seize in revendication or otherwise, such trees and the logs, timber or other product thereof where the same are found in the possession of any unauthorized person, and also to institute any action or suit at law or in equity against any wrongful possessor or trespasser, and to prosecute all trespassers and other offenders to punishment, and to recover damages, if any; and all proceedings pending at the expiration of any license may be continued to final termination as if the license had not expired.

59. Every person obtaining a license shall, at the expiration thereof, make to the officer or agent granting the same, or to the Superintendent-General, a return of the number and kinds of trees cut, and of the quantity and description of saw-logs, or of the number and description of sticks of square or other timber, manufactured and carried away under such license; and such statement shall be sworn to by the holder of the license, or his agent, or by his foreman: and any person refusing or neglecting to furnish such satement, or evading or attempting to evade any regulation made by Order in Council, shall be held to have cut without authority, and the timber or other product made shall be dealt with accordingly.

60. All trees cut, and the logs, timber or other products thereof, shall be liable for the payment of the dues thereon, so long as and

wheresoever the same or any part thereof may be found, whether in the original logs or manufactured into deals, boards or other stuff; and all officers or agents entrusted with the collection of such dues may follow and seize and detain the same wherever it is found, until the dues are paid or secured.

61. Any instrument or security taken for the dues, either before or after the cutting of the trees, as collateral security or to facilitate collection, shall not in any way affect the lien, but the lien shall subsist until the said dues are actually discharged.

62. If any timber so seized and detained for non-payment of dues remains more than twelve months in the custody of the agent or person appointed to guard the same, without the dues and expenses being paid,—then the Superintendent-General, may order a sale of the said timber to be made after sufficient notice; and the balance of the proceeds of such sale, after retaining the amount of dues and costs incurred, shall be handed over to the owner or claimant of such timber, upon his applying therefor and proving his right thereto.

63. If any person without authority cuts, or employs or induces any other person to cut, or assists in cutting any trees of any kind on Indian lands, or removes or carries away, or employs or induces or assists any other person to remove or carry away, any trees of any kind so cut from Indian lands aforesaid, he shall not acquire any right to the trees so cut, or any claim to any remuneration for cutting, preparing the same for market, or conveying the same to or towards market,—and when the trees or logs or timber, or other products thereof, have been removed, so that the same cannot, in the opinion of the Superintendent-General, conveniently be seized, he shall in addition to the loss of his labour and disbursements, forfeit a sum of three dollars for each tree (rafting stuff excepted), which he is proved to have cut or caused to be cut or carried away; and such sum shall be recoverable with costs, at the suit and in the name of the Superintendent-General or resident agent, in any court having jurisdiction in civil matters to the amount of the penalty: and in all such cases it shall be incumbent on the party charged to prove his authority to cut; and the averment of the party seizing or prosecuting, that he is duly employed under the authority of this Act, shall be sufficient proof thereof, unless the defendant proves the contrary.

64. Whenever satisfactory information, supported by affidavit made before a Justice of the Peace or before any other competent authority, is received by the Superintendent-General, or any other officer or agent acting under him, that any trees have been cut without authority on Indian lands, and describing where the same or the logs, timber or other products thereof can be found, the said Superintendent-General, officer or agent, or any one of them, may seize or cause to be seized the same in Her Majesty's name, wherever

found, and place the same under proper custody, until a decision can be had in the matter from competent authority:

2. And where the wood, timber, logs or other products thereof so reported to have been cut without authority on Indian lands, have been made up or intermingled with other wood, timber, logs or other products thereof into a crib, dram or raft, or in any other manner, so that it is difficult to distinguish the timber cut on reserves or Indian land without license, from the other timber with which it is made up or intermingled, the whole of the timber so made up or intermingled shall be held to have been cut without authority on Indian lands, and shall be seized and forfeited and sold by the Superintendent-General, or any other officer or agent acting under him, unless evidence satisfactory to him is adduced shewing the probable quantity not cut on Indian lands.

65. Any officer or person seizing trees, logs, timber or other products thereof, in the discharge of his duty under this Act, may, in the name of the Crown, call in any assistance necessary for securing and protecting the same; and whosoever, under any pretence, either by assault, force or violence, or by threat of such assault, force or violence, in any way resists or obstructs any officer or person acting in his aid, in the discharge of his duty under this Act, shall, on conviction thereof in a summary manner before a Justice of the Peace or other proper functionary, be liable to a fine not exceeding one hundred dollars, or to imprisonment not exceeding twelve months, or to both, in the discretion of the convicting justice or other functionary.

66. Whosoever, whether pretending to be the owner or not, either secretly or openly, and whether with or without force or violence, takes or carries away, or causes to be taken or carried away, without permission of the officer or person who seized the same, or of some competent authority, any trees, logs, timber or other product thereof, seized and detained as subject to forfeiture under this Act, before the same has been declared by competent authority to have been seized without due cause, shall be deemed to have stolen the same, as being the property of the Crown, and guilty of felony, and is liable to punishment accordingly:

2. And whenever any trees, logs, timber or other products thereof are seized for non-payment of Crown dues or for any other cause of forfeiture, or any prosecution is brought for any penalty or forfeiture under this Act, and any question arises whether the said dues have been paid or whether the same were cut on other than any of the lands aforesaid, the burden of proving payment, or on what land the same were cut, shall lie on the owner or claimant and not on the officer who seizes the same, or the party bringing such prosecution.

67. All trees, logs, timber or other products thereof seized under this Act shall be deemed to be condemned, unless the person from

whom the same are seized, or the owner thereof, within one month from the day of the seizure, gives notice to the seizing officer, or nearest officer or agent of the Superintendent-General, that he claims or intends to claim the same; failing such notice, the officer or agent seizing shall report the circumstances to the Superintendent-General, who may order the sale of the same by the said officer or agent:

2. And any judge of a superior, county or district court, or any Stipendiary Magistrate, may, in a summary way, and following the procedure on summary trials before Justices of the Peace out of sessions, try and determine such seizures, and may, pending the trial, order the delivery of the trees, logs, timber or other products thereof to the alleged owner, on receiving security by bond with two good and sufficient sureties, to be first approved by the said agent, to pay double the value in case of condemnation,—and such bond shall be taken in the name of the Superintendent-General, to Her Majesty's use, and shall be delivered up to and kept by the Superintendent-General; and if such seized trees, logs, timber or other products thereof are condemned, the value thereof shall be paid forthwith to the Superintendent-General, or agent, and the bond cancelled, otherwise the penalty of such bond shall be enforced and recovered.

68. Every person availing himself of any false statement or oath to evade the payment of dues under this Act, shall forfeit the timber on which dues are attempted to be evaded.

69. All moneys or securities of any kind applicable to the support or benefit of Indians, or any band of Indians, and all moneys accrued or hereafter to accrue from the sale of any Indian lands or of any timber on any reserves or Indian lands, shall, subject to the provisions of this Act, be applicable to the same purposes, and be dealt with in the same manner as they might have been applied to or dealt with before the passing of this Act.

70. The Governor in Council may, subject to the provisions of this Act, direct how, and in what manner, and by whom the moneys arising from sales of Indian lands, and from the property held or to be held in trust for the Indians, or from any timber on Indian lands or reserves, or from any other source for the benefit of Indians (with the exception of any small sum not exceeding ten per cent. of the proceeds of any lands, timber or property, which may be agreed at the time of the surrender to be paid to the members of the band interested therein), shall be invested from time to time, and how the payments or assistance to which the Indians may be entitled shall be made or given, and may provide for the general management of such moneys, and direct what percentage or proportion thereof shall be set apart from time to time, to cover the cost of and attendant upon the management of reserves, lands, property and moneys under the provisions of this Act, and for the construction or

repair of roads passing through such reserves or lands, and by way of contribution to schools frequented by such Indians.

71. The proceeds arising from the sale or lease of any Indian lands, or from the timber, hay, stone, minerals or other valuables thereon, or on a reserve, shall be paid to the Receiver-General to the credit of the Indian fund.

72. Whenever the Governor in Council deems it advisable for the good government of a band to introduce the election system of chiefs, he may by Order in Council provide that the chiefs of any band of Indians shall be elected, as hereinafter provided, at such time and place as the Superintendent-General may direct; and they shall, in such case, be elected for a period of three years, unless deposed by the Governor for dishonesty, intemperance, immorality or incompetency; and they may be in the proportion of one head chief and two second chiefs or councillors for every two hundred Indians: Provided, that no band shall have more than six head chiefs and twelve second chiefs, but any band composed of thirty Indians may have one chief: Provided always, that all life chiefs now living shall continue to hold the rank of chief until death or resignation, or until their removal by the Governor for dishonesty, intemperance, immorality or incompetency: Provided also, that in the event of His Excellency ordering that the chiefs of a band shall be elected, then and in such case the life chiefs shall not exercise the powers of chiefs unless elected under such order to the exercise of such powers.

73. At the election of a chief or chiefs, or the granting of any ordinary consent required of a band of Indians under this Act, those entitled to vote at the council or meeting thereof shall be the male members of the band of the full age of twenty-one years; and the vote of a majority of such members at a council or meeting of the band summoned according to their rules, and held in the presence of the Superintendent-General, or an agent acting under his instructions, shall be sufficient to determine such election, or grant such consent:

Provided that in the case of any band having a council of chiefs or councillors, any ordinary consent required of the band may be granted by a vote of a majority of such chiefs or councillors at a council summoned according to their rules, and held in the presence of the Superintendent-General or his agent.

74. The chief or chiefs of any band in council may frame, subject to confirmation by the Governor in Council, rules and regulations for the following subjects, viz:—

1. As to what religious denomination the teacher of the school established on the reserve shall belong to; provided always, that he shall be of the same denomination as the majority of the band; and provided that the Catholic or Protestant minor-

ity may likewise have a separate school with the approval of and under regulations to be made by the Governor in Council;

2. The care of the public health;
3. The observance of order and decorum at assemblies of the Indians in general council, or on other occasions;
4. The repression of intemperance and profligacy;
5. The prevention of trespass by cattle,—also for the protection of sheep, horses, mules and cattle;
6. The construction and maintenance of water-courses, roads, bridges, ditches and fences;
7. The construction and repair of school houses, council houses and other Indian public buildings;
8. The establishment of pounds and the appointment of pound-keepers;
9. The locating of the land in their reserves, and the establishment of a register of such locations;
10. The repression of noxious weeds;
11. The imposition of punishment, by fine or penalty, or by imprisonment, or both, for infraction of any of such rules or regulations; the fine or penalty in no case to exceed thirty dollars, and the imprisonment in no case to exceed thirty days; the proceedings for the imposition of such punishment to be taken in the usual summary way before a Justice of the Peace, following the procedure on summary trials before a justice out of sessions.

75. No Indian or non-treaty Indian shall be liable to be taxed for any real or personal property, unless he holds in his individual right real estate under a lease or in fee simple, or personal property, outside of the reserve or special reserve,—in which case he shall be liable to be taxed for such real or personal property at the same rate as other persons in the locality in which it is situate.

76. All land vested in the Crown, or in any person or body corporate, in trust for or for the use of any Indian or non-treaty Indian, or any band or irregular band of Indians or non-treaty Indians, shall be exempt from taxation.

77. No person shall take any security or otherwise obtain any lien or charge, whether by mortgage, judgment or otherwise, upon real or personal property of any Indian or non-treaty Indian within Canada, except on real or personal property subject to taxation under section seventy-five of this Act: Provided always, that any person selling any article to an Indian or non-treaty Indian may, notwithstanding this

section, take security on such article for any part of the price thereof which may be unpaid.

78. Indians and non-treaty Indians shall have the right to sue for debts due to them or in respect of any tort or wrong inflicted upon them, or to compel the performance of obligations contracted with them.

79. No pawn taken of any Indian or non-treaty Indian for any intoxicant shall be retained by the person to whom such pawn is delivered, but the thing so pawned may be sued for and recovered, with costs of suit, by the Indian or non-treaty Indian who has deposited the same, before any court of competent jurisdiction.

80. No presents given to Indians or non-treaty Indians, nor any property purchased or acquired with or by means of any annuities granted to Indians or any part thereof, and in the possession of any band of such Indians or of any Indian of any band or irregular band, shall be liable to be taken, seized or distrained for any debt, matter or cause whatsoever. Nor in the Province of British Columbia, the Province of Manitoba, the North-West Territories, or in the District of Keewatin, shall the same be sold, bartered, exchanged or given by any band or irregular band of Indians, or any Indian of any such band, to any person or Indian other than an Indian of such band; and any such sale, barter, exchange or gift shall be absolutely null and void, unless such sale, barter, exchange or gift be made with the written assent of the Superintendent-General or his agent; and whosoever buys or otherwise acquires any presents or property purchased as aforesaid, without the written consent of the Superintendent-General, or his agent, as aforesaid, is guilty of a misdemeanor, and is punishable by fine not exceeding two hundred dollars, or by imprisonment not exceeding six months, in any place of confinement other than a penitentiary. If any presents given to Indians or non-treaty Indians, or any property purchased or acquired with or by means of any annuities granted to Indians, be unlawfully in the possession of any person within the true intent and meaning of this section, any person acting under the authority (either general or special) of the Superintendent-General, may, with such assistance in that behalf as he may think necessary, seize and take possession of the same, and he shall deal therewith as the Superintendent-General may direct.

DISABILITIES AND PENALTIES.

81. No Indian or non-treaty Indian, resident in the Province of Manitoba, the North-West Territories or the District of Keewatin, shall be held capable of having acquired or acquiring a homestead or preemption right to a quarter section, or any portion of land in any surveyed or unsurveyed lands in the said Province of Manitoba, the

North-West Territories or the District of Keewatin, or the right to share in the distribution of any lands allotted to half-breeds, subject to the following exceptions:—

> (*a*) He shall not be disturbed in the occupation of any plot on which he has or may have permanent improvements prior to his becoming a party to any treaty with the Crown;
> (*b*) Nothing in this section shall prevent the Government of Canada, if found desirable, from compensating any Indian for his improvements on such a plot of land without obtaining a formal surrender therefor from the band;
> (*c*) Nothing in this section shall apply to any person who withdrew from any Indian treaty prior to the first day of October, in the year one thousand eight hundred and seventy-four.

82. Any Indian convicted of any crime punishable by imprisonment in any penitentiary or other place of confinement, shall, during such imprisonment, be excluded from participating in the annuities, interest money, or rents payable to the band of which he or she is a member; and whenever any Indian shall be convicted of any crime punishable by imprisonment in a penitentiary or other place of confinement, the legal costs incurred in procuring such conviction, and in carrying out the various sentences recorded, may be defrayed by the Superintendent-General, and paid out of any annuity or interest coming to such Indian, or to the band, as the case may be.

83. The Superintendent-General shall have power to stop the payment of the annuity and interest money of any Indian who may be proved, to the satisfaction of the Superintendent-General, to have been guilty of deserting his or her family, and the said Superintendent-General may apply the same towards the support of any family, woman or child so deserted; also to stop the payment of the annuity and interest money of any woman having no children, who deserts her husband and lives immorally with another man.

84. The Superintendent-General, in cases where sick or disabled, or aged and destitute persons are not provided for by the band of Indians of which they are members, may furnish sufficient aid from the funds of the band for the relief of such sick, disabled, aged or destitute persons.

85. Upon any inquest, or upon any enquiry into any matter involving a criminal charge, or upon the trial of any crime or offence whatsoever or by whomsoever committed, it shall be lawful for any court, judge, Stipendiary Magistrate, coroner or justice of the peace to receive the evidence of any Indian or non-treaty Indian, who is destitute of the knowledge of God and of any fixed and clear belief in religion or in a future state of rewards and punishments without administering the

usual form of oath to any such Indian, or non-treaty Indian, as aforesaid, upon his solemn affirmation or declaration to tell the truth, the whole truth and nothing but the truth, or in such form as may be approved by such court, judge, Stipendiary Magistrate, coroner or justice of the peace as most binding on the conscience of such Indian or non-treaty Indian.

86. Provided that in the case of any inquest, or upon any enquiry into any matter involving a criminal charge, or upon the trial of any crime or offence whatsoever, the substance of the evidence or information of any such Indian, or non-treaty Indian, as aforesaid, shall be reduced to writing and signed by the person (by mark if necessary) giving the same, and verified by the signature or mark of the person acting as interpreter (if any) and by the signature of the judge, Stipendiary Magistrate or coroner, or justice of the peace or person before whom such evidence or information has been given.

87. The court, judge, Stipendiary Magistrate or justice of the peace shall, before taking any such evidence, information or examination, caution every such Indian or non-treaty Indian, as aforesaid, that he will be liable to incur punishment if he do not so as aforesaid tell the truth.

88. The written declaration or examination, made, taken and verified in manner aforesaid, of any such Indian or non-treaty Indian as aforesaid, may be lawfully read and received as evidence upon the trial of any criminal suit or proceedings, when under the like circumstances the written affidavit, examination, deposition or confession of any other person, might be lawfully read and received as evidence.

89. Every solemn affirmation or declaration in whatever form made or taken by any Indian or non-treaty Indian as aforesaid shall be of the same force and effect as if such Indian or non-treaty Indian had taken an oath in the usual form, and he or she shall, in like manner, incur the penalty of perjury in case of falsehood.

90. Whoever sells, exchanges with, barters, supplies or gives to any Indian or non-treaty Indian in Canada, any kind of intoxicant, or causes or procures the same to be done, or connives or attempts thereat, or opens or keeps, or causes to be opened or kept on any reserve or special reserve, a tavern, house or building where any intoxicant is sold, bartered, exchanged or given, or is found in possession of any intoxicant in the house, tent, wigwam or place of abode of any Indian or non-treaty Indian, shall, on conviction thereof before any judge, Stipendiary Magistrate or two justices of the peace, upon the evidence of one credible witness other than the informer or prosecutor, or in the Province of Manitoba, in the District of Keewatin, in the North-West Territories or in the Province of British Columbia, upon the evidence of the informer alone if he be a credible person, be liable to imprisonment

for a period not less than one month nor exceeding six months, with or without hard labour, or be fined not less than fifty nor more than three hundred dollars, with costs of prosecution,—one moiety of the fine to go to the informer or prosecutor, and the other moiety to Her Majesty, to form part of the fund for the benefit of that body of Indians or non-treaty Indians, with respect to one or more members of which the offence was committed, or he shall be liable to both fine and imprisonment in the discretion of the convicting judge, Stipendiary Magistrate or justices of the peace; and the commander or person in charge of any steamer or other vessel, or boat, from or on board of which any intoxicant has been sold, bartered, exchanged, supplied or given to any Indian or non-treaty Indian, shall be liable, on conviction thereof before any judge, Stipendiary Magistrate or two justices of the peace, upon the evidence of one credible witness other than the informer or prosecutor, or in the Province of Manitoba, in the District of Keewatin, in the North-West Territories or in the Province of British Columbia, upon the evidence of the informer alone if he be a credible person, to be fined not less than fifty nor exceeding three hundred dollars for each such offence, with costs of prosecution,—the moieties of the fine to be applicable as hereinbefore mentioned; and in default of immediate payment of such fine and costs any person so fined shall be committed to any common gaol, house of correction, lock-up or other place of confinement by the judge, Stipendiary Magistrate or two justices of the peace before whom the conviction has taken place, for a period of not less than one nor more than six months, with or without hard labour, or until such fine and costs are paid; and any Indian or non-treaty Indian who makes or manufactures any intoxicant, or who has in his possession, or concealed, or who sells, exchanges with, barters, supplies or gives to any other Indian or non-treaty Indian in Canada any kind of intoxicant, shall, on conviction thereof, before any judge, Stipendiary Magistrate or two justices of the peace, upon the evidence of one credible witness other than the informer or prosecutor, or in the Province of Manitoba, in the District of Keewatin, in the North-West Territories or in the Province of British Columbia, upon the evidence of the informer alone if he be a credible person, be liable to imprisonment for a period of not less than one month nor more than six months, with or without hard labour, or a fine of not less than twenty-five or more than one hundred dollars, or to both fine and imprisonment in the discretion of the convicting judge, Stipendiary Magistrate or justices of the peace; and in all cases arising under this section, Indians or non-treaty Indians shall be competent witnesses: but no penalty shall be incurred in case of sickness where the intoxicant is made use of under the sanction of a medical man or under the directions of a minister of religion.

91. The keg, barrel, case, box, package or receptacle whence any intoxicant has been sold, exchanged, bartered, supplied or given, and as well that in which the original supply was contained as the vessel wherein any portion of such original supply was supplied as aforesaid, and the remainder of the contents thereof, if such barrel, keg, case, box, package, receptacle or vessel aforesaid respectively, can be identified,—and any intoxicant imported or manufactured or brought into and upon any reserve or special reserve, or into the house, tent, wigwam or place of abode, or on the person of any Indian or non-treaty Indian, may be searched for, and if found seized by any Indian superintendent, agent or bailiff, or other officer connected with the Indian Department, or by any constable wheresoever found on such land or in such place or on the person of such Indian or non-treaty Indian; and on complaint before any judge, Stipendiary Magistrate or justice of the peace, he may, on the evidence of any credible witness that this Act has been contravened in respect thereof, declare the same forfeited, and cause the same to be forthwith destroyed; and may condemn the Indian or other person in whose possession they were found to pay a penalty not exceeding one hundred dollars nor less than fifty dollars, and the costs of prosecution; and one-half of such penalty shall belong to the prosecutor and the other half to Her Majesty, for the purposes hereinbefore mentioned; and in default of immediate payment, the offender may be committed to any common gaol, house of correction, lock-up or other place of confinement, with or without hard labour, for any time not exceeding six nor less than two months, unless such fine and costs are sooner paid.

92. When it is proved before any judge, Stipendiary Magistrate or two justices of the peace that any vessel, boat, canoe or conveyance of any description upon the sea or sea coast, or upon any river, lake or stream in Canada, is employed in carrying any intoxicant, to be supplied to Indians or non-treaty Indians, such vessel, boat, canoe or conveyance so employed may be seized and declared forfeited, as in the next preceding section, and sold, and the proceeds thereof paid to Her Majesty for the purposes hereinbefore mentioned.

93. Every article, chattel, commodity or thing in the purchase, acquisition, exchange, trade or barter of which, in contravention of this Act, the consideration, either wholly or in part, may be any intoxicant, shall be forfeited to Her Majesty and shall be seized as in the ninety-first section in respect to any receptacle of any intoxicant, and may be sold, and the proceeds thereof paid to Her Majesty for the purposes hereinbefore mentioned.

94. It shall be lawful for any constable, without process of law, to arrest any Indian or non-treaty Indian whom he may find in a state of intoxication, and to convey him to any common gaol, house of correc-

tion, lock-up or other place of confinement, there to be kept until he shall have become sober; and such Indian or non-treaty Indian shall, when sober, be brought before any judge, Stipendiary Magistrate or justice of the peace, and if convicted of being so found in a state of intoxication shall be liable to imprisonment in any common gaol, house of correction, lock-up or other place of confinement, for any period not exceeding one month; and if any Indian or non-treaty Indian, having been so convicted as aforesaid, refuses upon examination to state or give information of the person, place and time from whom, where and when, he procured such intoxicant, and if from any other Indian or non-treaty Indian, then, if within his knowledge, from whom, where and when such intoxicant was originally procured or received, he shall be liable to imprisonment as aforesaid for a further period not exceeding fourteen days.

95. If any person, being the keeper of any house, allows or suffers any Indian woman to be or remain in such house, knowing, or having probable cause for believing, that such Indian woman is in or remains in such house with the intention of prostituting herself therein, such person shall be deemed guilty of an offence against this Act, and shall, on conviction thereof, in a summary way, before any Stipendiary Magistrate, police magistrate or justice of the peace, be liable to a fine of not less than ten dollars, or more than one hundred dollars, or to imprisonment in any gaol or place of confinement other than a penitentiary, for a term not exceeding six months.

96. Any person who appears, acts or behaves as master or mistress, or as the person having the care, government or management of any house in which any Indian woman is, or remains for the purpose of prostituting herself therein, shall be deemed and taken to be the keeper thereof, notwithstanding he or she may not in fact be the real keeper thereof.

97. No appeal shall lie from any conviction under the seven next preceding sections of this Act, except to a judge of any superior court of law, county, or circuit, or district court, or to the chairman or judge of the court of the sessions of the peace, having jurisdiction where the conviction was had; and such appeal shall be heard, tried, and adjudicated upon by such judge without the intervention of a jury; and no such appeal shall be brought after the expiration of thirty days from the conviction.

98. No prosecution, conviction or commitment under this Act shall be invalid on account of want of form, so long as the same is according to the true meaning of this Act.

ENFRANCHISEMENT.

99. Whenever any Indian man, or unmarried woman, of the full age of twenty-one years, obtains the consent of the band of which he or she is a member to become enfranchised, and whenever such Indian has been assigned by the band a suitable allotment of land for that purpose, the local agent shall report such action of the band, and the name of the applicant to the Superintendent-General; whereupon the Superintendent-General, if satisfied that the proposed allotment of land is equitable, shall authorize some competent person to report whether the applicant is an Indian who, from the degree of civilization to which he or she has attained, and the character for integrity, morality and sobriety which he or she bears, appears to be qualified to become a proprietor of land in fee simple; and upon the favorable report of such person, the Superintendent-General may grant such Indian a location ticket as a probationary Indian, for the land allotted to him or her by the band.

(1.) Any Indian who may be admitted to the degree of Doctor of Medicine, or to any other degree by any University of Learning, or who may be admitted in any Province of the Dominion to practice law either as an Advocate or as a Barrister or Counsellor, or Solicitor or Attorney or to be a Notary Public, or who may enter Holy Orders, or who may be licensed by any denomination of Christians as a Minister of the Gospel, may, upon petition to the Superintendent-General, *ipso facto* become and be enfranchised under this Act, and he shall then be entitled to all the rights and privileges to which any other member of the band to which he belongs would be entitled were he enfranchised under the provisions of this Act; and the Superintendent-General may give him a suitable allotment of land from the lands belonging to the band of which he is a member.

100. After the expiration of three years (or such longer period as the Superintendent-General may deem necessary in the event of such Indian's conduct not being satisfactory), the Governor may, on the report of the Superintendent-General, order the issue of letters patent, granting to such Indian in fee simple the land which had, with this object in view, been allotted to him or her by location ticket. And in such cases compliance with the provisions of sections thirty-six and thirty-seven and the sub-sections thereof shall not be necessary.

101. Every such Indian shall, before the issue of the letters patent mentioned in the next preceding section, declare to the Superintendent-General the name and surname by which he or she wishes to be enfranchised and thereafter known, and on his or her receiving such letters patent, in such name and surname, he or she shall be held to be

also enfranchised, and he or she shall thereafter be known by such name or surname, and if such Indian be a married man his wife and minor unmarried children also shall be held to be enfranchised; and from the date of such letters patent the provisions of this Act and of any Act or law making any distinction between the legal rights, privileges, disabilities and liabilities of Indians and those of Her Majesty's other subjects shall cease to apply to such Indian, or to the wife or minor unmarried children of such Indian as aforesaid, so declared to be enfranchised, who shall no longer be deemed Indians within the meaning of the laws relating to Indians, except in so far as their right to participate in the annuities and interest moneys, and rents and councils of the band of Indians to which they belonged, is concerned: Provided always, that any children of a probationary Indian, who being minors and unmarried when the probationary ticket was granted to such Indian, arrive at the full age of twenty one years before the letters patent are issued to such Indian, may, at the discretion of the Governor in Council, receive letters patent in their own names for their respective shares of the land allotted under the said ticket, at the same time that letters patent are granted to their parent; and provided, that if any Indian child having arrived at the full age of twenty-one years, during his or her parents' probationary period, be unqualified for enfranchisement, or if any child of such parent, having been a minor at the commencement of such period, be married during such period, then a quantity of land equal to the share of such child shall be deducted in such manner as may be directed by the Superintendent-General, from the allotment made to such Indian parent on receiving his probationary ticket.

102. If any probationary Indian should fail in qualifying to become enfranchised, or should die before the expiration of the required probation, his or her claim, or the claim of his or her heirs, to the land for which a probationary ticket was granted, or the claim of any unqualified Indian, or of any Indian who may marry during his or her parents' probationary period, to the land deducted under the operation of the next preceding section from his or her parents' probationary allotment, shall in all respects be the same as that conferred by an ordinary location ticket, as provided in the seventeenth, eighteenth, nineteenth and twentieth sections of this Act.

103. The children of any widow who becomes either a probationary or enfranchised Indian shall be entitled to the same privileges as those of a male head of a family in like circumstances.

104. In allotting land to probationary Indians, the quantity to be located to the head of a family shall be in proportion to the number of such family, compared with the total quantity of land in the reserve, and the whole number of the band; but any band may determine what quantity shall be allotted to each member for enfranchisement purposes, provided each female of any age, and each male member under

fourteen years of age, receive not less than one-half the quantity allotted to each male member of fourteen years of age and over.

105. Any Indian, not a member of the band, or any non-treaty Indian, who, with the consent of the band and the approval of the Superintendent-General, has been permitted to reside upon the reserve, or obtain a location thereon, may, on being assigned a suitable allot-ment of land by the band for enfranchisement, become enfranchised on the same terms and conditions as a member of the band; and such enfranchisement shall confer upon such Indian the same legal rights and privileges, and make such Indian subject to such disabilities and liabilities as affect Her Majesty's other subjects; but such enfranchise-ment shall not confer upon such Indian any right to participate in the annuities, interest moneys, rents or councils of the band.

106. Whenever any band of Indians, at a council summoned for the purpose according to their rules, and held in the presence of the Superintendent-General, or an agent duly authorized by him to attend such council, decides to allow every member of the band who chooses, and who may be found qualified, to become enfranchised, and to receive his or her share of the principal moneys of the band, and sets apart for such member a suitable allotment of land for the purpose, any applicant of such band, after such a decision, may be dealt with as provided in the seven next preceding sections until his or her enfran-chisement is attained; and whenever any member of the band, who for the three years immediately succeeding the date on which he or she was granted letters patent, (or for any longer period that the Super-intendent-General may deem necessary,) by his or her exemplary good conduct and management of property, proves that he or she is qualified to receive his or her share of such moneys, the Governor may, on the report of the Superintendent-General to that effect, order that the said Indian be paid his or her share of the capital funds at the credit of the band, or his or her share of the principal of the annuities of the band, estimated as yielding five per cent., out of such moneys as may be provided for the purpose by Parliament; and if such Indian be a married man then he shall also be paid his wife's and minor unmarried children's share of such funds and other principal moneys, and if such Indian be a widow, she shall also be paid her minor unmarried children's share; and the unmarried children of such married Indians, who become of age during the probationary period either for enfran-chisement or for payment of such moneys, if qualified by the character for integrity, morality and sobriety which they bear, shall receive their own share of such moneys when their parents are paid; and if not so qualified before they can become enfranchised or receive payment of such moneys they must themselves pass through the probationary periods; and all such Indians and their unmarried minor children who are paid their share of the principal moneys of their band as aforesaid,

shall thenceforward cease in every respect to be Indians of any class within the meaning of this Act, or Indians within the meaning of any other Act or law.

107. Sections ninety-nine to one hundred and six, both inclusive, of this Act, shall not apply to any band of Indians in the Province of British Columbia, the Province of Manitoba, the North-West Territories, or the District of Keewatin, save in so far as the said sections may, by proclamation of the Governor-General, be from time to time extended, as they may be, to any band of Indians in any of the said provinces or territories.

MISCELLANEOUS PROVISIONS.

108. All affidavits required under this Act, or intended to be used in reference to any claim, business or transaction in connection with Indian Affairs, may be taken before the Judge or Clerk of any County or Circuit Court, or any Justice of the Peace, or any Commissioner for taking affidavits in any of the Courts, or the Superintendent-General, or his Deputy, or any Inspector of Indian Agencies, or any Indian Agent, or any Surveyor duly licensed and sworn, appointed by the Superintendent-General to enquire into or take evidence or report in any matter submitted or pending before such Superintendent-General or if made out of Canada, before the Mayor or Chief Magistrate of, or the British Consul in, any city, town or municipality, or before any Notary Public; and any wilfully false swearing in any such affidavit shall be perjury.

109. Copies of any records, documents, books or papers belonging to or deposited in the Department of Indian Affairs attested under the signature of the Superintendent-General or of his Deputy shall be competent evidence in all cases in which the original records, documents, books or papers, could be evidence.

110. The Governor in Council may, by proclamation from time to time, exempt from the operation of this Act, or from the operation of any one or more of the sections of this Act, Indians or non-treaty Indians, or any of them, or any band or irregular band of them, or the reserves or special reserves, or Indian lands or any portions of them, in any Province, in the North-West Territories, or in the District of Keewatin, or in either of them, and may again, by proclamation from time to time, remove such exemption.

111. The Governor may, from time to time, appoint officers and agents to carry out this Act, and any Orders in Council made under it,—which officers and agents shall be paid in such manner and at such rates as the Governor in Council may direct out of any fund that may be appropriated by law for that purpose.

112. The Act passed in the thirty-ninth year of Her Majesty's reign and chaptered eighteen, and the Act passed in the forty-second year of Her Majesty's reign and chaptered thirty-four, are hereby repealed, with so much of any other Act or law as may be inconsistent with this Act, or as makes any provision in any matter provided for by this Act, except only as to things done, rights acquired, obligations contracted, or penalties incurred before the coming into force of this Act; and this Act shall be construed not as a new law but as a consolidation of those hereby repealed in so far as they make the same provision that is made by this Act in any matter hereby provided for.

113. No Act or enactment repealed by any Act hereby repealed shall revive by reason of such repeal.

C11.

54 Victoria (1891) Cap. 3 (Ontario). An Act for the Settlement of Questions between the Governments of Canada and Ontario Respecting Indian Lands. [assented to May 4, 1891]

HER Majesty, by and with the advice and consent of the Legislative Assembly of the Province of Ontario, enacts as follows:—

1. It shall be lawful for the Lieutenant-Governor in Council, if he shall see fit, to enter into an agreement with the Government of Canada in accordance with the terms of the draft of a proposed agreement contained in the schedule to this Act, with any modification or additional stipulations which may be agreed to by the two Governments, and such agreement, when entered into, and every matter and thing therein, shall be as binding on this Province as if the same were specified and set forth in an Act of this Legislature, and the Lieutenant-Governor in Council is hereby authorized to carry out the provisions of the agreement so to be entered into.

Schedule.

(Section 1.)

Agreement made by the   on behalf of the Government of Canada on the one part, and on behalf of the Government of Ontario on the other part subject, etc.

Whereas by Articles of a Treaty made on 3rd October, 1873, between Her Most Gracious Majesty the Queen, by Her commissioners the Honourable Alexander Morris, Lieutenant Governor of Manitoba and the North West territories, Joseph Albert Norbert Provencher and

Simon James Dawson, on the one part, and the Saulteaux Tribe of the Ojibbeway Indians, inhabitants of the country within the limits there-inafter defined and described, by their chiefs, chosen and named as thereinafter mentioned, of the other part; which said Treaty is usually known as the North West Angle Treaty, No. 3; The Saulteaux tribe of the Ojibbeway Indians and all other the Indians inhabiting the country therein defined and described surrendered to Her Majesty all their rights, titles and privileges whatsoever to the lands therein defined and described on certain terms and considerations therein men-tioned.

And whereas by the said Treaty out of the lands so surrendered, Reserves were to be selected and laid aside for the benefit of the said Indians; and the said Indians were amongst other things hereinafter provided to have the right to pursue their avocations of hunting and fishing throughout the tract surrendered, subject to such regulations as might from time to time be made by the Government of the Dominion of Canada, and saving and excepting such tracts as might from time to time be required or taken up for settlement, mining, lumbering or other purposes by the said Government of the Dominion of Canada or by any of the subjects duly authorized therefor by the said Government.

And whereas the true boundaries of Ontario have since been ascer-tained and declared to include part of the territory surrendered by the said Treaty, and other territory north of the height of land with respect to which Indians are understood to make a claim as being occupants thereof, according to their mode of occupying, and as not having yet surrendered their claim thereto or interest therein.

And whereas before the true boundaries had been declared as aforesaid, the Government of Canada had selected and set aside certain Reserves for the Indians in intended pursuance of the said treaty, and the said Government of Ontario was no party to the selection, and has not yet concurred therein.

And whereas it is deemed desirable for the Dominion of Canada and the Province of Ontario to come to a friendly and just understanding in respect of the said matters, it is, therefore, agreed as follows; subject to confirmation as already mentioned:—

1. With respect to the tracts to be from time to time taken up for settlement, mining, lumbering or other purposes and to the regulations required in that behalf as in the said Treaty mentioned, it is hereby conceded and declared that, as the Crown lands in the surrendered treaty have been decided to belong to the Province of Ontario, or to Her Majesty in right of the said Province, the rights of hunting and fishing by the Indians throughout the tract surrendered, not including the Reserves to be made thereunder, do not continue with reference to any tracts which have been, or from time to time may be, required or taken

up for settlement, mining, lumbering or other purposes by the Government of Ontario or persons duly authorized by the said Government of Ontario; and that the concurrence of the Province of Ontario is required in the selection of the said Reserves.

2. That to avoid dissatisfaction or discontent among the Indians, full enquiry will be made by the government of Ontario as to the reserves heretofore laid out in the territory, with a view of acquiescing in the location and extent thereof unless some good reason presents itself for a different course.

3. That in case the government of Ontario after such enquiry is dissatisfied with the reserves or any of them already selected, or in case other reserves in the said territory are to be selected, a joint commission or joint commissions shall be appointed by the two governments of Canada and Ontario to settle and determine any question or all questions relating to such reserves or proposed reserves.

4. That in case of all Indian reserves so to be confirmed or hereafter selected, the waters within the lands laid out or to be laid out as Indian reserves in the said territory, including the land covered with water lying between the projecting headlands of any lake or sheets of water, not wholly surrounded by an Indian reserve or reserves, shall be deemed to form part of such reserve, including islands wholly within such headlands, and shall not be subject to the public common right of fishery by others than Indians of the band to which the reserve belongs.

5. That this agreement is made without prejudice to the jurisdiction of the parliament of Canada, with respect to inland fisheries under the British North America Act, 1867, in case the same shall be decided to apply to the said fisheries herein mentioned.

6. That any future treaties with the Indians in respect of territory in Ontario to which they have not hitherto surrendered their claim aforesaid, shall be deemed to require the concurrence of the government of Ontario.

C12.

20 and 21 George V (1930) Cap. 29 (Canada). An Act Respecting the Transfer of the Natural Resources of Manitoba. /assented to May 30, 1930/ (Extract)

* * *

INDIAN RESERVES

11. All lands included in Indian reserves within the Province, includ-

ing those selected and surveyed but not yet confirmed, as well as those confirmed, shall continue to be vested in the Crown and administered, by the Government of Canada for the purposes of Canada, and the Province will from time to time, upon the request of the Superintendent General of Indian Affairs, set aside, out of the unoccupied Crown lands hereby transferred to its administration, such further areas as the said Superintendent General may, in agreement with the Minister of Mines and Natural Resources of the Province, select as necessary to enable Canada to fulfil its obligations under the treaties with the Indians of the Province, and such areas shall thereafter be administered by Canada in the same way in all respects as if they had never passed to the Province under the provisions hereof.

12. The provisions of paragraphs one to six inclusive and of paragraph eight of the agreement made between the Government of the Dominion of Canada and the Government of the Province of Ontario on the 24th day of March, 1924, which said agreement was confirmed by Statute of Canada, fourteen and fifteen George the Fifth chapter forty-eight, shall (except so far as they relate to the *Bed of Navigable Waters Act*) apply to the lands included in such Indian reserves as may hereafter be set aside under the last preceding clause as if the said agreement had been made between the parties hereto, and the provisions of the said paragraphs shall likewise apply to the lands included in the reserves heretofore selected and surveyed, except that neither the said lands nor the proceeds of the disposition thereof shall in any circumstances become administrable by or be paid to the Province.

13. In order to secure to the Indians of the Province the continuance of the supply of game and fish for their support and subsistence, Canada agrees that the laws respecting game in force in the Province from time to time shall apply to the Indians within the boundaries thereof, provided, however, that the said Indians shall have the right, which the Province hereby assures to them, of hunting, trapping and fishing game and fish for food at all seasons of the year on all unoccupied Crown lands and on any other lands to which the said Indians may have a right of access.

* * *

C13.

20 and 21 George V (1930) Cap. 37 (Canada). An Act Respecting the Transfer of the Railway Belt and the Peace River Block. /assented to May 30, 1930/ (Extract)

* * *

INDIAN RESERVES

13. Nothing in this agreement shall extend to the lands included within Indian reserves in the Railway Belt and the Peace River Block, but the said reserves shall continue to be vested in Canada in trust for the Indians on the terms and conditions set out in a certain order of the Governor General of Canada in Council approved on the 3rd day of February, 1930 (P.C. 208).

* * *

C14.

20 and 21 George V (1930) Cap. 41 (Canada). An Act Respecting the Transfer of the Natural Resources of Saskatchewan. /assented to May 30, 1930/ (Extract)

* * *

INDIAN RESERVES

10. All lands included in Indian reserves within the Province, including those selected and surveyed but not yet confirmed, as well as those confirmed, shall continue to be vested in the Crown and administered by the Government of Canada for the purposes of Canada, and the Province will from time to time, upon the request of the Superintendent General of Indian Affairs, set aside, out of the unoccupied Crown lands hereby transferred to its administration, such further areas as the said Superintendent General may, in agreement with the appropriate Minister of the Province, select as necessary to enable Canada to fulfil its obligations under the treaties with the Indians of the Province, and such areas shall thereafter be administered by Canada in the same way in all respects as if they had never passed to the Province under the provisions hereof.

11. The provisions of paragraphs one to six inclusive and of

paragraph eight of the agreement made between the Government of the Dominion of Canada and the Government of the Province of Ontario on the 24th day of March, 1924, which said agreement was confirmed by Statute of Canada, fourteen and fifteen George the Fifth chapter forty-eight, shall (except so far as they relate to the *Bed of Navigable Waters Act*) apply to the lands included in such Indian reserves as may hereafter be set aside under the last preceding clause as if the said agreement had been made between the parties hereto, and the provisions of the said paragraphs shall likewise apply to the lands included in the reserves heretofore selected and surveyed, except that neither the said lands nor the proceeds of the disposition thereof shall in any circumstances become administrable by or be paid to the Province.

12. In order to secure to the Indians of the Province the continuance of the supply of game and fish for their support and subsistence, Canada agrees that the laws respecting game in force in the Province from time to time shall apply to the Indians within the boundaries thereof, provided, however, that the said Indians shall have the right, which the Province hereby assures to them, of hunting, trapping and fishing game and fish for food at all seasons of the year on all unoccupied Crown lands and on any other lands to which the said Indians may have a right of access.

* * *

C15.

14 and 15 George VI (1951 and as amended to 1970) Cap. 29 (Canada). An Act Respecting Indians (The Indian Act 1951).

SHORT TITLE

1. This Act may be cited as the *Indian Act*. R.S., c. 149, s. 1.

INTERPRETATION

2. (1) In this Act
"band" means a body of Indians
    (*a*) for whose use and benefit in common, lands, the legal title to which is vested in Her Majesty, have been set apart before, on or after the 4th day of September 1951,
    (*b*) for whose use and benefit in common, moneys are held by Her Majesty, or
    (*c*) declared by the Governor in Council to be a band for the purposes of this Act;

"child" includes a legally adopted Indian child;

"council of the band" means

(a) in the case of a band to which section 74 applies, the council established pursuant to that section,

(b) in the case of a band to which section 74 does not apply, the council chosen according to the custom of the band, or, where there is no council, the chief of the band chosen according to the custom of the band;

"Department" means the Department of Indian Affairs and Northern Development;

"elector" means a person who

(a) is registered on a Band List,

(b) is of the full age of twenty-one years, and

(c) is not disqualified from voting at band elections;

"estate" includes real and personal property and any interest in land;

"Indian" means a person who pursuant to this Act is registered as an Indian or is entitled to be registered as an Indian;

"Indian moneys" means all moneys collected, received or held by Her Majesty for the use and benefit of Indians or bands;

"intoxicant" includes alcohol, alcoholic, spirituous, vinous, fermented or other intoxicating liquor or combination of liquors and mixed liquor a part of which is spirituous, vinous, fermented or otherwise intoxicating and all drinks or drinkable liquids and all preparations or mixtures capable of human consumption that are intoxicating;

"member of a band" means a person whose name appears on a Band List or who is entitled to have his name appear on a Band List;

"mentally incompetent Indian" means Indian who, pursuant to the laws of the province in which he resides, has been found to be mentally defective or incompetent for the purpose of any laws of that province providing for the administration of estates of mentally defective or incompetent persons;

"Minister" means the Minister of Indian Affairs and Northern Development;

"registered" means registered as an Indian in the Indian Register;

"Registrar" means the officer of the Department who is in charge of the Indian Register;

"reserve" means a tract of land, the legal title to which is vested in Her Majesty, that has been set apart by Her Majesty for the use and benefit of a band;

"superintendent" includes a commissioner, regional supervisor, Indian superintendent, assistant Indian superintendent and any other person declared by the Minister to be a superintendent for the purposes of this Act, and with reference to a band or a reserve, means the superintendent for that band or reserve;

"surrendered lands" means a reserve or part of a reserve or any interest therein, the legal title to which remains vested in Her Majesty, that has been released or surrendered by the band for whose use and benefit and may by proclamation revoke any such declaration.

(3) Sections 114 to 123 and, unless the Minister otherwise orders, sections 42 to 52 do not apply to or in respect of any Indian who does not ordinarily reside on a reserve or on lands belonging to Her Majesty in right of Canada or a province. R.S., c. 149, s. 4; 1956, c. 40, s. 1.

DEFINITION AND REGISTRATION OF INDIANS

5. An Indian Register shall be maintained in the Department, which shall consist of Band Lists and General Lists and in which shall be recorded the name of every person who is entitled to be registered as an Indian. R.S., c. 149, s. 5.

6. The name of every person who is a member of a band and is entitled to be registered shall be entered in the Band List for that band, and the name of every person who is not a member of a band and is entitled to be registered shall be entered in a General List. R.S., c. 149, s. 6.

7. (1) The Registrar may at any time add to or delete from a Band List or a General List the name of any person who, in accordance with this Act, is entitled or not entitled, as the case may be, to have his name included in that List.

(2) The Indian Register shall indicate the date on which each name was added thereto or deleted therefrom. R.S., c. 149, s. 7.

8. The band lists in existence in the Department on the 4th day of September 1951 shall constitute the Indian Register, and the applicable lists shall be posted in a conspicuous place in the superintendent's office that serves the band or persons to whom the List relates and in all other places where band notices are ordinarily displayed. R.S., c. 149, s. 8.

9. (1) Within six months after a list has been posted in accordance with section 8 or within three months after the name of a person has been added to or deleted from a Band List or a General List pursuant to section 7.

(a) in the case of a Band List, the council of the band, any ten electors of the band, or any three electors if there are less than ten electors in the band,

(b) in the case of a posted portion of a General List, any adult person whose name appears on that posted portion, and

(c) the person whose name was included in or omitted from the List referred to in section 8, or whose name was added to or deleted from a Band List or a General List,

may, by notice in writing to the Registrar, containing a brief statement of the grounds therefor, protest the inclusion, omission, addition, or deletion, as the case may be, of the name of that person, and the onus of establishing those grounds lies on the person making the protest.

(2) Where a protest is made to the Registrar under this section he shall cause an investigation to be made into the matter and shall render a decision, and subject to a reference under subsection (3), the decision of the Registrar is final and conclusive.

(3) Within three months from the date of a decision of the Registrar under this section

(a) the council of the band affected by the Registrar's decision, or

(b) the person by or in respect of whom the protest was made,

may, by notice in writing, request the Registrar to refer the decision to a judge for review, and thereupon the Registrar shall refer the decision, together with all material considered by the Registrar in making his decision, to the judge of the county or district court of the county or district in which the band is situated or in which the person in respect of whom the protest was made resides, or such other county or district as the Minister may designate, or in the Province of Quebec, to the judge of the Superior Court for the district in which the band is situated or in which the person in respect of whom the protest was made resides, or such other district as the Minister may designate.

(4) The judge of the county, district or Superior Court, as the case may be, shall inquire into the correctness of the Registrar's decision, and for such purposes may exercise all the powers of a commissioner under Part I of the *Inquiries Act*; the judge shall decide whether the person in respect of whom the protest was made is, in accordance with this Act, entitled or not entitled, as the case may be, to have his name included in the Indian Register, and the decision of the judge is final and conclusive.

(5) Not more than one reference of a Registrar's decision in respect of a protest may be made to a judge under this section.

(6) Where a decision of the Registrar has been referred to a judge for review under this section, the burden of establishing that the decision of the Registrar is erroneous is on the person who requested that the decision be so referred. R.S., c. 149, s. 9; 1965, c. 40, s. 2.

10. Where the name of a male person is included in, omitted from, added to or deleted from a Band List or a General List, the names

of his wife and his minor children shall also be included, omitted, added or deleted, as the case may be. R.S., c. 149, s. 10.

11. (1) Subject to section 12, a person is entitled to be registered if that person

(a) on the 26th day of May 1874 was, for the purposes of *An Act providing for the organization of the Department of the Secretary of State of Canada, and for the management of Indian and Ordnance Lands,* being chapter 42 of the Statutes of Canada, 1868, as amended by section 6 of chapter 6 of the Statutes of Canada, 1869, and section 8 of chapter 21 of the Statutes of Canada, 1874, considered to be entitled to hold, use or enjoy the lands and other immovable property belonging to or appropriated to the use of the various tribes, bands or bodies of Indians in Canada;

(b) is a member of a band

(i) for whose use and benefit, in common, lands have been set apart or since the 26th day of May 1874, have been agreed by treaty to be set apart, or

(ii) that has been declared by the Governor in Council to be a band for the purposes of this Act;

(c) is a male person who is a direct descendant in the male line of a male person described in paragraph (a) or (b);

(d) is the legitimate child of

(i) a male person described in paragraph (a) or (b), or

(ii) a male person described in paragraph (c);

(e) is the illegitimate child of a female person described in paragraph (a), (b) or (d); or

(f) is the wife or widow of a person who is entitled to be registered by virtue of paragraph (a), (b), (c), (d) or (e).

(2) Paragraph (1) (e) applies only to persons born after the 13th day of August 1956. R.S., c. 149, s. 11; 1956, c. 40, s. 3.

12. (1) The following persons are not entitled to be registered, namely,

(a) a person who

(i) has received or has been allotted half-breed lands or money scrip,

(ii) is a descendant of a person described in subparagraph (i),

(iii) is enfranchised, or

(iv) is a person born of a marriage entered into after the 4th day of September 1951 and has attained the age of twenty-one years, whose mother and whose father's mother are not persons described in paragraph 11 (1) (a), (b) or (d) or entitled to be registered by virtue of paragraph 11 (1) (e), unless, being a woman, that person is the wife or widow of a person described in section 11, and

(b) a woman who married a person who is not an Indian, unless that woman is subsequently the wife or widow of a person described in section 11.

(2) The addition to a Band List of the name of an illegitimate child described in paragraph 11 (1) (e) may be protested at any time within twelve months after the addition, and if upon the protest it is decided that the father of the child was not an Indian, the child is not entitled to be registered under that paragraph.

(3) The Minister may issue to any Indian to whom this Act ceases to apply, a certificate to that effect.

(4) Subparagraphs (1) (a) (i) and (ii) do not apply to a person who

(a) pursuant to this Act is registered as an Indian on the 13th day of August 1958, or

(b) is a descendant of a person described in paragraph (a) of this subsection.

(5) Subsection (2) applies only to persons born after the 13th day of August 1956. R.S., c. 149, s. 12; 1956, c. 40, ss. 3, 4; 1958, c. 19, s. 1.

13. Subject to the approval of the Minister and, if the Minister so directs, to the consent of the admitting band,

(a) a person whose name appears on a General List may be admitted into membership of a band with the consent of the council of the band, and

(b) a member of a band may be admitted into membership of another band with the consent of the council of the latter band. 1956, c. 40, s. 5.

14. A woman who is a member of a band ceases to be a member of that band if she marries a person who is not a member of that band, but if she marries a member of another band, she thereupon becomes a member of the band of which her husband is a member. R.S., c. 149, s. 14.

15. (1) Subject to subsection (2), an Indian who becomes enfranchised or who otherwise ceases to be a member of a band is entitled to receive from Her Majesty

(a) one per capita share of the capital and revenue moneys held by Her Majesty on behalf of the band, and

(b) an amount equal to the amount that in the opinion of the Minister he would have received during the next succeeding twenty years under any treaty then in existence between the band and Her Majesty if he had continued to be a member of the band.

(2) A person is not entitled to receive any amount under subsection (1)

(a) if his name was removed from the Indian register pursuant to a protest made under section 9, or

(b) if he is not entitled to be a member of a band by reason of the application of paragraph 11 (1) (e) or subparagraph 12 (1) (a) (iv).

(3) Where by virtue of this section moneys are payable to a person who is under the age of twenty-one, the Minister may

(a) pay the moneys to the parent, guardian or other person having the custody of that person or to the public trustee, public administrator or other like official for the province in which that person resides, or

(b) cause payment of the moneys to be withheld until that person reaches the age of twenty-one.

(4) Where the name of a person is removed from the Indian Register and he is not entitled to any payment under subsection (1), the Minister shall, if he considers it equitable to do so, authorize payment, out of moneys appropriated by Parliament, of such compensation as the Minister may determine for any permanent improvements made by that person on lands in a reserve.

(5) Where, prior to the 4th day of September 1951, any woman became entitled, under section 14 of the *Indian Act*, chapter 98 of the Revised Statutes of Canada, 1927, or any prior provisions to the like effect, to share in the distribution of annuities, interest moneys or rents, the Minister may, in lieu thereof, pay to such woman out of the moneys of the band an amount equal to ten times the average annual amounts of such payments made to her during the ten years last preceding or, if they were paid for less than ten years, during the years they were paid. R.S., c. 149, s. 15; 1956, c. 40, s. 6.

16. (1) Section 15 does not apply to a person who ceases to be a member of one band by reason of his becoming a member of another band, but, subject to subsection (3), there shall be transferred to the credit of the latter band the amount to which that person would, but for this section, have been entitled under section 15.

(2) A person who ceases to be a member of one band by reason of his becoming a member of another band is not entitled to any interest in the lands or moneys held by Her Majesty on behalf of the former band, but he is entitled to the same interest in common in lands and moneys held by Her Majesty on behalf of the latter band as other members of that band.

(3) Where a woman who is a member of one band becomes a member of another band by reason of marriage, and the per capita share

of the capital and revenue moneys held by Her Majesty on behalf of the first-mentioned band is greater than the per capita share of such moneys so held for the second-mentioned band, there shall be transferred to the credit of the second-mentioned band an amount equal to the per capita share held for that band, and the remainder of the money to which the woman would, but for this section, have been entitled under section 15 shall be paid to her in such manner and at such times as the Minister may determine. R.S., c. 149, s. 16.

17. (1) The Minister may, whenever he considers it desirable,
    (a) constitute new bands and establish Band Lists with respect thereto from existing Band Lists or General Lists, or both,
    (b) amalgamate bands that, by a vote of a majority of their electors, request to be amalgamated, and
    (c) where a band has applied for enfranchisement, remove any name from the Band List and add it to the General List.

(2) Where pursuant to subsection (1) a new band has been established from an existing band or any part thereof, such portion of the reserve lands and funds of the existing band as the Minister determines shall be held for the use and benefit of the new band.

(3) No protest may be made under section 9 in respect of the deletion from or addition to a list consequent upon the exercise by the Minister of any of his powers under subsection (1). R.S., c. 149, s. 17; 1956, c. 40, s. 7.

RESERVES

18. (1) Subject to this Act, reserves are held by Her Majesty for the use and benefit of the respective bands for which they were set apart; and subject to this Act and to the terms of any treaty or surrender, the Governor in Council may determine whether any purpose for which lands in a reserve are used or are to be used is for the use and benefit of the band.

(2) The Minister may authorize the use of lands in a reserve for the purpose of Indian schools, the administration of Indian affairs, Indian burial grounds, Indian health projects or, with the consent of the council of the band, for any other purpose for the general welfare of the band, and may take any lands in a reserve required for such purposes, but where an individual Indian, immediately prior to such taking, was entitled to the possession of such lands, compensation for such use shall be paid to the Indian, in such amount as may be agreed between the Indian and the Minister, or, failing agreement, as may be determined in such manner as the Minister may direct. R.S., c. 149, s. 18; 1956, c. 40, s. 8.

19. The Minister may

(a) authorize surveys of reserves and the preparation of plans and reports with respect thereto,

(b) divide the whole or any portion of a reserve into lots or other subdivisions, and

(c) determine the location and direct the construction of roads in a reserve. R.S., c. 149, s. 19.

POSSESSION OF LANDS IN RESERVES

20. (1) No Indian is lawfully in possession of land in a reserve unless, with the approval of the Minister, possession of the land has been allotted to him by the council of the band.

(2) The Minister may issue to an Indian who is lawfully in possession of land in a reserve a certificate, to be called a Certificate of Possession, as evidence of his right to possession of the land described therein.

(3) For the purposes of this Act, any person who, on the 4th day of September 1951, held a valid and subsisting Location Ticket issued under *The Indian Act, 1880*, or any statute relating to the same subject-matter, shall be deemed to be lawfully in possession of the land to which the location ticket relates and to hold a Certificate of Possession with respect thereto.

(4) Where possession of land in a reserve has been allotted to an Indian by the council of the band, the Minister may, in his discretion, withhold his approval and may authorize the Indian to occupy the land temporarily and may prescribe the conditions as to use and settlement that are to be fulfilled by the Indian before the Minister approves of the allotment.

(5) Where the Minister withholds approval pursuant to subsection (4), he shall issue a Certificate of Occupation to the Indian, and the Certificate entitles the Indian, or those claiming possession by devise or descent, to occupy the land in respect of which it is issued for a period of two years from the date thereof.

(6) The Minister may extend the term of a Certificate of Occupation for a further period not exceeding two years, and may, at the expiration of any period during which a Certificate of Occupation is in force

(a) approve the allotment by the council of the band and issue a Certificate of Possession if in his opinion the conditions as to use and settlement have been fulfilled, or

(b) refuse approval of the allotment by the council of the band and declare the land in respect of which the Certificate of Occupation was issued to be available for reallotment by the council of the band. c.149, s. 20.

21. There shall be kept in the Department a register, to be known as the Reserve Land Register, in which shall be entered particulars relating to Certificates of Possession and Certificates of Occupation and other transactions respecting lands in a reserve. R.S., c. 149, s. 21.

22. Where an Indian who is in possession of lands at the time they are included in a reserve, made permanent improvements thereon before that time, he shall be deemed to be in lawful possession of such lands at the time they are so included. R.S., c. 149, s. 22.

23. An Indian who is lawfully removed from lands in a reserve upon which he has made permanent improvements may, if the Minister so directs, be paid compensation in respect thereof in an amount to be determined by the Minister, either from the person who goes into possession or from the funds of the band, at the discretion of the Minister. R.S., c. 149, s. 23.

24. An Indian who is lawfully in possession of lands in a reserve may transfer to the band or to another member of the band the right to possession of the land, but no transfer or agreement for the transfer of the right to possession of lands in a reserve is effective until it is approved by the Minister. R.S., c. 149, s. 24.

25. (1) An Indian who ceases to be entitled to reside on a reserve may, within six months or such further period as the Minister may direct, transfer to the band or another member of the band the right to possession of any lands in the reserve of which he was lawfully in possession.

(2) Where an Indian does not dispose of his right of possession in accordance with subsection (1), the right to possession of the land reverts to the band, subject to the payment to the Indian who was lawfully in possession of the land, from the funds of the band, of such compensation for permanent improvements as the Minister may determine. R.S., c. 149, s. 25.

26. Whenever a Certificate of Possession or Occupation or a Location Ticket issued under *The Indian Act, 1880*, or any statute relating to the same subject-matter was, in the opinion of the Minister, issued to or in the name of the wrong person, through mistake, or contains any clerical error or misnomer, or wrong description of any material fact therein, the Minister may cancel the Certificate or Location Ticket and issue a corrected Certificate in lieu thereof. 1956, c. 40, s. 9.

27. The Minister may, with the consent of the holder thereof, cancel any Certificate of Possession or Occupation or Location Ticket referred to in section 26, and may cancel any Certificate of Possession or Occupation or Location Ticket that in his opinion was issued through fraud or in error. 1956, c. 40, s. 9.

28. (1) Subject to subsection (2), a deed, lease, contract, instrument, document or agreement of any kind whether written or oral, by which a band or a member of a band purports to permit a person other than a member of that band to occupy or use a reserve or to reside or otherwise exercise any rights on a reserve is void.

(2) The Minister may by permit in writing authorize any person for a period not exceeding one year, or with the consent of the council of the band for any longer period, to occupy or use a reserve or to reside or otherwise exercise rights on a reserve. R.S., c. 149, s. 28; 1956, c. 40, s. 10.

29. Reserve lands are not subject to seizure under legal process. R.S., c. 149, s. 29.

TRESPASS ON RESERVES

30. A person who trespasses on a reserve is guilty of an offence and is liable on summary conviction to a fine not exceeding fifty dollars or to imprisonment for a term not exceeding one month, or to both. R.S., c. 149, s. 30.

31. (1) Without prejudice to section 30, where an Indian or a band alleges that persons other than Indians are or have been

(a) unlawfully in occupation or possession of,

(b) claiming adversely the right to occupation or possession of, or

(c) trespassing upon

a reserve or part of a reserve, the Attorney General of Canada may exhibit an Information in the Exchequer Court of Canada claiming, on behalf of the Indian or the band, the relief or remedy sought.

(2) An Information exhibited under subsection (1) shall, for all purposes of the *Exchequer Court Act*, be deemed to be an action or suit by the Crown within the meaning of paragraph 29(d) of that Act.

(3) Nothing in this section shall be construed to impair, abridge or otherwise affect any right or remedy that, but for this section, would be available to Her Majesty or to an Indian or a band. R.S., c. 149, s. 31.

SALE OR BARTER OF PRODUCE

32. (1) A transaction of any kind whereby a band or a member thereof purports to sell, barter, exchange, give or otherwise dispose of cattle or other animals, grain or hay, whether wild or cultivated, or root crops or plants or their products from a reserve in Manitoba, Saskatchewan or Alberta, to a person other than a member of that band, is void unless the superintendent approves the transaction in writing.

(2) The Minister may at any time by order exempt a band and the

members thereof or any member thereof from the operation of this section, and may revoke any such order. R.S., c. 149, s. 32.

33. Every person who enters into a transaction that is void under subsection 32(1) is guilty of an offence. R.S., c. 149, s. 33.

ROADS AND BRIDGES

34. (1) A band shall ensure that the roads, bridges, ditches and fences within the reserve occupied by that band are maintained in accordance with instructions issued from time to time by the superintendent.

(2) Where, in the opinion of the Minister, a band has not carried out the instructions of the superintendent given under subsection (1), the Minister may cause the instructions to be carried out at the expense of the band or any member thereof and may recover the cost thereof from any amounts that are held by Her Majesty and are payable to the band or such member. R.S., c. 149, s. 34.

LANDS TAKEN FOR PUBLIC PURPOSES

35. (1) Where by an Act of the Parliament of Canada or a provincial legislature, Her Majesty in right of a province, a municipal or local authority or a corporation is empowered to take or to use lands or any interest therein without the consent of the owner, the power may, with the consent of the Governor in Council and subject to any terms that may be prescribed by the Governor in Council, be exercised in relation to lands in a reserve or any interest therein.

(2) Unless the Governor in Council otherwise directs, all matters relating to compulsory taking or using of lands in a reserve under subsection (1) are governed by the statute by which the powers are conferred.

(3) Whenever the Governor in Council has consented to the exercise by a province, authority or corporation of the powers referred to in subsection (1), the Governor in Council may, in lieu of the province, authority or corporation taking or using the lands without the consent of the owner, authorize a transfer or grant of such lands to the province, authority or corporation, subject to any terms that may be prescribed by the Governor in Council.

(4) Any amount that is agreed upon or awarded in respect of the compulsory taking or using of land under this section or that is paid for a transfer or grant of land pursuant to this section shall be paid to the Receiver General for the use and benefit of the band or for the use and benefit of any Indian who is entitled to compensation or payment as a

result of the exercise of the powers referred to in subsection (1). R.S., c. 149, s. 35.

SPECIAL RESERVES

36. Where lands have been set apart for the use and benefit of a band and legal title thereto is not vested in Her Majesty, this Act applies as though the lands were a reserve within the meaning of this Act. R.S., c. 149, s. 36.

SURRENDERS

37. Except where this Act otherwise provides, lands in a reserve shall not be sold, alienated, leased or otherwise disposed of until they have been surrendered to Her Majesty by the band for whose use and benefit in common the reserve was set apart. R.S., c. 149, s. 37.

38. (1) A band may surrender to Her Majesty any right or interest of the band and its members in a reserve.

(2) A surrender may be absolute or qualified, conditional or unconditional. R.S., c. 149, s. 38.

39. (1) A surrender is void unless

   (a) it is made to Her Majesty,

   (b) it is assented to by a majority of the electors of the band

      (i) at a general meeting of the band called by the council of the band,

      (ii) at a special meeting of the band called by the Minister for the purpose of considering a proposed surrender, or

      (iii) by a referendum as provided in the regulations, and

   (c) it is accepted by the Governor in Council.

(2) Where a majority of the electors of a band did not vote at a meeting or referendum called pursuant to subsection (1) of this section or pursuant to section 51 of the *Indian Act*, chapter 98 of the Revised Statutes of Canada, 1927, the Minister may, if the proposed surrender was assented to by a majority of the electors who did vote, call another meeting by giving thirty days notice thereof or another referendum as provided in the regulations.

(3) Where a meeting is called pursuant to subsection (2) and the proposed surrender is assented to at the meeting or referendum by a majority of the electors voting, the surrender shall be deemed, for the purpose of this section, to have been assented to by a majority of the electors of the band..

(4) The Minister may, at the request of the council of the band or

whenever he considers it advisable, order that a vote at any meeting under this section shall be by secret ballot.

(5) Every meeting under this section shall be held in the presence of the superintendent or some other officer of the Department designated by the Minister. R.S., c. 149, s. 39; 1956, c. 40, s. 11.

40. When a proposed surrender has been assented to by the band in accordance with section 39, it shall be certified on oath by the superintendent or other officer who attended the meeting and by the chief or a member of the council of the band, and shall then be submitted to the Governor in Council for acceptance or refusal. R.S., c. 149, s. 40.

41. A surrender shall be deemed to confer all rights that are necessary to enable Her Majesty to carry out the terms of the surrender. R.S., c. 149, s. 41.

DESCENT OF PROPERTY

42. (1) Unless otherwise provided in this Act, all jurisdiction and authority in relation to matters and causes testamentary, with respect to deceased Indians, is vested exclusively in the Minister, and shall be exercised subject to and in accordance with regulations of the Governor in Council.

(2) The Governor in Council may make regulations for providing that a deceased Indian who at the time of his death was in possession of land in a reserve shall, in such circumstances and for such purposes as the regulations prescribe, be deemed to have been at the time of his death lawfully in possession of that land.

(3) Regulations made under this section may be made applicable to estates of Indians who died before, on or after the 4th day of September 1951. R.S., c. 149, s. 42; 1956, c. 40, s. 12.

43. Without restricting the generality of section 42, the Minister may

(*a*) appoint executors of wills and administrators of estates of deceased Indians, remove them and appoint others in their stead;

(*b*) authorize executors to carry out the terms of the wills of deceased Indians;

(*c*) authorize administrators to administer the property of Indians who die intestate;

(*d*) carry out the terms of wills of deceased Indians and administer the property of Indians who die intestate; and

(*e*) make or give any order, direction or finding that in his opinion it is necessary or desirable to make or give with respect to any matter referred to in section 42. R.S., c. 149, s. 43.

44. (1) The court that would have jurisdiction if the deceased

were not an Indian may, with the consent of the Minister, exercise, in accordance with this Act, the jurisdiction and authority conferred upon the Minister by this Act in relation to testamentary matters and causes and any other powers, jurisdiction and authority ordinarily vested in that court.

(2) The Minister may direct in any particular case that an application for the grant of probate of the will or letters of administration shall be made to the court that would have jurisdiction if the deceased were not an Indian, and the Minister may refer to such court any question arising out of any will or the administration of any estate.

(3) A court that is exercising any jurisdiction or authority under this section shall not without the consent in writing of the Minister enforce any order relating to real property on a reserve. R.S., c. 149, s. 44.

WILLS

45. (1) Nothing in this Act shall be construed to prevent or prohibit an Indian from devising or bequeathing his property by will.

(2) The Minister may accept as a will any written instrument signed by an Indian in which he indicates his wishes or intention with respect to the disposition of his property upon his death.

(3) No will executed by an Indian is of any legal force or effect as a disposition of property until the Minister has approved the will or a court has granted probate thereof pursuant to this Act. R.S., c. 149, s. 45.

46. (1) The Minister may declare the will of an Indian to be void in whole or in part if he is satisfied that

(a) the will was executed under duress or undue influence;

(b) the testator at the time of execution of the will lacked testamentary capacity;

(c) the terms of the will would impose hardship on persons for whom the testator had a responsibility to provide;

(d) the will purports to dispose of land in a reserve in a manner contrary to the interest of the band or contrary to this Act;

(e) the terms of the will are so vague, uncertain or capricious that proper administration and equitable distribution of the estate of the deceased would be difficult or impossible to carry out in accordance with this Act; or

(f) the terms of the will are against the public interest.

(2) Where a will of an Indian is declared by the Minister or by a court to be wholly void, the person executing the will shall be deemed to have died intestate, and where the will is so declared to be void in part

only, any bequest or devise affected thereby, unless a contrary intention appears in the will, shall be deemed to have lapsed. R.S., c. 149, s. 46.

APPEALS

47. (1) A decision of the Minister made in the exercise of the jurisdiction or authority conferred upon him by section 42, 43 or 46 may, within two months from the date thereof, be appealed by any person affected thereby to the Exchequer Court of Canada, if the amount in controversy in the appeal exceeds five hundred dollars or if the Minister consents to an appeal.

(2) The judges of the Exchequer Court may make rules respecting the practice and procedure governing appeals under this section. R.S., c. 149, s. 47.

DISTRIBUTION OF PROPERTY ON INTESTACY

48. (1) Where the net value of the estate of an intestate does not, in the opinion of the Minister, exceed in value two thousand dollars, the estate shall go to the widow.

(2) Where the net value of the estate of an intestate, in the opinion of the Minister, is two thousand dollars or more, two thousand dollars shall go to the widow, and the remainder shall go as follows, namely:

(a) if the intestate left no issue, the remainder shall go to the widow;

(b) if the intestate left one child, one-half of the remainder shall go to the widow; and

(c) if the intestate left more than one child, one-third of the remainder shall go to the widow;

and where a child has died leaving issue and such issue is alive at the date of the intestate's death, the widow shall take the same share of the estate as if the child had been living at that date.

(3) Notwithstanding subsections (1) and (2),

(a) where in any particular case the Minister is satisfied that any children of the deceased will not be adequately provided for, he may direct that all or any part of the estate that would otherwise go to the widow shall go to the children, and

(b) the Minister may direct that the widow shall have the right, during her widowhood, to occupy any lands on a reserve that were occupied by her deceased husband at the time of his death.

(4) Where an intestate dies leaving issue his estate shall be distributed, subject to the rights of the widow, if any, *per stirpes* among such issue.

(5) Where an intestate dies leaving no widow or issue his estate shall go to his father and mother in equal shares if both are living, but if either of them is dead the estate shall go to the survivor.

(6) Where an intestate dies leaving no widow or issue or father or mother his estate shall go to his brothers and sisters in equal shares, and if any brother or sister is dead the children of the deceased brother or sister shall take the share heir parent would have taken if living, but where the only persons entitled are children of deceased brothers and sisters, they shall take per capita.

(7) Where an intestate dies leaving no widow, issue, father, mother, brother or sister, and no children of any deceased brother or sister, his estate shall go to his next-of-kin.

(8) Where the estate goes to the next-of-kin it shall be distributed equally among the next-of-kin of equal degree of consanguinity to the intestate and those who legally represent them, but in no case shall representation be admitted after brothers' and sisters' children, and any interest in land in a reserve shall vest in Her Majesty for the benefit of the band if the nearest of kin of the intestate is more remote than a brother or sister.

(9) For the purposes of this section, degrees of kindred shall be computed by counting upward from the intestate to the nearest common ancestor and then downward to the relative, and the kindred of the half-blood shall inherit equally with those of the whole-blood in the same degree.

(10) Descendants and relatives of the intestate begotten before his death but born thereafter shall inherit as if they had been born in the lifetime of the intestate and had survived him.

(11) All such estate as is not disposed of by will shall be distributed as if the testator had died intestate and had left no other estate.

(12) No widow is entitled to dower in the land of her deceased husband dying intestate, and no husband is entitled to an estate by curtesy in the land of his deceased wife so dying, and there is no community of real or personal property situated on a reserve.

(13) Illegitimate children and their issue shall inherit from the mother as if the children were legitimate, and shall inherit as if the children were legitimate, through the mother, if dead, any real or personal property that she would have taken, if living, by gift, devise or descent from any other person.

(14) Where an intestate, being an illegitimate child, dies leaving no widow or issue, his estate shall go to his mother, if living, but if the mother is dead his estate shall go to the other children of the same mother in equal shares, and where any child is dead the children of the deceased child shall take the share their parent would have taken if

living; but where the only persons entitled are children of deceased children of the mother, they shall take per capita.

(15) This section applies in respect of an intestate woman as it applies in respect of an intestate male, and for the purposes of this section the word "widow" includes "widower".

(16) In this section "child" includes a legally adopted child and a child adopted in accordance with Indian custom. R.S., c. 149, s. 48; 1956, c. 40, s. 13.

49. A person who claims to be entitled to possession or occupation of lands in a reserve by devise or descent shall be deemed not to be in lawful possession or occupation of that land until the possession is approved by the Minister. R.S., c. 149, s. 49.

50. (1) A person who is not entitled to reside on a reserve does not by devise or descent acquire a right to possession or occupation of land in that reserve.

(2) Where a right to possession or occupation of land in a reserve passes by devise or descent to a person who is not entitled to reside on a reserve, that right shall be offered for sale by the superintendent to the highest bidder among persons who are entitled to reside on the reserve and the proceeds of the sale shall be paid to the devisee or descendant, as the case may be.

(3) Where no tender is received within six months or such further period as the Minister may direct after the date when the right to possession or occupation is offered for sale under subsection (2), the right shall revert to the band free from any claim on the part of the devisee or descendant, subject to the payment, at the discretion of the Minister, to the devisee or descendant, from the funds of the band, of such compensation for permanent improvements as the Minister may determine.

(4) The purchaser of a right to possession or occupation of land under subsection (2) shall be deemed not to be in lawful possession or occupation of the land until the possession is approved by the Minister. R.S., c. 149, s. 50.

MENTALLY INCOMPETENT INDIANS

51. (1) Subject to this section, all jurisdiction and authority in relation to the property of mentally incompetent Indians is vested exclusively in the Minister.

(2) Without restricting the generality of subsection (1), the Minister may

(a) appoint persons to administer the estates of mentally incompetent Indians;

(b) order that any property of a mentally incompetent Indian shall be sold, leased, alienated, mortgaged, disposed of or otherwise dealt with for the purpose of

  (i) paying his debts or engagements,

  (ii) discharging encumbrances on his property,

  (iii) paying debts or expenses incurred for his maintenance or otherwise for his benefit, or

  (iv) paying or providing for the expenses of future maintenance; and

(c) make such orders and give such directions as he considers necessary to secure the satisfactory management of the estates of mentally incompetent Indians.

(3) The Minister may order that any property situated off a reserve and belonging to a mentally incompetent Indian shall be dealt with under the laws of the province in which the property is situated. R.S., c. 149, s. 51.

GUARDIANSHIP

52. The Minister may administer or provide for the administration of any property to which infant children of Indians are entitled, and may appoint guardians for such purpose. R.S., c. 149, s. 52.

MANAGEMENT OF RESERVES AND SURRENDERED LANDS

53. (1) The Minister or a person appointed by him for the purpose may manage, sell, lease or otherwise dispose of surrendered lands in accordance with this Act and the terms of the surrender.

(2) Where the original purchaser of surrendered lands is dead and the heir, assignee or devisee of the original purchaser applies for a grant of the lands, the Minister may, upon receipt of proof in such manner as he directs and requires in support of any claim for the grant and upon being satisfied that the claim has been equitably and justly established, allow the claim and authorize a grant to issue accordingly.

(3) No person who is appointed to manage, sell, lease or otherwise dispose of surrendered lands or who is an officer or servant of Her Majesty employed in the Department may, except with the approval of the Governor in Council, acquire directly or indirectly any interest in surrendered lands. R.S., c. 149, s. 53.

54. Where surrendered lands have been agreed to be sold or otherwise disposed of and letters patent relating thereto have not issued, or where surrendered lands have been leased, the purchaser, lessee or other person having an interest in the surrendered lands may, with the

approval of the Minister, assign his interest in the surrendered lands or a part thereof to any other person. R.S., c. 149, s. 54.

55. (1) There shall be kept in the Department a register, to be known as the Surrendered Lands Register, in which shall be entered particulars in connection with any lease or other disposition of surrendered lands by the Minister or any assignment thereof.

(2) A conditional assignment shall not be registered.

(3) Registration of an assignment may be refused until proof of its execution has been furnished.

(4) An assignment registered under this section is valid against an unregistered assignment or an assignment subsequently registered. R.S., c. 149, s. 55.

56. Where an assignment is registered there shall be endorsed on the original copy thereof a certificate of registration signed by the Minister or by an officer of the Department authorized by him to sign such certificates. R.S., c. 149, s. 56.

57. The Governor in Council may make regulations

(a) authorizing the Minister to grant licences to cut timber on surrendered lands, or, with the consent of the council of the band, on reserve lands;

(b) imposing terms, conditions and restrictions with respect to the exercise of rights conferred by licences granted under paragraph (a);

(c) providing for the disposition of surrendered mines and minerals underlying lands in a reserve;

(d) prescribing the penalty not exceeding one hundred dollars or imprisonment for a term of three months, or both, that may be imposed on summary conviction for violation of any regulation made under this section; and

(e) providing for the seizure and forfeiture of any timber or minerals taken in violation of any regulation made under this section. R.S., c. 149, s. 57.

58. (1) Where land in a reserve is uncultivated or unused, the Minister may, with the consent of the council of the band,

(a) improve or cultivate such land and employ persons therefor, and authorize and direct the expenditure of so much of the capital funds of the band as he considers necessary for such improvement or cultivation including the purchase of such stock, machinery or material or for the employment of such labour as the Minister considers necessary;

(b) where the land is in the lawful possession of any individual, grant a lease of such land for agricultural or grazing purposes or for any purpose that is for the benefit of the person in possession; and

(c) where the land is not in the lawful possession of any individual, grant for the benefit of the band a lease of such land for agricultural or grazing purposes.

(2) Out of the proceeds derived from the improvement or cultivation of lands pursuant to paragraph (1) (b), a reasonable rent shall be paid to the individual in lawful possession of the lands or any part thereof, and the remainder of the proceeds shall be placed to the credit of the band, but if improvements are made on the lands occupied by an individual, the Minister may deduct the value of such improvements from the rent payable to such individual under this subsection.

(3) The Minister may lease for the benefit of any Indian upon his application for that purpose, the land of which he is lawfully in possession without the land being surrendered.

(4) Notwithstanding anything in this Act, the Minister may, without a surrender

(a) dispose of wild grass or dead or fallen timber, and

(b) with the consent of the council of the band, dispose of sand, gravel, clay and other non-metallic substances upon or under lands in a reserve, or, where such consent cannot be obtained without undue difficulty or delay, may issue temporary permits for the taking of sand, gravel, clay and other non-metallic substances upon or under lands in a reserve, renewable only with the consent of the council of the band,

and the proceeds of such transactions shall be credited to band funds or shall be divided between the band and the individual Indians in lawful possession of the lands in such shares as the Minister may determine. R.S., c. 149, s. 58; 1956, c. 40, s. 14.

59. The Minister may, with the consent of the council of a band,

(a) reduce or adjust the amount payable to Her Majesty in respect of a sale, lease or other disposition of surrendered lands or a lease or other disposition of lands in a reserve or the rate of interest payable thereon, and

(b) reduce or adjust the amount payable to the band by an Indian in respect of a loan made to the Indian from band funds. R.S., c. 149, s. 59.

60. (1) The Governor in Council may at the request of a band grant to the band the right to exercise such control and management over lands in the reserve occupied by that band as the Governor in Council considers desirable.

(2) The Governor in Council may at any time withdraw from a band a right conferred upon the band under subsection (1). R.S., c. 149, s. 60.

MANAGEMENT OF INDIAN MONEYS

61. (1) Indian moneys shall be expended only for the benefit of the Indians or bands for whose use and benefit in common the moneys are received or held, and subject to this Act and to the terms of any treaty or surrender, the Governor in Council may determine whether any purpose for which Indian moneys are used or are to be used is for the use and benefit of the band.

(2) Interest upon Indian moneys held in the Consolidated Revenue Fund shall be allowed at a rate to be fixed from time to time by the Governor in Council. R.S., c. 149, s. 61.

62. All Indian moneys derived from the sale of surrendered lands or the sale of capital assets of a band shall be deemed to be capital moneys of the band and all Indian moneys other than capital moneys shall be deemed to be revenue moneys of the band. R.S., c. 149, s. 62.

63. Notwithstanding the *Financial Administration Act*, where moneys to which an Indian is entitled are paid to a superintendent under any lease or agreement made under this Act, the superintendent may pay the moneys to the Indian. R.S., c. 149, s. 63.

64. With the consent of the council of a band, the Minister may authorize and direct the expenditure of capital moneys of the band

(a) to distribute per capita to the members of the band an amount not exceeding fifty per cent of the capital moneys of the band derived from the sale of surrendered lands;

(b) to construct and maintain roads, bridges, ditches and water courses on the reserves or on surrendered lands;

(c) to construct and maintain outer boundary fences on reserves;

(d) to purchase land for use by the band as a reserve or as an addition to a reserve;

(e) to purchase for the band the interest of a member of the band in lands on a reserve;

(f) to purchase livestock and farm implements, farm equipment, or machinery for the band;

(g) to construct and maintain on or in connection with a reserve such permanent improvements or works as in the opinion of the Minister will be of permanent value to the band or will constitute a capital investment;

(h) to make to members of the band, for the purpose of promoting the welfare of the band, loans not exceeding one-half of the total value of

(i) the chattels owned by the borrower, and

(ii) the land with respect to which he holds or is eligible to receive a Certificate of Possession,

and may charge interest and take security therefor;

(*i*) to meet expenses necessarily incidental to the management of lands on a reserve, surrendered lands and any band property;

(*j*) to construct houses for members of the band, to make loans to members of the band for building purposes with or without security and to provide for the guarantee of loans made to members of the band for building purposes; and

(*k*) for any other purpose that in the opinion of the Minister is for the benefit of the band. R.S. c. 149, s. 64; 1956, c. 40, s. 15.

65. The Minister may pay from capital moneys

(*a*) compensation to an Indian in an amount that is determined in accordance with this Act to be payable to him in respect of land compulsorily taken from him for band purposes, and

(*b*) expenses incurred to prevent or suppress grass or forest fires or to protect the property of Indians in cases of emergency. R.S., c. 149, s. 65.

66. (1) With the consent of the council of a band, the Minister may authorize and direct the expenditure of revenue moneys for any purpose that in his opinion will promote the general progress and welfare of the band or any member of the band.

(2) The Minister may make expenditures out of the revenue moneys of the band to assist sick, disabled, aged or destitute Indians of the band and to provide for the burial of deceased indigent members of the band and to provide for the payment of contributions under the *Unemployment Insurance Act* on behalf of employed persons who are paid in respect of their employment out of moneys of the band.

(3) The Minister may authorize the expenditure of revenue moneys of the band for all or any of the following purposes, namely:

(*a*) for the destruction of noxious weeds and the prevention of the spreading or prevalence of insects, pests or diseases that may destroy or injure vegetation on Indian reserves;

(*b*) to prevent, mitigate and control the spread of diseases on reserves, whether or not the diseases are infectious or communicable;

(*c*) to provide for the inspection of premises on reserves and the destruction, alteration or renovation thereof;

(*d*) to prevent overcrowding of premises on reserves used as dwellings;

(*e*) to provide for sanitary conditions in private premises on reserves as well as in public places on reserves; and

(*f*) for the construction and maintenance of boundary fences. R.S., c. 149, s. 66; 1956, c. 40, s. 16.

67. Where money is expended by Her Majesty for the purpose of raising or collecting Indian moneys, the Minister may authorize the

recovery of the amount so expended from the moneys of the band. 1956, c. 40, s. 17.

68. (1) Where the Minister is satisfied that a male Indian

(a) has deserted his wife or family without sufficient cause,

(b) has conducted himself in such a manner as to justify the refusal of his wife or family to live with him, or

(c) has been separated by imprisonment from his wife and family, he may order that payments of any annuity or interest money to which that Indian is entitled shall be applied to the support of the wife or family or both the wife and family of that Indian.

(2) Where the Minister is satisfied that a female Indian has deserted her husband or family, he may order that payments of any annuity or interest money to which that Indian is entitled shall be applied to the support of her family.

(3) Where the Minister is satisfied that one or both of the parents of an illegitimate child is an Indian, he may stop payments out of any annuity or interest moneys to which either or both of the parents would otherwise be entitled and apply the moneys to the support of the child, but not so as to prejudice the welfare of any legitimate child of either Indian. R.S., c. 149, s. 67.

69. (1) The Governor in Council may by order permit a band to control, manage and expend in whole or in part its revenue moneys and may amend or revoke any such order.

(2) The Governor in Council may make regulations to give effect to subsection (1) and may declare therein the extent to which this Act and the *Financial Administration Act* shall not apply to a band to which an order made under subsection (1) applies. R.S., c. 149, s. 68.

LOANS TO INDIANS

70. (1) The Minister of Finance may from time to time authorize advances to the Minister out of the Consolidated Revenue Fund of such sums of money as the Minister may require to enable him

(a) to make loans to bands, groups of Indians or individual Indians for the purchase of farm implements, machinery, livestock, motor vehicles, fishing equipment, seed grain, fencing materials, materials to be used in native handicrafts, any other equipment, and gasoline and other petroleum products, or for the making of repairs or the payment of wages, or for the clearing and breaking of land within reserves,

(b) to expend or to lend money for the carrying out of cooperative projects on behalf of Indians, or (*c*) to provide for any other matter prescribed by the Governor in Council.

(2) The Governor in Council may make regulations to give effect to subsection (1).

(3) Expenditures that are made under subsection (1) shall be accounted for in the same manner as public moneys.

(4) The Minister shall pay to the Receiver General all moneys that he receives from bands, groups of Indians or individual Indians by way of repayments of loans made under subsection (1).

(5) The total amount of outstanding advances to the Minister under this section shall not at any one time exceed six million and fifty thousand dollars.

(6) The Minister shall within fifteen days after the termination of each fiscal year or, if Parliament is not then in session, within fifteen days after the commencement of the next ensuing session, lay before Parliament a report setting out the total number and amount of loans made under subsection (1) during that year. R.S., c. 149, s. 69; 1952-53, c. 41, s. 4; 1956, c. 40, s. 18; 1968-69, c. 28, s. 185; 1969-70, c. 2, Sch. vote L50a. [*See* 1969-70, c. 24, Sch. vote L53b.]

FARMS

71. (1) The Minister may operate farms on reserves and may employ such persons as he considers necessary to instruct Indians in farming and may purchase and distribute without charge, pure seed to Indian farmers.

(2) The Minister may apply any profits that result from the operation of farms pursuant to subsection (1) on reserves to extend farming operations on the reserves or to make loans to Indians to enable them to engage in farming or other agricultural operations or he may apply such profits in any way that he considers to be desirable to promote the progress and development of the Indians. R.S., c. 149, s. 70.

TREATY MONEY

72. Moneys that are payable to Indians or to Indian bands under a treaty between Her Majesty and the band and for the payment of which the Government of Canada is responsible, may be paid out of the Consolidated Revenue Fund. R.S., c. 149, s. 71.

REGULATIONS

73. (1) The Governor in Council may make regulations

(*a*) for the protection and preservation of fur-bearing animals, fish and other game on reserves;

(*b*) for the destruction of noxious weeds and the prevention of the spreading or prevalence of insects, pests or diseases that may destroy or injure vegetation on Indian reserves;

(*c*) for the control of the speed, operation and parking of vehicles on roads within reserves;

(*d*) for the taxation, control and destruction of dogs and for the protection of sheep on reserves;

(*e*) for the operation, supervision and control of pool rooms, dance halls and other places of amusement on reserves;

(*f*) to prevent, mitigate and control the spread of diseases on reserves, whether or not the diseases are infectious or communicable;

(*g*) to provide medical treatment and health services for Indians;

(*h*) to provide compulsory hospitalization and treatment for infectious diseases among Indians;

(*i*) to provide for the inspection of premises on reserves and the destruction, alteration or renovation thereof;

(*j*) to prevent overcrowding of premises on reserves used as dwellings;

(*k*) to provide for sanitary conditions in private premises on reserves as well as in public places on reserves;

(*l*) for the construction and maintenance of boundary fences; and

(*m*) for empowering and authorizing the council of a band to borrow money for band projects or housing purposes and providing for the making of loans out of moneys so borrowed to members of the band for housing purposes.

(2) The Governor in Council may prescribe the penalty, not exceeding a fine of one hundred dollars or imprisonment for a term not exceeding three months, or both, that may be imposed on summary conviction for violation of a regulation made under subsection (1).

(3) The Governor in Council may make orders and regulations to carry out the purposes and provisions of this Act. R.S., c. 149, s. 72; 1956, c. 40, s. 19.

ELECTIONS OF CHIEFS AND BAND COUNCILS

74. (1) Whenever he deems it advisable for the good government of a band, the Minister may declare by order that after a day to be named therein the council of the band, consisting of a chief and councillors, shall be selected by elections to be held in accordance with this Act.

(2) Unless otherwise ordered by the Minister, the council of a

band in respect of which an order has been made under subsection (1) shall consist of one chief, and one councillor for every one hundred members of the band, but the number of councillors shall not be less than two nor more than twelve and no band shall have more than one chief.

(3) The Governor in Council may, for the purposes of giving effect to subsection (1), make orders or regulations to provide

(a) that the chief of a band shall be elected by

    (i) a majority of the votes of the electors of the band, or

    (ii) a majority of the votes of the elected councillors of the band from among themselves, but the chief so elected shall remain a councillor; and

(b) that the councillors of a band shall be elected by

    (i) a majority of the votes of the electors of the band, or

    (ii) a majority of the votes of the electors of the band in the electoral section in which the candidate resides and that he proposes to represent on the council of the band.

(4) A reserve shall for voting purposes consist of one electoral section, except that where the majority of the electors of a band who were present and voted at a referendum or a special meeting held and called for the purpose in accordance with the regulations have decided that the reserve should for voting purposes be divided into electoral sections and the Minister so recommends, the Governor in Council may make orders or regulations to provide that the reserve shall for voting purposes be divided into not more than six electoral sections containing as nearly as may be an equal number of Indians eligible to vote and to provide for the manner in which electoral sections so established shall be distinguished or identified. R.S., c. 149, s. 73; 1956, c. 40, s. 20.

75. (1) No person other than an elector who resides in a section may be nominated for the office of councillor to represent that section on the council of the band.

(2) No person may be a candidate for election as chief or councillor unless his nomination is moved and seconded by persons who are themselves eligible to be nominated. R.S., c. 149, s. 74.

76. (1) The Governor in Council may make orders and regulations with respect to band elections and, without restricting the generality of the foregoing, may make regulations with respect to

(a) meetings to nominate candidates;

(b) the appointment and duties of electoral officers;

(c) the manner in which voting shall be carried out;

(d) election appeals; and

(e) the definition of residence for the purpose of determining the eligibility of voters.

(2) The regulations made under paragraph (1) (c) shall make provision for secrecy of voting. R.S., c. 149, s. 75.

77. (1) A member of a band who is of the full age of twenty-one years and is ordinarily resident on the reserve is qualified to vote for a person nominated to be chief of the band, and where the reserve for voting purposes consists of one section, to vote for persons nominated as councillors.

(2) A member of a band who is of the full age of twenty-one years and is ordinarily resident in a section that has been established for voting purposes is qualified to vote for a person nominated to be councillor to represent that section. R.S., c. 149, s. 76.

78. (1) Subject to this section, chiefs and councillors hold office for two years.

(2) The office of chief or councillor becomes vacant when

(a) the person who holds that office

    (i) is convicted of an indictable offence,

    (ii) dies or resigns his office, or

    (iii) is or becomes ineligible to hold office by virtue of this Act; or

(b) the Minister declares that in his opinion the person who holds that office

    (i) is unfit to continue in office by reason of his having been convicted of an offence,

    (ii) has been absent from meetings of the council for three consecutive meetings without being authorized to do so, or

    (iii) was guilty, in connection with an election, of corrupt practice, accepting a bribe, dishonesty or malfeasance.

(3) The Minister may declare a person who ceases to hold office by virtue of subparagraph (2) (b) (iii) to be ineligible to be a candidate for chief or councillor for a period not exceeding six years.

(4) Where the office of chief or councillor becomes vacant more than three months before the date when another election would ordinarily be held, a special election may be held in accordance with this Act to fill the vacancy. R.S., c. 149, s. 77.

79. The Governor in Council may set aside the election of a chief or a councillor on the report of the Minister that he is satisfied that

(a) there was corrupt practice in connection with the election;

(b) there was a violation of this Act that might have affected the result of the election; or

(c) a person nominated to be a candidate in the election was ineligible to be a candidate. R.S., c. 149, s. 78.

80. The Governor in Council may make regulations with respect to band meetings and council meetings and, without restricting the

generality of the foregoing, may make regulations with respect to
    (*a*) presiding officers at such meetings;
    (*b*) notice of such meetings;
    (*c*) the duties of any representative of the Minister at such meetings; and
    (*d*) the number of persons required at the meeting to constitute a quorum. R.S., c. 149, s. 79.

POWERS OF THE COUNCIL

81. The council of a band may make bylaws not inconsistent with this Act or with any regulation made by the Governor in Council or the Minister, for any or all of the following purposes, namely:
    (*a*) to provide for the health of residents on the reserve and to prevent the spreading of contagious and infectious diseases;
    (*b*) the regulation of traffic;
    (*c*) the observance of law and order;
    (*d*) the prevention of disorderly conduct and nuisances;
    (*e*) the protection against and prevention of trespass by cattle and other domestic animals, the establishment of pounds, the appointment of pound-keepers, the regulation of their duties and the provision for fees and charges for their services;
    (*f*) the construction and maintenance of water courses, roads, bridges, ditches, fences and other local works;
    (*g*) the dividing of the reserve or a portion thereof into zones and the prohibition of the construction or maintenance of any class of buildings or the carrying on of any class of business, trade or calling in any such zone;
    (*h*) the regulation of the construction, repair and use of buildings, whether owned by the band or by individual members of the band;
    (*i*) the survey and allotment of reserve lands among the members of the band and the establishment of a register of Certificates of Possession and Certificates of Occupation relating to allotments and the setting apart of reserve lands for common use, if authority therefor has been granted under section 60;
    (*j*) the destruction and control of noxious weeds;
    (*k*) the regulation of bee-keeping and poultry raising;
    (*l*) the construction and regulation of the use of public wells, cisterns, reservoirs and other water supplies;
    (*m*) the control and prohibition of public games, sports, races, athletic contests and other amusements;

(n) the regulation of the conduct and activities of hawkers, peddlers or others who enter the reserve to buy, sell or otherwise deal in wares or merchandise;

(o) the preservation, protection and management of fur-bearing animals, fish and other game on the reserve;

(p) the removal and punishment of persons trespassing upon the reserve or frequenting the reserve for prescribed purposes;

(q) with respect to any matter arising out of or ancillary to the exercise of powers under this section; and

(r) the imposition on summary conviction of a fine not exceeding one hundred dollars or imprisonment for a term not exceeding thirty days, or both, for violation of a bylaw made under this section. R.S., c. 149, s. 80.

82. (1) A copy of every by-law made under the authority of section 81 shall be forwarded by mail by the chief or a member of the council of the band to the Minister within four days after it is made.

(2) A by-law made under section 81 comes into force forty days after a copy thereof is forwarded to the Minister pursuant to subsection (1), unless it is disallowed by the Minister within that period, but the Minister may declare the by-law to be in force at any time before the expiration of that period. R.S., c. 149, s. 81.

83. (1) Without prejudice to the powers conferred by section 81, where the Governor in Council declares that a band has reached an advanced stage of development, the council of the band may, subject to the approval of the Minister, make by-laws for any or all of the following purposes, namely

(a) the raising of money by

    (i) the assessment and taxation of interests in land in the reserve of persons lawfully in possession thereof, and

    (ii) the licensing of businesses, callings, trades and occupations;

(b) the appropriation and expenditure of moneys of the band to defray band expenses;

(c) the appointment of officials to conduct the business of the council, prescribing their duties and providing for their remuneration out of any moneys raised pursuant to paragraph (a);

(d) the payment of remuneration, in such amount as may be approved by the Minister, to chiefs and councillors, out of any moneys raised pursuant to paragraph (a);

(e) the imposition of a penalty for non-payment of taxes imposed pursuant to this section, recoverable on summary conviction, not exceeding the amount of the tax or the amount remaining unpaid;

(*f*) the raising of money from band members to support band projects; and

(*g*) with respect to any matter arising out of or ancillary to the exercise of powers under this section.

(2) No expenditure shall be made out of moneys raised pursuant to paragraph (1) (*a*) except under the authority of a by-law of the council of the band. R.S., c. 149, s. 82; 1956, c. 40, s. 21.

84. Where a tax that is imposed upon an Indian by or under the authority of a by-law made under section 83 is not paid in accordance with the by-law, the Minister may pay the amount owing together with an amount equal to one-half of one per cent thereof out of moneys payable out of the funds of the band to the Indian. R.S., c. 149, s. 83.

85. The Governor in Council may revoke a declaration made under section 83 whereupon that section no longer applies to the band to which it formerly applied, but any by-law made under the authority of that section and in force at the time the declaration is revoked shall be deemed to continue in force until it is revoked by the Governor in Council. R.S., c. 149, s. 84.

86. A copy of a by-law made by the council of a band under this Act, if it is certified to be a true copy by the superintendent, is evidence that the by-law was duly made by the council and approved by the Minister, without proof of the signature or official character of the superintendent, and no such by-law is invalid by reason of any defect in form. R.S., c. 149, s. 85.

TAXATION

87. Notwithstanding any other Act of the Parliament of Canada or any Act of the legislature of a province, but subject to subsection (2) and to section 83, the following property is exempt from taxation, namely:

(*a*) the interest of an Indian or a band in reserve or surrendered lands; and

(*b*) the personal property of an Indian or band situated on a reserve;

and no Indian or band is subject to taxation in respect of the ownership, occupation, possession or use of any property mentioned in paragraph (*a*) or (*b*) or is otherwise subject to taxation in respect of any such property; and no succession duty, inheritance tax or estate duty is payable on the death of any Indian in respect of any such property or the succession thereto if the property passes to an Indian, nor shall any such property be taken into account in determining the duty payable under the *Dominion Succession Duty Act*, being chapter 89 of the Revised Statutes of Canada, 1952, or the tax payable under the *Estate Tax Act*, on or in respect of other property passing to an Indian. R.S., c. 149, s. 86; 1958, c. 29, s. 59; 1960, c. 8, s. 1.

LEGAL RIGHTS

88. Subject to the terms of any treaty and any other Act of the Parliament of Canada, all laws of general application from time to time in force in any province are applicable to and in respect of Indians in the province, except to the extent that such laws are inconsistent with this Act or any order, rule, regulation or by-law made thereunder, and except to the extent that such laws make provision for any matter for which provision is made by or under this Act. R.S., c. 149, s. 87.

89. (1) Subject to this Act, the real and personal property of an Indian or a band situated on a reserve is not subject to charge, pledge, mortgage, attachment, levy, seizure, distress or execution in favour or at the instance of any person other than an Indian.

(2) A person who sells to a band or a member of a band a chattel under an agreement whereby the right of property or right of possession thereto remains wholly or in part in the seller, may exercise his rights under the agreement notwithstanding that the chattel is situated on a reserve. R.S., c. 149, s. 88.

90. (1) For the purposes of sections 87 and 89, personal property that was

(a) purchased by Her Majesty with Indian moneys or moneys appropriated by Parliament for the use and benefit of Indians or bands, or

(b) given to Indians or to a band under a treaty or agreement between a band and Her Majesty,

shall be deemed always to be situated on a reserve.

(2) Every transaction purporting to pass title to any property that is by this section deemed to be situated on a reserve, or any interest in such property, is void unless the transaction is entered into with the consent of the Minister or is entered into between members of a band or between the band and a member thereof.

(3) Every person who enters into any transaction that is void by virtue of subsection (2) is guilty of an offence, and every person who, without the written consent of the Minister, destroys personal property that is by this section deemed to be situated on a reserve, is guilty of an offence. R.S., c. 149, s. 89.

TRADING WITH INDIANS

91. (1) No person may, without the written consent of the Minister, acquire title to any of the following property situated on a reserve, namely:

(a) an Indian grave house;

(b) a carved grave pole;

(c) a totem pole;

(d) a carved house post; or

(*e*) a rock embellished with paintings or carvings.

(2) Subsection (1) does not apply to chattels referred to therein that are manufactured for sale by Indians.

(3) No person shall remove, take away, mutilate, disfigure, deface or destroy any chattel referred to in subsection (1) without the written consent of the Minister.

(4) A person who violates this section is guilty of an offence and is liable on summary conviction to a fine not exceeding two hundred dollars or to imprisonment for a term not exceeding three months. R.S., c. 149, s. 90.

92. (1) No person who is

(*a*) an officer or employee in the Department,

(*b*) a missionary engaged in mission work among Indians, or

(*c*) a school teacher on a reserve,

shall, without a license from the Minister or his duly authorized representative, trade for profit with an Indian or sell to him directly or indirectly goods or chattels, but no such licence shall be issued to a full-time officer or employee in the Department.

(2) The Minister or his duly authorized representative may at any time cancel a licence given under this section.

(3) A person who violates subsection (1) is guilty of an offence and is liable on summary conviction to a fine not exceeding five hundred dollars.

(4) Without prejudice to subsection (3), an officer or employee in the Department who contravenes subsection (1) may be dismissed from office. R.S., c. 149, s. 91.

REMOVAL OF MATERIALS FROM RESERVES

93. A person who, without the written permission of the Minister or his duly authorized representative,

(*a*) removes or permits anyone to remove from a reserve

(i) minerals, stone, sand, gravel, clay or soil, or

(ii) trees, saplings, shrubs, underbrush, timber, cordwood or hay, or

(*b*) has in his possession anything removed from a reserve contrary to this section,

is guilty of an offence and is liable on summary conviction to a fine not exceeding five hundred dollars or to imprisonment for a term not exceeding three months, or to both. 1956, c. 40, s. 22.

94. A person who directly or indirectly by himself or by any other person on his behalf knowingly

(*a*) sells, barters, supplies or gives an intoxicant to
    (i) any person on a reserve, or
    (ii) an Indian outside a reserve,
(*b*) opens or keeps or causes to be opened or kept on a reserve a dwelling-house, building, tent, or place in which intoxicants are sold, supplied or given to any person, or
(*c*) makes or manufactures intoxicants on a reserve,
is guilty of an offence and is liable on summary conviction to a fine of not less than fifty dollars and not more than three hundred dollars or to imprisonment for a term of not less than one month and not more than six months, with or without hard labour, or to both fine and imprisonment. R.S., c. 149, s. 93.

95. An Indian who
(*a*) has intoxicants in his possession,
(*b*) is intoxicated, or
(*c*) makes or manufactures intoxicants, off a reserve, is guilty of an offence and is liable on summary conviction to a fine of not less than ten dollars and not more than fifty dollars or to imprisonment for a term not exceeding three months or to both fine and imprisonment. R.S., c. 149, s. 94.

96. (1) Subsection (2) or subsection (3) comes into force, or ceases to be in force, in a province or in a part thereof only if a proclamation declaring it to be in force, or to cease to be in force, as the case may be, in the province or part thereof is issued by the Governor in Council at the request of the lieutenant governor in council of the province.

(2) No offence is committed against subparagraph 94(*a*) (ii) or paragraph 95(*a*) if intoxicants are sold to an Indian for consumption in a public place in accordance with the law of the province where the sale takes place.

(3) No offence is committed against sub-paragraph 94(*a*) (ii) or paragraph 95(*a*) if intoxicants are sold to or had in possession by an Indian in accordance with the law of the province where the sale takes place or the possession is had. 1956, c. 40, s. 23.

97. A person who is found
(*a*) with intoxicants in his possession, or
(*b*) intoxicated,
on a reserve, is guilty of an offence and is liable on summary conviction to a fine of not less than ten dollars and not more than fifty dollars or to imprisonment for a term not exceeding three months or to both fine and imprisonment. R.S., c. 149, s. 96.

98. (1) Subsection (2) comes into force, or ceases to be in force,

in a reserve only if a proclamation declaring it to be in force, or to cease to be in force, as the case may be, in the reserve, is issued by the Governor in Council.

(2) No offence is committed against paragraph 97(*a*) if intoxicants are had in possession by any person in accordance with the law of the province where the possession is had.

(3) A proclamation in respect of a reserve shall not be issued under subsection (1) except in accordance with the wishes of the band, as expressed at a referendum of the electors of the band by a majority of the electors who voted thereat.

(4) The Governor in Council may make regulations

(*a*) respecting the taking of votes and the holding of a referendum for the purposes of this section, and

(*b*) defining a reserve for the purposes of subsection (1) to consist of one or more reserves or any part thereof.

(5) No proclamation bringing subsection (2) into force in a reserve shall be issued unless the council of the band has transmitted to the Minister a resolution of the council requesting that subsection (2) be brought into force in the reserve, and either

(*a*) the reserve is situated in a province or part thereof in which subsection 96(3) is in force, or

(*b*) the Minister has communicated the contents of the resolution to the attorney general of the province in which the reserve is situated, the lieutenant governor in council of the province has not, within sixty days after such communication, objected to the granting of the request, and the Governor in Council has directed that the wishes of the band with respect thereto be ascertained by a referendum of the electors of the band.

(6) Where subsection (2) is in force in a reserve no offence is committed against subparagraph 94(*a*) (ii) or paragraph 95(*a*) if intoxicants are sold to or had in possession by a member of the band in accordance with the law of the province in which the reserve is situated. 1956, c. 40, s. 23.

99. The provisions of this Act relating to intoxicants do not apply where the intoxicant is used or is intended to be used in cases of sickness or accident. R.S., c. 149, s. 97.

100. In any prosecution under this Act the burden of proof that an intoxicant was used or was intended to be used in a case of sickness or accident is upon the accused. R.S., c. 149, s. 98.

101. In every prosecution under this Act a certificate of analysis furnished by an analyst employed by the Government of Canada or by a province shall be accepted as evidence of the facts stated therein and of the authority of the person giving or issuing the certificate, without proof of the signature of the person appearing to have signed the

certificate or his official character, and without further proof thereof. R.S., c. 149, s. 99.

102. Every person who is guilty of an offence against any provision of this Act or any regulation made by the Governor in Council or the Minister for which a penalty is not provided elsewhere in this Act or the regulations, is liable on summary conviction to a fine not exceeding two hundred dollars or to imprisonment for a term not exceeding three months, or to both. R.S., c. 149, s. 100.

FORFEITURES AND PENALTIES

103. (1) Whenever a peace officer or a superintendent or a person authorized by the Minister believes on reasonable grounds that an offence against section 33, 90, 93, 94, 95 or 97 has been committed, he may seize all goods and chattels by means of or in relation to which he reasonably believes the offence was committed.

(2) All goods and chattels seized pursuant to subsection (1) may be detained for a period of three months following the day of seizure unless during that period proceedings under this Act in respect of such offence are undertaken, in which case the goods and chattels may be further detained until such proceedings are finally concluded.

(3) Where a person is convicted of an offence against the sections mentioned in subsection (1), the convicting court or judge may order that the goods and chattels by means of or in relation to which the offence was committed, in addition to any penalty imposed, are forfeited to Her Majesty and may be disposed of as the Minister directs.

(4) A justice who is satisfied by information upon oath that there is reasonable ground to believe that there are upon a reserve or in any building, receptacle or place any goods or chattels by means of or in relation to which an offence against any of the sections mentioned in subsection (1) has been, is being or is about to be committed, may at any time issue a warrant under his hand authorizing a person named therein or a peace officer at any time to search the reserve, building, receptacle or place for any such goods or chattels. R.S., c. 149, s. 101; 1952-53, c. 41, s. 5; 1956, c. 40, s. 24.

104. Every fine, penalty or forfeiture imposed under this Act belongs to Her Majesty for the benefit of the band with respect to which or to one or more members of which the offence was committed or to which the offender, if an Indian, belongs, but the Governor in Council may from time to time direct that the fine, penalty or forfeiture shall be paid to a provincial, municipal or local authority that bears in whole or in part the expense of administering the law under which the fine, penalty or forfeiture is imposed, or that the fine, penalty or forfeiture

shall be applied in the manner that he considers will best promote the purposes of the law under which the fine, penalty or forfeiture is imposed, or the administration of that law. R.S., c. 149, s. 102.

105. In any order, writ, warrant, summons or proceeding issued under this Act it is sufficient if the name of the person or Indian referred to therein is the name given to or is the name by which the person or Indian is known by, the person who issues the order, writ, warrant, summons or proceedings, and if no part of the name of the person is given to or known by the person issuing the order, writ, warrant, summons or proceedings, it is sufficient if the person or Indian is described in any manner by which he may be identified. R.S., c. 149, s. 103.

106. A police magistrate or a stipendiary magistrate has and may exercise, with respect to matters arising under this Act, jurisdiction over the whole county, union of counties or judicial district in which the city, town or other place for which he is appointed or in which he has jurisdiction under provincial laws is situated. R.S., c. 149, s. 104.

107. The Governor in Council may appoint persons to be, for the purposes of this Act, justices of the peace and those persons have and may exercise the powers and authority of two justices of the peace with regard to

(c) offences under this Act, and

(b) any offence against the provisions of the *Criminal Code* relating to cruelty to animals, common assault, breaking and entering and vagrancy, where the offence is committed by an Indian or relates to the person or property of an Indian. R.S., c. 149, s. 105; 1956, c. 40, s. 25.

108. For the purposes of this Act or any matter relating to Indian affairs

(a) persons appointed by the Minister for the purpose,

(b) superintendents, and

(c) the Minister, Deputy Minister and the chief officer in charge of the branch of the Department relating to Indian affairs, are *ex officio* commissioners for the taking of oaths. R.S., c. 149, s. 107.

ENFRANCHISEMENT

109. (1) On the report of the Minister that an Indian has applied for enfranchisement and that in his opinion the Indian

(a) is of the full age of twenty-one years,

(b) is capable of assuming the duties and responsibilities of citizenship, and

(c) when enfranchised, will be capable of supporting himself and his dependants, the Governor in Council may by order declare that the Indian and his wife and minor unmarried children are enfranchised.

(2) On the report of the Minister that an Indian woman married a person who is not an Indian, the Governor in Council may by order declare that the woman is enfranchised as of the date of her marriage and, on the recommendation of the Minister may by order declare that all or any of her children are enfranchised as of the date of the marriage or such other date as the order may specify.

(3) Where, in the opinion of the Minister, the wife of an Indian is living apart from her husband, the names of his wife and his minor children who are living with the wife shall not be included in an order under subsection (1) that enfranchises the Indian unless the wife has applied for enfranchisement, but where the Governor in Council is satisfied that such wife is no longer living apart from her husband, the Governor in Council may by order declare that the wife and the minor children are enfranchised.

(4) A person is not enfranchised unless his name appears in an order of enfranchisement made by the Governor in Council. R.S., c. 149, s. 108; 1956, c. 40, s. 26.

110. A person with respect to whom an order for enfranchisement is made under this Act shall, from the date thereof, or from the date of enfranchisement provided for therein, be deemed not to be an Indian within the meaning of this Act or any other statute or law. 1956, c. 40, s. 27.

111. (1) Upon the issue of an order of enfranchisement, any interest in land and improvements on an Indian reserve of which the enfranchised Indian was in lawful possession or over which he exercised rights of ownership, at the time of his enfranchisement, may be disposed of by him by gift or private sale to the band or another member of the band, but if not so disposed of within thirty days after the date of the order of enfranchisement such land and improvements shall be offered for sale by tender by the superintendent and sold to the highest bidder and the proceeds of such sale paid to him; and if no bid is received and the property remains unsold after six months from the date of such offering, the land, together with improvements, shall revert to the band free from any interest of the enfranchised person therein, subject to the payment, at the discretion of the Minister, to the enfranchised Indian, from the funds of the band, of such compensation for permanent improvements as the Minister may determine.

(2) When an order of enfranchisement issues or has issued, the Governor in Council may, with the consent of the council of the band, by order declare that any lands within a reserve of which the enfranchised Indian had formerly been in lawful possession shall cease to be Indian reserve lands.

(3) When an order has been made under subsection (2), the enfranchised Indian is entitled to occupy such lands for a period of ten years from the date of his enfranchisement, and the enfranchised Indian shall pay to the funds of the band, or there shall, out of any money payable to the enfranchised Indian under this Act, be transferred to the funds of the band, such amount per acre for the lands as the Minister considers to be the value of the common interest of the band in the lands.

(4) At the end of the ten-year period referred to in subsection (3) the Minister shall cause a grant of the lands to be made to the enfranchised Indian or to his legal representatives. R.S., c. 149, s. 110.

112. (1) Where the Minister reports that a band has applied for enfranchisement, and has submitted a plan for the disposal or division of the funds of the band and the lands in the reserve, and in his opinion the band is capable of managing its own affairs as a municipality or part of a municipality, the Governor in Council may by order approve the plan, declare that all the members of the band are enfranchised, either as of the date of the order or such later date as may be fixed in the order, and may make regulations for carrying the plan and the provisions of this section into effect.

(2) An order for enfranchisement may not be made under subsection (1) unless more than fifty per cent of the electors of the band signify, at a meeting of the band called for the purpose, their willingness to become enfranchised under this section, and their approval of the plan.

(3) The Governor in Council may, for the purpose of giving effect to this section, authorize the Minister to enter into an agreement with a province or a municipality, or both, upon such terms as may be agreed upon by the Minister and the province or municipality, or both.

(4) Without restricting the generality of subsection (3), an agreement made thereunder may provide for financial assistance to be given to the province or the municipality or both to assist in the support of indigent, infirm or aged persons to whom the agreement applies, and such financial assistance, or any part thereof, shall, if the Minister so directs, be paid out of moneys of the band, and any such financial assistance not paid out of moneys of the band shall be paid out of moneys appropriated by Parliament. R.S., c. 149, s. 111.

113. (1) Where a band has applied for enfranchisement within the meaning of this Act and has submitted a plan for the disposal or division of the funds of the band and the lands in the reserve, the Minister may appoint a committee to inquire into and report upon any or all of the following matters, namely:

(a) the desirability of enfranchising the band;

(b) the adequacy of the plan submitted by it; and

(*c*) any other matter relating to the application for enfranchisement or to the disposition thereof.

(2) A committee appointed under subsection (1) shall consist of

(*a*) a judge or retired judge of a superior, surrogate, district or county court,

(*b*) an officer of the Department, and

(*c*) a member of the band to be designated by the council of the band. 1960-61, c. 9, s. 1.

SCHOOLS

114. (1) The Governor in Council may authorize the Minister, in accordance with this Act, to enter into agreements on behalf of Her Majesty for the education in accordance with this Act of Indian children, with

(*a*) the government of a province,

(*b*) the Commissioner of the Northwest Territories,

(*c*) the Commissioner of the Yukon Territory,

(*d*) a public or separate school board, and

(*e*) a religious or charitable organization.

(2) The Minister may, in accordance with this Act, establish, operate and maintain schools for Indian children. 1956, c. 40, s. 28.

115. The Minister may

(*a*) provide for and make regulations with respect to standards for buildings, equipment, teaching, education, inspection and discipline in connection with schools;

(*b*) provide for the transportation of children to and from school;

(*c*) enter into agreements with religious organizations for the support and maintenance of children who are being educated in schools operated by those organizations; and

(*d*) apply the whole or any part of moneys that would otherwise be payable to or on behalf of a child who is attending a residential school to the maintenance of that child at that school. R.S., c. 149, s. 114.

116. (1) Subject to section 117, every Indian child who has attained the age of seven years shall attend school.

(2) The Minister may

(*a*) require an Indian who has attained the age of six years to attend school;

(*b*) require an Indian who becomes sixteen years of age during the school term to continue to attend school until the end of that term; and

(*c*) require an Indian who becomes sixteen years of age to attend school for such further period as the Minister considers advisable, but no Indian shall be required to attend school after he becomes eighteen years of age. R.S., c. 149, s. 115; 1956, c. 40, s. 29.

117. An Indian child is not required to attend school if the child

(a) is, by reason of sickness or other unavoidable cause that is reported promptly to the principal, unable to attend school;

(b) is, with the permission in writing of the superintendent, absent from school for a period not exceeding six weeks in each term for the purpose of assisting in husbandry or urgent and necessary household duties;

(c) is under efficient instruction at home or elsewhere, within one year after the written approval by the Minister of such instruction; or

(d) is unable to attend school because there is insufficient accommodation in the school that the child is entitled or directed to attend. R.S., c. 149, s. 116; 1956, c. 40, s. 30.

118. Every Indian child who is required to attend school shall attend such school as the Minister may designate, but no child whose parent is a Protestant shall be assigned to a school conducted under Roman Catholic auspices and no child whose parent is a Roman Catholic shall be assigned to a school conducted under Protestant auspices, except by written direction of the parent. R.S., c. 149, s. 117.

119. (1) The Minister may appoint persons, to be called truant officers, to enforce the attendance of Indian children at school, and for that purpose a truant officer has the powers of a peace officer.

(2) Without restricting the generality of subsection (1), a truant officer may

(a) enter any place where he believes, on reasonable grounds, that there are Indian children who are between the ages of seven and sixteen years of age, or who are required by the Minister to attend school;

(b) investigate any case of truancy; and

(c) serve written notice upon the parent, guardian or other person having the care or legal custody of a child to cause the child to attend school regularly thereafter.

(3) Where a notice has been served in accordance with paragraph (2) (c) with respect to a child who is required by this Act to attend school, and the child does not within three days after the service of notice attend school and continue to attend school regularly thereafter, the person upon whom the notice was served is guilty of an offence and is liable on summary conviction to a fine of not more than five dollars or to imprisonment for a term not exceeding ten days, or to both.

(4) Where a person has been served with a notice in accordance with paragraph (2) (c) , it is not necessary within a period of twelve

months thereafter to serve that person with any other notice in respect of further non-compliance with the provisions of this Act, and whenever such person within the period of twelve months fails to cause the child with respect to whom the notice was served or any other child of whom he has charge or control to attend school and continue in regular attendance as required by this Act, such person is guilty of an offence and liable to the penalties imposed by subsection (3) as if he had been served with the notice.

(5) A child who is habitually late for school shall be deemed to be absent from school.

(6) A truant officer may take into custody a child whom he believes on reasonable grounds to be absent from school contrary to this Act and may convey the child to school, using as much force as the circumstances require. R.S., c. 149, s. 118.

120. An Indian child who

(a) is expelled or suspended from school, or

(b) refuses or fails to attend school regularly, shall be deemed to be a juvenile delinquent within the meaning of the *Juvenile Delinquents Act*. R.S., c. 149, s. 119.

121. (1) Where the majority of the members of a band belongs to one religious denomination, the school established on the reserve that has been set apart for the use and benefit of that band shall be taught by a teacher of that denomination.

(2) Where the majority of the members of a band are not members of the same religious denomination and the band by a majority vote of those electors of the band who were present at a meeting called for the purpose requests that day schools on the reserve should be taught by a teacher belonging to a particular religious denomination, the school on that reserve shall be taught by a teacher of that denomination. R.S., c. 149, s. 120.

122. A Protestant or Roman Catholic minority of any band may, with the approval of and under regulations to be made by the Minister, have a separate day school or day school classroom established on the reserve unless, in the opinion of the Governor in Council, the number of children of school age does not so warrant. R.S., c. 149, s. 121.

123. In sections 114 to 122

"child" means an Indian who has attained the age of six years but has not attained the age of sixteen years, and a person who is required by the Minister to attend school;

"school" includes a day school, technical school, high school and residential school;

"truant officer" includes

(a) a member of the Royal Canadian Mounted Police,

(*b*) a special constable appointed for police duty on a reserve; and
(*c*) a school teacher and a chief of the band, when authorized by
the superintendent. R.S., c. 149, s. 122.

PRIOR GRANTS

124. Where, prior to the 4th day of September 1951, a reserve or portion of a reserve was released or surrendered to the Crown pursuant to Part I of the *Indian Act*, chapter 98 of the Revised Statutes of Canada, 1927, or pursuant to the provisions of the statutes relating to the release or surrender of reserves in force at the time of the release or surrender, and

(*a*) prior to that date Letters Patent under the Great Seal were issued purporting to grant a reserve or portion of a reserve so released or surrendered, or any interest therein, to any person, and the Letters Patent have not been declared void or inoperative by any Court of competent jurisdiction, or

(*b*) prior to that date a reserve or portion of a reserve so released or surrendered, or any interest therein, was sold or agreed to be sold by the Crown to any person, and the sale or agreement for sale has not been cancelled or by any Court of competent jurisdiction declared void or inoperative,

the Letters Patent or the sale or agreement for sale, as the case may be, shall, for all purposes, be deemed to have been issued or made at the date thereof under the direction of the Governor in Council. 1952-53, c. 41, s. 6.

Section D

Pre-Confederation and Post-Confederation Treaties, 1811-1921

D1 (a).

The Selkirk Treaty, 1817.

THIS indenture, made on the eighteenth day of July, in the fifty-seventh year of the reign of our Sovereign Lord King George the Third, and in the year of our Lord eighteen hundred and seventeen, between the undersigned Chiefs and warriors of the Chippeway or Saulteaux Nation and of the Killistine or Cree Nation, on the one part, and the Right Honorable Thomas Earl of Selkirk, on the other part:

Witnesseth, that for and in consideration of the annual present or quit rent hereinafter mentioned, the said Chiefs have given, granted and confirmed, and do, by these presents, give, grant and confirm unto our Sovereign Lord the King all that tract of land adjacent to Red River and Ossiniboyne River, beginning at the mouth of Red River and extending along same as far as Great Forks at the mouth of Red Lake River, and along Ossiniboyne River, otherwise called Rivière des Champignons, and extending to the distance of six miles from Fort Douglas on every side, and likewise from Fort Doer, and also from the Great Forks and in other parts extending in breadth to the distance of two English statute miles back from the banks of the said rivers, on each side, together with all the appurtenances whatsoever of the said tract of land, to have and to hold forever the said tract of land and appurtenances to the use of the said Earl of Selkirk, and of the settlers being established thereon, with the consent and permission of our Sovereign Lord the King, or of the said Earl of Selkirk. Provided always, and these presents are under the express condition that the said Earl, his heirs and successors, or their agents, shall annually pay to the Chiefs and warriors of the Chippeway or Saulteaux Nation, the present or quit rent consisting of one hundred pounds weight of good and merchantable tobacco, to be delivered on or before the tenth day of October at the forks of Ossiniboyne River—and to the Chiefs and warriors of the Killistine or Cree Nation, a like present or quit rent of one hundred pounds of tobacco, to be delivered to them on or before the said tenth day of October, at Portage de la Prairie, on the banks of Ossiniboyne River. Provided always that the traders hitherto established upon any part of the above-mentioned tract of land shall not be molested in the possession of the lands which they have already cultivated and improved, till His Majesty's pleasure shall be known.

In witness whereof the Chiefs aforesaid have set their marks, at the Forks of Red River on the day aforesaid.

(Signed)   SELKIRK.

MACHE WHESEAB,   His x mark.
   Le Sonnant.

MECHKADDEWIKONAIE,   " x "
   La robe noire.

KAYAJIESKEBINOA,   " x "
   L'Homme Noir.

PEGOWIS.   " x "

OUCKIDOAT,   " x "
   Le Premier.

Signed in presence of
   THOMAS THOMAS.
   JAMES BIRD.
   F. MATTHEY,
      Captain.
   P. D. ORSONNENS.
      Captain.
   MILES MACDONELL.
   J. BTE. CHARLES DE LORIMIER
   LOUIS NOLIN,
      Interpreter.

D1 (b).

Indenture of Sale from the Hudson's Bay Company to the Earl of Selkirk, 1811.

THIS INDENTURE, made the twelfth day of June, in the fifty-first year of the reign of Our Sovereign Lord George the Third, by the grace of God, of the United Kingdom of Great Britain and Ireland, King, Defender of the Faith, and in the year of our Lord one thousand eight hundred and eleven, between the Governor and Company of Adventurers of England, trading into Hudson's Bay, of the one part, and the Right Honorable Thomas Earl of Selkirk, of the other part:

Whereas the said Governor and Company are seized to them and their successors in fee simple, as absolute lords and proprietors of all the lands and territories situate upon the coasts and confines of the seas, streights, bays, lakes, rivers, creeks, and sounds, within the entrance of the streights commonly called Hudson's Streights, in the north-west part of America, and which lands and territories are reputed as one of the plantations or colonies belonging or annexed to the United Kingdom of Great Britain and Ireland, and are called Rupert's Land.

And whereas the said Governor and Company have, for divers good and valuable causes and considerations them thereunto moving, agreed to convey and assure a certain tract or parcel of the said lands and territories hereinafter described, unto and to the use of the said Earl of Selkirk, his heirs and assigns, under and subject to certain conditions hereinafter expressed and contained. Now, therefore, this indenture witnesseth, that in pursuance of such agreement, and in consideration of the sum of ten shillings of lawful money of Great Britain to the said Governor and Company, well and truly paid by the said Earl of Selkirk, at or before the execution of these presents (the receipt whereof is hereby acknowledged), and for divers good and other valuable causes and considerations, them, the said Governor and Company hereunto moving, the said Governor and Company have given, granted, aliened, enfeoffed and confirmed, and by these presents do give, grant, alien, enfeoff, and confirm unto the said Earl of Selkirk, his heirs and assigns, all that tract of land or territory, being within and forming part of the aforesaid lands and territories of the said Governor and Company, bounded by an imaginary line running as follows, that is to say: beginning on the western shore of the Lake Winnipie, otherwise Winnipey, at a point in fifty-two degrees, and thirty north latitude, and thence running due west to the Lake Winnipegoos, otherwise called Little Winnipey, then in a southerly direction through the said lake so as to strike its western shore in latitude fifty-two degrees, then due west to the place where the parallel of fifty-two degrees, then due west to the place where the parallel of fifty-two degrees north latitude intersects the western branch of Red River, otherwise called Assiniboyne River, then due south from that point of intersection to the height of land which separates the waters running into Hudson's Bay, from those of the Missouri and Mississippi, then in an easterly direction along the said height of land to the source of the River Winnipie, or Winnipey (meaning by such last named river, the principal branch of the waters which unite in Lake Saginagus), thence along the main stream of these waters and the middle of the several lakes through which they flow to the mouth of the Winnipie River, and thence in a northerly direction through the middle of Lake Winnipie to the place of beginning.

In witness whereof the said parties to these presents have hereunto set their hands and seals the day and year first above written.

(Signed)   SELKIRK.   [L. S.]
              ALEXANDER LEAN,   [L. S.]
                 Secretary of the Hudson's Bay Company.

Indorsed.-Sealed under the common seal of the within mentioned Governor and Company, and signed and delivered by Alexander Lean, their Secretary, pursuant to their order and appointment, and signed, sealed and delivered by the within mentioned Thomas, Earl of Selkirk (being first duly stamped), in the presence of

ALEXANDER MUNDELL,
   Parliament Street, Westminister.

EDWARD ROBERTS,
   Hudson's Bay House.

Suit l'attestation écrite et assermentie du premier de ces deux temoins, Alex. Mundell, en presence du Maire de Londres.

Sworn at the Mansion House,   London, this twenty-third day
         (Signed)   ALEXANDER MUNDELL.
of April, 1819, before me,

JOHN AIKINS,   [L.S.]
   Mayor.

Puis, Attestation notariée, in testimonium veritatis.

(Signed)   WILLIAM DUFF,
              Notary Public.

Be it remembered that on the fourth day of September, in the year 1812, at the Forks of Red River, peaceable possession of the land and hereditaments by the within written indenture, granted and enfeoffed, or otherwise assured or expressed, and intended so to be, was taken, had, and delivered, by the within named William Hillier, one of the attorneys for that purpose appointed, unto the within named Miles Macdonell, Esquire, who was duly authorized to receive the same, to and for the use of the within named Earl of Selkirk, his heirs and assigns, according to the form and effect of the within written indenture in the presence of

(Signed)   JOHN McLEOD,
RODERICK McKENZIE.

D2.

The Robinson Superior Treaty, 1850.

THE ROBINSON SUPERIOR TREATY.

THIS AGREEMENT, made and entered into on the seventh day of September, in the year of Our Lord one thousand eight hundred and fifty, at Sault Ste. Marie, in the Province of Canada, between the Honorable William Benjamin Robinson, of the one part, on behalf of Her Majesty the Queen, and Joseph Peandechat, John Iuinway, Mishe-Muckqua, Totomencie, Chiefs, and Jacob Warpela, Ahmutchiwagabou, Michel Shelageshick, Manitoshainse, and Chiginans, principal men of the Ojibewa Indians inhabiting the Northern Shore of Lake Superior, in the said Province of Canada, from Batchewananng Bay to Pigeon River, at the western extremity of said lake, and inland throughout the extent to the height of land which separates the territory covered by the charter of the Honorable the Hudson's Bay Company from the said tract, and also the islands in the said lake within the boundaries of the British possessions therein, of the other part, witnesseth:

That for and in consideration of the sum of two thousand pounds of good and lawful money of Upper Canada, to them in hand paid, and for the further perpetual annuity of five hundred pounds, the same to be paid and delivered to the said Chiefs and their tribes at a convenient season of each summer, not later than the first day of August at the Honorable the Hudson's Bay Company's Posts of Michipicoton and Fort William, they the said Chiefs and principal men do freely, fully and voluntarily surrender, cede, grant and convey unto Her Majesty, Her heirs and successors forever, all their right, title and interest in the whole of the territory above described, save and except the reservations set forth in the schedule hereunto annexed, which reservations shall be held and occupied by the said Chiefs and their tribes in common, for the purposes of residence and cultivation,—and should the said Chiefs and their respective tribes at any time desire to dispose of any mineral or other valuable productions upon the said reservations, the same will be at their request sold by order of the Superintendent-General of the

Indian Department for the time being, for their sole use and benefit, and to the best advantage.

And the said William Benjamin Robinson of the first part, on behalf of Her Majesty and the Government of this Province, hereby promises and agrees to make the payments as before mentioned; and further to allow the said Chiefs and their tribes the full and free privilege to hunt over the territory now ceded by them, and to fish in the waters thereof as they have heretofore been in the habit of doing, saving and excepting only such portions of the said territory as may from time to time be sold or leased to individuals, or companies of individuals, and occupied by them with the consent of the Provincial Government. The parties of the second part futher promise and agree that they will not sell, lease, or otherwise dispose of any portion of their reservations without the consent of the Superintendent-General of Indian Affairs being first had and obtained; nor will they at any time hinder or prevent persons from exploring or searching for minerals or other valuable productions in any part of the territory hereby ceded to Her Majesty as before mentioned. The parties of the second part also agree that in case the Government of this Province should before the date of this agreement have sold, or bargained to sell, any mining locations or other property on the portions of the territory hereby reserved for their use and benefit, then and in that case such sale, or promise of sale, shall be perfected, if the parties interested desire it, by the Government, and the amount accruing therefrom shall be paid to the tribe to whom the reservation belongs. The said William Benjamin Robinson on behalf of Her Majesty, who desires to deal liberally and justly with all her subjects, further promises and agrees that in case the territory hereby ceded by the parties of the second part shall at any future period produce an amount which will enable the Government of this Province without incurring loss to increase the annuity hereby secured to them, then, and in that case, the same shall be augmented from time to time, provided that the amount paid to each individual shall not exceed the sum of one pound provincial currency in any one year, or such further sum as Her Majesty may be graciously pleased to order; and provided further that the number of Indians entitled to the benefit of this treaty shall amount to two-thirds of their present numbers (which is twelve hundred and forty) to entitle them to claim the full benefit thereof, and should their numbers at any future period not amount to two-thirds of twelve hundred and forty, the annuity shall be diminished in proportion to their actual numbers.

Schedule of Reservations made by the above named and subscribing Chiefs and principal men.

First—Joseph Pean-de-chat and his tribe, the reserve to commence about two miles from Fort William (inland), on the right bank of the River Kiministiquia; thence westerly six miles, parallel to the shores of the lake; thence northerly five miles, thence easterly to the right bank of the said river, so as not to interfere with any acquired rights of the Honorable Hudson's Bay Company.

Second—Four miles square at Gros Cap, being a valley near the Honorable Hudson's Bay Company's post of Michipicoton, for Totominai and tribe.

Third—Four miles square on Gull River, near Lake Nipigon, on both sides of said river, for the Chief Mishimuckqua and tribe.

(Signed)

W. B. ROBINSON.		
JOSEPH PEAN-DE-CHAT.	His x mark.	[L.S.]
JOHN MINWAY.	" x "	[L.S.]
MISHE-MUCKQUA.	" x "	[L.S.]
TOTOMINAI.	" x "	[L.S.]
JACOB WAPELA.	" x "	[L.S.]
AH-MUTCHINAGALON.	" x "	[L.S.]
MICHEL SHELAGESHICK.	" x "	[L.S.]
MANITOU SHAINSE.	" x "	[L.S.]
CHIGINANS.	" x "	[L.S.]

Signed, sealed and delivered at Sault-Ste. Marie, the day and year first above written, in presence of—

(Signed)   GEORGE IRONSIDE,
                S. I. Affairs.
           ASTLEY P. COOPER,
                Capt. Com. Rifle Brig.
           H. M. BALFOUR,
                2nd Lieut. Rifle Brig.
           JOHN SWANSTON,
                C. F. Hon. Hud. Bay Co.
           GEORGE JOHNSTON
                Interpreter
           F. W. KEATING.

D3.

Treaty Number One, 1871.

ARTICLES OF A TREATY, made and concluded this third day of August, in the year of our Lord, one thousand eight hundred and seventy-one, between Her Most Gracious Majesty the Queen of Great Britain and Ireland, by Her Commissioner Wemyss M. Simpson, Esquire, of the one part, and the Chippewa and Swampy Cree Tribes of Indians, inhabitants of the country within the limits hereinafter defined and described by their chiefs, chosen and named as hereinafter mentioned, of the other part:

Whereas, all the Indians inhabiting the said country have, pursuant to an appointment made by the said Commissioner, been convened at the Stone Fort, otherwise called Lower Fort Garry, to deliberate upon certain matters of interest to Her Most Gracious Majesty of the one part, and to the said Indians of the other; and whereas the said Indians have been notified and informed by Her Majesty's said Commissioner, that it is the desire of Her Majesty to open up to settlement and immigration a tract of country bounded and described as hereinafter mentioned, and to obtain the consent thereto of her Indian subjects inhabiting the said tract and to make a treaty and arrangements with them, so that there may be peace and good will between them and Her Majesty, and that they may know and be assured of what allowance they are to count upon and receive, year by year, from Her Majesty's bounty and benevolence.

And whereas the Indians of the said tract, duly convened in Council as aforesaid, and being requested by Her Majesty's said Commissioner to name certain Chiefs and head men, who should be authorized on their behalf to conduct such negotiations, and sign any treaty to be founded thereon, and to become responsible to Her Majesty for the faithful performance, by their respective bands, of such obligations as should be assumed by them the said Indians, have thereupon named the following persons for that purpose, that is to say: Mis-koo-kenew, or Red Eagle, (Henry Prince); Ka-ke-ka-penais, or Bird for ever; Na-sha-ke-penais, or Flying down Bird; Na-na-wa-nana, or Centre of Bird's Tail; Ke-we-tayash, or Flying round; Wa-ko-wush, or Whip-poor-Will; Oo-za-we-kwun, or Yellow Quill; and thereupon, in open Council, the different bands have presented their respective Chiefs to His Excellency the Lieutenant-Governor of the Province of Manitoba, and of the North-West Territory, being present at such Council, and to the said Commissioner, as the Chiefs and head men for the purposes aforesaid, of the respective bands of Indians inhabiting the said District, hereinafter described; and whereas the said Lieutenant-Governor and the said Commissioner, then and there received and acknowledged the persons so presented as Chiefs and head men, for the purpose aforesaid; and whereas the said Commissioner has proceeded to negotiate a treaty with the said Indians, and the same has finally been agreed upon and concluded as follows, that is to say:

The Chippewa and Swampy Cree Tribes of Indians, and all other the Indians inhabiting the district hereinafter described and defined, do hereby cede, release, surrender, and yield up to Her Majesty the Queen, and her successors for ever, all the lands included within the following limits, that is to say: Beginning at the International boundary line near its junction with the Lake of the Woods, at a point due north from the centre of Roseau Lake, thence to run due north to the centre of Roseau Lake; thence northward to the centre of White Mouth Lake, otherwise called White Mud Lake; thence by the middle of the lake and the middle of the river issuing therefrom, to the mouth thereof in Winnipeg River; thence by the Winnipeg River to its mouth; thence westwardly, including all the islands near the south end of the lake, across the lake to the mouth of the Drunken River; thence westwardly, to a point on Lake Manitoba, half way between Oak Point and the mouth of Swan Creek; thence across Lake Manitoba, on a line due west to its western shore; thence in a straight line to the crossing of the Rapids on the Assiniboine; thence due south to the International boundary line, and thence easterly by the said line to the place of beginning; to have and to hold the same to Her said Majesty the Queen, and her successors for ever; and Her Majesty the Queen, hereby agrees and undertakes to lay aside and reserve for the sole and exclusive use of the Indians, the following tracts of land, that is to say: For the use of the Indians belonging to the band of which Henry Prince, otherwise called Mis-koo-ke-new, is the Chief, so much of land on both sides of the Red River, beginning at the south line of St. Peter's Parish, as will furnish one hundred and sixty acres for each family of five, or in that proportion for larger or smaller families; and for the use of the Indians of whom Na-sha-ke-penais, Na-na-wa-nanan, Ke-we-tayash, and Wa-ko-wush, are the Chiefs, so much land on the Roseau River, as will furnish one hundred and sixty acres for each family of five, or in that proportion for larger or smaller families, beginning from the mouth of the river; and for the use of the Indians, of which Ka-ke-ka-penais is the Chief, so much land on the Winnipeg River, above Fort Alexander, as will furnish one hundred and sixty acres for each family of five, or in that proportion for larger or smaller families; beginning at a distance of a mile or thereabout above the Fort; and for the use of the Indians, of whom Oo-za-we-Kwun is Chief, so much land on the south and east side of the Assiniboine, about twenty miles above the Portage, as will furnish one hundred and sixty acres for each family of five, or in that proportion for larger or smaller families, reserving also a further tract enclosing said reserve, to comprise an equivalent to twenty-five square miles of equal breadth, to be laid out round the reserve; it is being understood, however, that if at the date of the execution of this treaty, there are any settlers within the bounds of any lands reserved by any band, Her Majesty reserves the right to deal with such settlers as she shall deem just, so as not to diminish the extent of land allotted to the Indians.

And with a view to show the satisfaction of Her Majesty with the behaviour and good conduct of her Indians, parties to this treaty, she hereby, through her Commissioner, makes them a present of three dollars for each Indian man, woman and child belonging to the bands here represented.

And further, Her Majesty agrees to maintain a school on each reserve hereby made, whenever the Indians of the reserve should desire it.

Within the boundary of Indian Reserves, until otherwise enacted by the proper legislative authority, no intoxicating liquor shall be allowed to be introduced or sold, and all laws now in force or hereafter to be enacted to preserve Her Majesty's Indian subjects, inhabiting the reserves or living elsewhere, from the evil influence of the use of intoxicating liquors, shall be strictly enforced.

Her Majesty's Commissioner shall, as soon as possible after the execution of this treaty, cause to be taken an accurate census of all the Indians inhabiting the district above described, distributing them in families, and shall in every year ensuring the date hereof, at some period during the month of July in each year, to be duly notified to the Indians, and at or near the respective reserves, pay to each Indian family of five persons the sum of fifteen dollars Canadian currency, or in like proportion for a larger or smaller family, such payment to be made in such articles as the Indians shall require of blankets, clothing, prints (assorted colors), twine or traps, at the current cost price in Montreal, or otherwise, if Her Majesty shall deem the same desirable in the interests of Her Indian people, in cash.

And the undersigned Chiefs do hereby bind and pledge themselves and their people strictly to observe this treaty, and to maintain perpetual peace between themselves and Her Majesty's white subjects, and not to interfere with the property or in any way molest the persons of Her Majesty's white or other subjects.

In witness whereof Her Majesty's said Commissioner and the said

Indian Chiefs have hereunto subscribed and set their hand and seal, at the Lower Fort Garry, this day and year herein first above mentioned.

(Signed)	WEMYSS M. SIMPSON,	[L.S.]
	Indian Commissioner.	
	MIS-KOO-KE-NEW (or Red Eagle)	His x mark.
	(Henry Prince).	
	KA.KE-KA-PENAIS (or Bird Forever)	" x "
	(William Pennefather).	
	NA-SHA-KE-PENAIS (or Flying down Bird).	" x "
	NA-NA-WA-NANAN (or Centre of Bird's Tail).	" x "
	KE-WE-TAY-ASH (or Flying Round).	" x "
	WA-KO-WUSH (or Whip-poor-will).	" x "
	OI-ZA-WE-KWUN (or Yellow Quill).	" x "

Signed, sealed and delivered in the presence of (the same having been first read and explained)—

(Signed)	ADAMS G. ARCHIBALD,
	Lieut.-Gov. of Manitoba and the N.-W. Territories.
	JAMES McKAY, P.L.C.
	A. G. IRVINE,
	Major.
	ABRAHAM COWLEY.
	DONALD GUNN, M.L.C.
	THOMAS HOWARD.
	HENRY COCHRANE.
	JAMES McARRISTER.
	HUGH McARRISTER.
	E. ALICE ARCHIBALD.
	HENRY BOUTHILLIER.

D4.

Treaty Number Eleven, 1921, with Subsequent Adhesions.

ARTICLES OF A TREATY made and concluded on the several dates mentioned therein in the year of Our Lord One thousand Nine hundred and Twenty-One, between His Most Gracious Majesty George V, King of Great Britain and Ireland and of the British Dominions beyond the Seas, by His Commissioner, Henry Anthony Conroy, Esquire, of the

City of Ottawa, of the One Part, and the Slave, Dogrib, Loucheux, Hare and other Indians, inhabitants of the territory within the limits hereinafter defined and described, by their Chiefs and Headmen, hereunto subscribed, of the other part:—

WHEREAS, the Indians inhabiting the territory hereinafter defined have been convened to meet a commissioner representing His Majesty's Government of the Dominion of Canada at certain places in the said territory in this present year of 1921, to deliberate upon certain matters of interest to His Most Gracious Majesty, of the one part, and the said Indians of the other.

AND WHEREAS, the said Indians have been notified and informed by His Majesty's said commissioner that it is His desire to open for settlement, immigration, trade, travel, mining, lumbering and such other purposes as to His Majesty may seem meet, a tract of country bounded and described as hereinafter set forth, and to obtain the consent thereto of His Indian subjects inhabiting the said tract, and to make a treaty, so that there may be peace and goodwill between them and His Majesty's other subjects, and that His Indian people may know and be assured of what allowances they are to expect and receive from His Majesty's bounty and benevolence.

AND WHEREAS, the Indians of the said tract, duly convened in council at the respective points named hereunder, and being requested by His Majesty's Commissioner, to name certain Chiefs and Headmen, who should be authorized on their behalf to conduct such negotiations and sign any treaty to be founded thereon, and to become responsible to His Majesty for the faithful performance by their respective bands of such obligations as shall be assumed by them, the said Indians have therefore acknowledged for that purpose the several chiefs and Headmen who have subscribed thereto.

AND WHEREAS the said Commissioner has proceeded to negotiate a treaty with the Slave, Dogrib, Loucheux, Hare and other Indians inhabiting the district hereinafter defined and described, which has been agreed upon and concluded by the respective bands at the dates mentioned hereunder, the said Indians do hereby cede, release, surrender and yield up to the Government of the Dominion of Canada, for His Majesty the King and His Successors forever, all their rights, titles, and privileges whatsoever to the lands included within the following limits, that is to say:

Commencing at the northwesterly corner of the territory ceded under the provisions of Treaty Number Eight; thence northeasterly along the height-of-land to the point where it intersects the boundary between the Yukon Territory and the Northwest Territories; thence northwesterly along the said boundary to the shore of the Arctic ocean; thence easterly along the said shore to the mouth of the Coppermine river; thence southerly and southeasterly along the left bank of the said river to Lake Gras by way of Point lake; thence along the southern shore of Lake Gras to a point situated northwest of the most western extremity of Aylmer lake; thence along the southern shore of Aylmer lake and following the right bank of the Lockhart river to Artillery lake; thence along the western shore of Artillery lake and following the right bank of the Lockhart river to the site of Old Fort Reliance where the said river enters Great Slave lake, this being the northeastern corner of the territory ceded under the provisions of Treaty Number Eight; thence westerly along the northern boundary of the said territory so ceded to the point of commencement; comprising an area of approximately three hundred and seventy-two thousand square miles.

AND ALSO, the said Indian rights, titles and privileges whatsoever to all other lands wherever situated in the Yukon Territory, the Northwest Territories or in any other portion of the Dominion of Canada.

To have and to hold the same to His Majesty the King and His Successors forever.

AND His Majesty the King hereby agrees with the said Indians that they shall have the right to pursue their usual vocations of hunting, trapping and fishing throughout the tract surrendered as heretofore described, subject to such regulations as may from time to time be made by the Government of the Country acting under the authority of His Majesty, and saving and excepting such tracts as may be required or taken up from time to time for settlement, mining, lumbering, trading or other purposes.

AND His Majesty the King hereby agrees and undertakes to lay aside reserves for each band, the same not to exceed in all one square mile for each family of five, or in that proportion for larger or smaller families;

PROVIDED, however, that His Majesty reserves the right to deal with any settlers within the boundaries of any lands reserved for any band as He may see fit; and also that the aforesaid reserves of land, or any interest therein, may be sold or otherwise disposed of by His Majesty's Government for the use and benefit of the said Indians entitled thereto, with their consent first had and obtained; but in no wise shall the said Indians, or any of them, be entitled to sell or otherwise alienate any of the lands allotted to them as reserves.

It is further agreed between His Majesty and His Indian subjects that such portions of the reserves and lands above indicated as may at any time be required for public works, buildings, railways, or roads of whatsoever nature may be appropriated for that purpose by His Majesty's Government of the Dominion of Canada, due compensation being made to the Indians for the value of any improvements thereon, and an equivalent in land, money or other consideration for the area of the reserve so appropriated.

And in order to show the satisfaction of His Majesty with the behaviour and good conduct of His Indian subjects, and in extinguishment of all their past claims hereinabove mentioned, He hereby, through his Commissioner, agrees to give to each Chief a present of thirty-two dollars in cash, to each Headman, twenty-two dollars, and to every other Indian of whatever age of the families represented, at the time and place of payment, twelve dollars.

HIS MAJESTY, also agrees that during the coming year, and annually thereafter, He will cause to be paid to the said Indians in cash, at suitable places and dates, of which the said Indians shall be duly notified, to each Chief twenty-five dollars, to each Headman fifteen dollars, and to every other Indian of whatever age five dollars, to be paid only to heads of families for the members thereof, it being provided for the purposes of this Treaty that each band having at least thirty members may have a Chief, and that in addition to a Chief, each band may have Councillors or Headmen in the proportion of two to each two hundred members of the band.

FURTHER, His Majesty agrees that each Chief shall receive once and for all a silver medal, a suitable flag and a copy of this Treaty for the use of his band; and during the coming year, and every third year thereafter, each Chief and Headman shall receive a suitable suit of clothing.

FURTHER, His Majesty agrees to pay the salaries of teachers to instruct the children of said Indians in such manner as His Majesty's Government may deem advisable.

FURTHER, His Majesty agrees to supply once and for all to each Chief of a band that selects a reserve, ten axes, five hand-saws, five augers, one grind-stone, and the necessary files and whetstones for the use of the band.

FURTHER, His Majesty agrees that, each band shall receive once and for all equipment for hunting, fishing and trapping to the value of fifty dollars for each family of such band, and that there shall be distributed annually among the Indians equipment, such as twine for nets, ammunition and trapping to the value of three dollars per head for each Indian who continues to follow the vocation of hunting, fishing and trapping.

FURTHER, His Majesty agrees that, in the event of any of the

Indians aforesaid being desirous of following agricultural pursuits, such Indians shall receive such assistance as is deemed necessary for that purpose.

AND the undersigned Slave, Dogrib, Loucheux, Hare and other Chiefs and Headmen, on their own behalf and on behalf of all the Indians whom they represent, do hereby solemnly promise and engage to strictly observe this Treaty, and also to conduct and behave themselves as good loyal subjects of His Majesty the King.

THEY promise and engage that they will, in all respects, obey and abide by the law; that they will maintain peace between themselves and others of His Majesty's subjects, whether Indians, half-breeds or whites, now inhabiting and hereafter to inhabit any part of the said ceded territory; that they will not molest the person or property of any inhabitant of such ceded tract, or of any other district or country, or interfere with, or trouble any person passing or travelling through the said tract or any part thereof, and that they will assist the officers of His Majesty in bringing to justice and punishment any Indian offending against the stipulations of this Treaty, or infringing the law in force in the country so ceded.

IN WITNESS WHEREOF, His Majesty's said Commissioner and the said Chiefs and Headmen have hereunto set their hands at the places and times set forth in the year herein first above written.

SIGNED AT PROVIDENCE on the twenty-seventh day of June, 1921, by His Majesty's Commissioner and the Chiefs and Headmen in the presence of the undersigned witnesses, after having been first interpreted and explained.

WITNESSES:

W. V. BRUCE, *Insp. R.C.M.P.*

F. H. KITTO,

A. H. MILLER,

G. BREYNAT, O.M.I., *Bishop of Adr.*,
    Vic. Apost. of Mackenzie,

J. A. R. BALSILLIE.

H. A. CONROY, *Comm.*

PAUL LAFOIN x *Chief*,
            his
            mark

HARRY FRANCIS x *Headman*,
            his
            mark

BAPTISTE SABOURINE x *Headman*.
            his
            mark

SIGNED at Simpson on the eleventh day of July, 1921, by His Majesty's Commissioner and the Chiefs and Headmen in the presence

of the undersigned witnesses, after having been first interpreted and
explained.

WITNESSES: H. A. CONROY, *Comm.*
(Sgd.)
G. BREYNAT, O.M.I., *Bishop of Adr.,*   (ANTOINE) (signed in syllabics)
   Vic. Apost. of Mackenzie,
JOHN G. CORRY,   (KORWERGEN) (signed in syllabics)
W. V. BRUCE, *Insp. R.C.M.P.,*   his
A. F. CAMSELL,   BEDSEDIA x
T. W. HARRIS.   mark

SIGNED at Wrigley on the thirteenth day of July, 1921, by His
Majesty's Commissioner and the Chiefs and Headmen in the presence
of the undersigned witnesses, after having been first interpreted and
explained.

WITNESSES:
(Sgd.)
G. BREYNAT, O.M.I., *Bishop of Adr.,*   H. A. CONROY, *Comm.*
   Vic. Apost. of Mackenzie,
W. V. BRUCE, *Insp. R.C.M.P.,*   (YENDO) (signed in syllabics)
A. L. McDONALD.
F. H. BACON.

SIGNED at Norman on the fifteenth day of July, 1921, by His
Majesty's Commissioner and the Chiefs and Headmen in the presence
of the undersigned witnesses, after having been first interpreted and
explained.

WITNESSES:
(Sgd.)   H. A. CONROY, *Comm.*
G. BREYNAT, O.M.I., *Bishop of Adr.,*
   Vic. Apost. of Mackenzie,   ALBERT WRIGHT,
W. V. BRUCE, *Insp. R.C.M.P.,*   his
GEO. P. JOHNSTON,   SAUL BLONDIN x
G. H. M. CAMPBELL, *Const. R.C.M.P.*   mark

SIGNED at Good Hope on the twenty-first day of July, 1921, by
His Majesty's Commissioner and the Chiefs and Headmen in the

presence of the undersigned witnesses, after having been first interpreted and explained.

WITNESSES:
(Sgd.)

G. BREYNAT, O.M.I., *Bishop of Adr.*,
   Vic. Apost. of Mackenzie
W. V. BRUCE, *Insp. R.C.M,.P.*
F. H. BACON,
J. H. BRASHAR, *Cpl. R.C.M.P.*

H. A. CONROY, *Comm.*
     his
SIMEON X
     mark
     his
FRANCOIS X NATEGAL.
     mark

SIGNED at Arctic Red River on the twenty-sixth day of July, 1921, by His Majesty's Commissioner and the Chiefs and Headmen in the presence of the undersigned witnesses, after having been first interpreted and explained.

WITNESSES:
(Sgd.)

G. BREYNAT, O.M.I., *Bishop of Adr.*,
   Vic. Apost. of Mackenzie,
W. V. BRUCE, *Insp. R.C.M.P.*,
J. LECUYER, Pr. O.M.I.
J. PARSONS.

H. A. CONROY, *Comm.*
     his
PAUL X
     mark
NIDE APHI,
FABIEN-LALOO.

SIGNED at McPherson on the twenty-eighth day of July, 1921, by His Majesty's Commissioner and the Chiefs and Headmen in the presence of the undersigned witnesses, after having been first interpreted and explained.

WITNESSES:
(Sgd.)

W. V. BRUCE, *Insp. R.C.M.P.*,
J. PARSONS,
F. H. BACON,
JAMES FIRTH.

H. A. CONROY, *Comm.*

JABY LALO,

JOHNNIE KIKAWCHIK.

SIGNED at Rae on the twenty-second day of August, 1921, by His Majesty's Commissioner and the Chiefs and Headmen in the presence of the undersigned witnesses, after having been first interpreted and explained.

WITNESSES:	H. A. CONROY, *Comm.*,
(Sgd.)	his
G. BREYNAT, O.M.I., *Bishop of Adr.*,	MORPHY x
Vic. Apost. of Mackenzie,	mark
W. J. O'DONNELL,	his
W. V. BRUCE, *Insp. R.C.M.P.*,	JERMAIN x
ED. HERON, H. B. Co.	mark
	his
CLAUDE WM. LAFOUNTAIN,	JOSUE x BEAULIEU.
	mark

SIGNED at Liard on the seventeenth day of July, 1922, by His Majesty's Commissioner and the Chiefs and Headmen in the presence of the undersigned witnesses, after having been first interpreted and explained.

WITNESSES:	(Sgd.)
(Sgd.)	THOMAS WILLIAM HARRIS, *Comm.*
	his
G. BREYNAT, O.M.I., *Bishop of Adr.*,	THOMAS E. KINLA x *Chief*,
Vic. Ap. of Mackenzie	mark
	his
F. MOISAN, O.M.I. *Ptre.*	JOSEPH FANTASQUR x *Headman*,
A. BORBIN, *Const. R.C.M.P.*,	mark
JOSEPH BERRAULT, *Interpreter*.	his
	DAVID CELIBETA x *Headman*.
	mark

List of Sources
and References

A1.　　Adam Shortt and Arthur G. Doughty, *Documents Relating to the Constitutional History of Canada 1759-1791* 2nd. rev. ed., Parts 1-2 (Ottawa: King's Printer, 1918), pp.26, 33, 34 (Part 1).

A2.　　Adam Shortt and Arthur G. Doughty, *op.cit.*, Part 1, pp.166-168.

A3.　　Adam Shortt and Arthur G. Doughty, *op.cit.*, Part 1, pp.199-200.

A4(a).　Adam Shortt and Arthur G. Doughty, *op.cit.*, Part 1, p.199.

A4(b).　Adam Shortt and Arthur G. Doughty, *op.cit.*, Part 2, pp.614-620.

A5.　　Adam Shortt and Arthur G. Doughty, *op.cit.*, Part 2, pp.814-815.

A6.　　Arthur G. Doughty and Duncan A. McArthur, *Documents Relating to the Constitutional History of Canada 1791-1818* (Ottawa: King's Printer, 1914), p.46.

A7.　　*American State Papers, Foreign Relations*, vol. 1 (Washington, 1832), p.520.

A8(a-c).　Arthur G. Doughty and Duncan A. McArthur, *op.cit.*, pp.187-191.

A9.　　Edward Hertslet, *The Map of Europe by Treaty* (London: Butterworth's, Harrison, 1875), p.58.

A10(a-d).　Arthur G. Story and Norah Story, *Documents Relating to the Constitutional History of Canada 1819-1828* (Ottawa: King's Printer, 1935), pp.174-178.

B1.　　*Arrêts et Regléments du Conseil Supérieur de Quebec, et Ordonnances et Jugements des Intendants du Canada*, vol. 2 (Quebec: Fréchette, 1855), p.6.

B2.　　*Ibid.*, p.16.

B3.　　*Ibid.*, p.152.

B4.　　*Ibid.*, p.262.

B5.　　*Ibid.*, p.271.

B6-B16.　References and texts of this legislation may be found in:
　(a) *Statutes of the Province of Canada* (Toronto and Quebec: Stewart Derbshire and George Desbarats, 1851-1857); *Consolidated Statutes of the Province of Canada* (Toronto and Quebec: Stewart Derbshire and George Desbarats, 1859); *Revised Statutes of Canada 1952 and 1970*, Appendices.

B17-B18.　*Acts of the Legislatures of the Provinces now Comprised in the Dominion and of Canada* (Ottawa: Brown Chamberlin, 1887), pp.600,602.

B19.　　*The Consolidated Statutes of Newfoundland 1916* (Third Series), 4 vols. (St. John's: Robinson and Company, 1919), vol. 1, p.572.

C1.　　*Revised Statutes of Canada*, 1952 and 1970, Appendices; also in Maurice Ollivier, *British North America Acts and Selected Statutes 1867-1962* (Ottawa: Queen's Printer, 1963).

C2.　　*Statutes of Canada*, 1868.

C3.   *Statutes of Canada*, 1869.

C4.   *Statutes of Canada*, 1870.

C5.   *Consolidated Orders-in-Council of Canada* (Ottawa: Queen's Printer, 1889).

C6.   *Ibid*.

C7.   *Statutes of Canada*, 1874.

C8.   *Statutes of Canada*, 1876.

C9.   *Statutes of Canada*, 1876.

C10. *Statutes of Canada*, 1880.

C11. *Statutes of Ontario*, 1891.

C12-C14. *Statutes of Canada*, 1930.

C15. *Statutes of Canada*, 1951 and 1970.

D1a-b.   Alexander Morris, *The Treaties of Canada with the Indians of Manitoba and the Northwest Territories* (Toronto: Belfords, Clarke and Co., 1880), pp.301-302.

D2.   *Ibid*., pp.302-304.

D3.   *Indian Treaties and Surrenders from 1680-1890*, 2 vols. (Ottawa: Brown Chamberlin [Queen's Printer], 1891), vol. 1, pp.282-285.

D4.   *Treaty No.11 (June 27, 1921) and Adhesion (July 17, 1922) with Reports etc*. (Ottawa: Queen's Printer, 1926).

Suggestions for Further Reading

A. Canadian Indian Legal and Administrative History

Alvord, Clarence W., *The Genesis of the Proclamation of 1763* (Michigan Pioneer and Historical Society, 1908).

British Columbia Papers Connected with the Indian Land Question, 1850-1875 (Victoria: Wolfenden, 1875).

Brown, Elizabeth G., "British Statutues in the Emergent Nations of North America: 1606-1649," *American Journal of Legal History*, vol. 7 (1963), pp.95-135.

Canada: Parliament of Canada. "Special Joint Committee of the Senate and House of Commons Appointed to Examine and Consider the Indian Act," Minutes of the Proceedings and Evidence, nos.1-506, *Select and Standing Committies of the House of Commons*, vol. VI (Ottawa, 1946).

Canada: Parliament of Canada. "Special Joint Committee of the Senate and House of Commons to Continue and Complete the Examination and Consideration of the Indian Act," Minutes of Proceedings and Evidence, nos. 21-41, *Select and Standing Committees of the Senate and the House of Commons*, vol. II parts 1 and 2 (Ottawa, 1947); nos. 1-5, vol. II (Ottawa, 1948).

Cumming, Peter A. and Neil H. Mickenberg. *Native Rights in Canada*, 2nd. ed. (Toronto: Indian-Eskimo Association and General Publishing, 1972).

Drucker, Philip., *The Native Brotherhoods: Modern Intertribal Organizations on the Northwest Coast*, Smithsonian Institution, Bureau of American Ethnology Bulletin 168 (Washington: U.S. Government Printing Bureau, 1958). (cf. esp. pp. 78-152).

Duff, Wilson. "The Fort Victoria Treaties," *British Columbia Studies*, No.3 (Fall, 1969), pp. 3-57.

Gates, L.F. *Land Policies of Upper Canada* (Toronto: University of Toronto Press, 1968).

Green, L.C., "Canada's Indians: Federal Policy, International, and Constitutional Law," *Ottawa Law Review*, vol.4 (1970), pp.101-131.

Harper, Allan G., "Canada's Indian Administration: The Treaty System," *America Indigena*, vols. V, VI, VII (1945-1947).

Hodgetts, J.E. *Pioneer Public Service - An Administrative History of the United Canadas, 1841-1867* (Toronto: University of Toronto Press, 1955).

Indian Treaties and Surrenders from 1680 to 1890, 2 vols. (Ottawa: Queen's Printer, 1891) [reprinted, Toronto: Cole's, 1971].

Kerr, J.A., "The Indian Treaties of 1876," *Dalhousie Review*, vol.17 (1937-1938), pp.187-195.

Laviolette, F.E., *The Struggle for Survival: Indian Cultures and the Protestant Ethic in British Columbia* (Toronto: University of Toronto Press, 1961).

Lysyk, Kenneth, "Indian Hunting Rights: Constitutional Considerations and the Role of Indian Treaties in British Columbia," *University of British Columbia Law Review*, vol.2 (1966), pp.401 ff.

Lysyk, Kenneth, "The Unique Constitutional Position of the Canadian Indian," *Canadian Bar Review*, vol.45 (1967), pp.513 ff.

MacFarlane, R.O. "British Indian Policy in Nova Scotia to 1760," *Canadian Historical Review*, vol.19 (June, 1938), pp.154-167.

MacInnes, T.R.L., "History of Indian Administration in Canada," *Canadian Journal of Economics and Political Science*, vol. XII (1946), pp.387-394.

MacInnes, T.R.L., "Report on the Indian Title in Canada with Special Reference to British Columbia," *House of Commons, Sessional Papers* (no.47) (Ottawa: King's Printer, 1914).

MacInnes, T.R.L., "The History and Policies of Indian Administration in Canada," in *The North American Indian Today*, eds. C.T. Loram and T.F. McIlwraith (Toronto: University of Toronto Press, 1943).

Martin, Chester, "The Colonial Policy of the Dominion," *Transactions of the Royal Society of Canada*, Series III, vol. XVI (1922), pp.35-47.

McNickle, D'Arcy, "Indian and European: Indian-White Relations from Discovery to 1887," *Annals of the American Academy of Political and Social Science*, vol. 311 (1957), pp.1-11.

Mickenberg, Neil H. "Aboriginal Rights in Canada and the United States," *Osgoode Hall Law Journal*, vol.9 (1971), pp.119 ff.

Morris, Alexander. *The Treaties of Canada* (Toronto: Belfords, Clarke, 1880). [Reprinted, Toronto: Coles, 1971].

Palmer, C.A.G., "The Unilateral Abrogation of Indian and Eskimo Treaty Rights," *Criminal Reports*, vol.47 (1966), pp.395-400.

Patterson, E. Palmer, *The Canadian Indian: A History Since 1500* (Don Mills, Ont.: Collier-Macmillan, 1972).

Richards, J.H., "Lands and Policies: Attitudes and Controls in the Alienation of Lands in Ontario during the First Century of Settlement," *Ontario History*, vol.50 (1958), pp.193-209.

Riddell, R.G., "A Study in the Land Policy of the Colonial Office, 1763-1853," *Canadian Historical Review*, vol.18 (1937), pp.385-405.

Schweiser, D.A., "Indians, Eskimos and the Law," *Saskatchewan Law Review*, vol.33 (1968), pp.19-40.

Scott, Duncan Campbell, "Indian Affairs, 1763-1841," in *Canada and its Provinces*, eds. Adam Shortt and A.G. Doughty, vol.4 (Toronto: Publisher's Association of Canada, 1914).

Scott, Duncan Campbell, "Indian Affairs, 1840-1867," in *Canada and its Provinces*, eds. Adam Shortt and A.G. Doughty, vol.5, (Toronto: Publisher's Association of Canada, 1913).

Scott, Duncan Campbell, *The Administration of Indian Affairs in Canada* (Toronto: Canadian Institute of International Affairs, 1931).

Stanlyey G.F.G., "The Indian Background of Canadian History," *Canadian Historical Association Annual Report*, 1952, pp.14-21.

Trelease, A. *Indian Affairs in Colonial New York: The Seventeenth Century* (Ithaca: Cornell University Press, 1960).

Wraxall, P., *An Abridgement of the Indian Affairs Transacted in New York from 1678-1751* (New York: Benjamin Blom, 1968).

B. The Sociology of Law

Aubert, Vilhelm (ed.), *Sociology of Law; Selected Readings* (Baltimore: Penguin, 1969).

Auerbach, C. "Legal Tasks for the Sociologist," *Law and Society Review*, vol. 1 (Nov. 1966), pp.91-104.

Cairns, Huntington, *Law and the Social Sciences* (New York: Brace and World, 1935).

Chambliss, William J. and Robert B. Seidman, *Sociology of the Law: A Research Bibliography* (Berkeley: Glendessary Press, 1970).

Davis, F., "Treatment of Law in American Sociology," *Sociology and Social Research*, vol.42 (Nov. 1957), pp.99-105.

Ehrlich, Eugen, *Fundamental Principles of the Sociology of Law*, (trans. Walter L. Moll) (New York: Russell and Russell, 1962).

Ehrlich, Eugen, "Sociology of Law," (trans. N. Isaacs), *Harvard Law Review*, vol.36 (1921-1922), pp.129 ff.

Evan, William M. (ed.), *Law and Sociology*. (New York: Free Press of Glencoe, 1962).

Evan, William M., "Towards a Sociological Almanac of Legal Systems," *International Social Science Journal*, vol.17 (1965), pp.335-338.

Gibbs, J., "The Sociology of Law and Normative Phenomena," *American Sociological Review*, vol.31 (June 1966), pp.315-325.

Glegvad, B. (ed.), "Contributions to the Sociology of Law," *Acta Sociologica*, vol. 10 (1966), pp.1-190.

Gurvitch, Georges, *Sociology of Law* (London: Routledge and Kegan Paul, 1947).

Jones, Ernest M., "Impact Research and Sociology of Law: Some Tentative Proposals," *Wisconsin Law Review*, 1966 (Spring 1966), pp.331-339.

Llewellyn, K.N. "Law and the Social Sciences— Especially Sociology," *American Sociological Review*, vol. 14 (1949), pp.451-462.

Llewellyn, K.N., "The Normative, The Legal and the Law-Jobs: The Problem of Juristic Method, Being also an Effort to Integrate the "Legal" into Sociological and Political Theory," *Yale Law Journal*, vol.49 (1940), pp.1335-1340.

Ormrod, Robert, "The Developing Relations between the Law and the Social Sciences," *British Journal of Criminology*, vol.4 (April 1964), pp.320-331.

Rheinstein, Max (ed.), *Max Weber on Law and Economy in Society*, trans. Edward Shils and Max Rheinstein (Cambridge, Mass.: Harvard University Press, 1954).

Reisman, David. "Law and Social Science," *Yale Law Journal*, vol.50 (1941), pp.636-653.

Riesman, David. "Law and Sociology," *Indian Journal of Social Research*, vol.4 (Jan. 1963), pp.102-104.

Sawer, G., *Law in Society*. (Oxford: Oxford University Press,, 1965).

Schelsky, Helmut, "System-Functional, Anthropological, and Person-Functional Approaches to the Sociology of Law," *International Journal of Sociology*, vol. 1 no.4 (1971-1972), pp.336-414.

Simpson, Sidney Post and Julius Stone, *Cases and Readings on Law and Society*, 4 vols., American Casebook Series, (St. Paul, Minn.: West Publishing, 1948-1949).

Skolnick, J., "The Sociology of Law in America," *Law and Society* (supp., Summer 1965), pp.4-39.

Timasheff, N.S., *Introduction to the Sociology of Law*, Harvard Sociological Studies No.3, (Cambridge, Mass.: Harvard University Press, 1939).

Timasheff, N.S., "The Sociological Place of Law," *American Journal of Sociology*, vol.44 (Sept. 1938).

Timasheff, N.S., "What is 'Sociology of Law'?", *American Journal of Sociology*, vol.43 (1937), pp.225 ff.

THE CARLETON LIBRARY